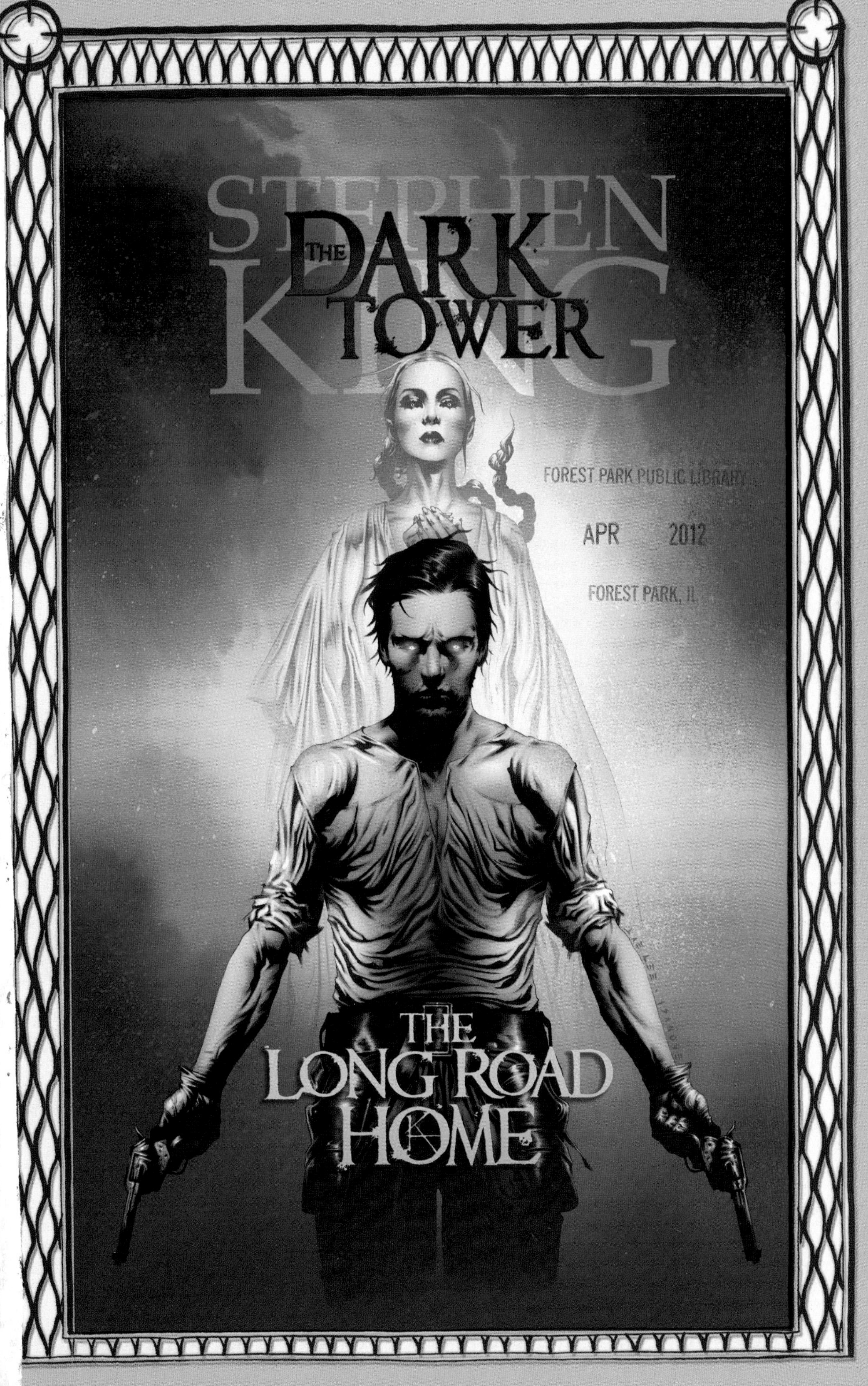
STEPHEN KING
THE DARK TOWER
THE LONG ROAD HOME

STEPHEN KING

THE DARK TOWER

THE LONG ROAD HOME

CREATIVE DIRECTOR AND EXECUTIVE DIRECTOR
STEPHEN KING

PLOTTING AND CONSULTATION
ROBIN FURTH

SCRIPT
PETER DAVID

ART
JAE LEE AND RICHARD ISANOVE

LETTERING
CHRIS ELIOPOULOS

ASSISTANT EDITOR
LAUREN SANKOVITCH

EDITOR
NICOLE BOOSE

SENIOR EDITOR
RALPH MACCHIO

COLLECTION EDITOR
MARK D. BEAZLEY

ASSISTANT EDITORS
JOHN DENNING AND CORY LEVINE

EDITOR, SPECIAL PROJECTS
JENNIFER GRUNWALD

SENIOR EDITOR, SPECIAL PROJECTS
JEFF YOUNGQUIST

SENIOR VICE PRESIDENT OF SALES
DAVID GABRIEL

SENIOR VICE PRESIDENT OF STRATEGIC DEVELOPMENT
RUWAN JAYATILLEKE

PRODUCTION
JERRY KALINOWSKI

EDITOR IN CHIEF
JOE QUESADA

PUBLISHER
DAN BUCKLEY

SPECIAL THANKS TO CHUCK VERRILL, MARSHA DEFILLIPO,
RALPH VICINANZA, BARBARA ANN MCINTYRE, BRIAN STARK, JIM
NAUSEDAS, JIM MCCANN, ARUNE SINGH, CHRIS ALLO, JEFF SUTER,
JIM CALAFIORE AND ANTHONY FLAMINI

FOR MORE INFORMATION ON DARK TOWER COMICS, VISIT MARVEL.COM/DARKTOWER.

TO FIND MARVEL COMICS AT A LOCAL COMIC SHOP, CALL 1-888-COMICBOOK.

DARK TOWER: THE LONG ROAD HOME. Contains material originally published in magazine form as DARK TOWER: THE LONG ROAD HOME #1-5. First printing 2008. ISBN# 978-0-7851-2709-3. Published by MARVEL PUBLISHING, INC., a subsidiary of MARVEL ENTERTAINMENT, INC. OFFICE OF PUBLICATION: 417 5th Avenue, New York, NY 10016. Copyright © 2008 Stephen King. All rights reserved. $24.99 per copy in the U.S. and $26.50 in Canada (GST #R127032852); Canadian Agreement #40668537. All characters featured in this issue and the distinctive names and likenesses thereof, and all related indicia are trademarks of Stephen King. No similarity between any of the names, characters, persons, and/or institutions in this magazine with those of any living or dead person or institution is intended, and any such similarity which may exist is purely coincidental. **Printed in the U.S.A.** ALAN FINE, CEO Marvel Toys & Publishing Divisions and CMO Marvel Characters, Inc.; DAVID GABRIEL, SVP of Publishing Sales & Circulation; DAVID BOGART, SVP of Business Affairs & Talent Management; MICHAEL PASCIULLO, VP of Merchandising & Communications; JIM O'KEEFE, VP of Operations & Logistics; DAN CARR, Executive Director of Publishing Technology; JUSTIN F. GABRIE, Director of Editorial Operations; SUSAN CRESPI, Editorial Operations Manager; OMAR OTIEKU, Production Manager; STAN LEE, Chairman Emeritus. For information regarding advertising in Marvel Comics or on Marvel.com, please contact Mitch Dane, Advertising Director, at mdane@marvel.com. For Marvel subscription inquiries, please call 800-217-9158.

10 9 8 7 6 5 4 3 2 1

A STUDY IN CRIMSON

It's a truism that to have a great super hero comic, you need a great villain. And that dictum may apply to much of mainstream literature, as well. The Master, Stephen King, has provided his Dark Tower novels with a real headliner in that regard—The Crimson King!

This grotesque gent is so horrifying that, in his own words: Were I to confront you with my true "impressive" form, your mind would leak from your ears. Not a man you want to mess with.

What's fascinating about this awe-inspiring entity of evil is how identifiable he is to us all. He speaks to the darkest impulses in humanity, the often overpowering urge to utterly destroy, raze and rend whatever displeases or angers you. He doesn't want to do the routine Doctor Doom trip and just take over the world because he can run it better than blah blah... The Crimson King wants to reach the Dark Tower so he can shatter the very fulcrum of reality and return the endless multiverse to its primal chaos.

He isn't interested in ruling the world as it is. He wants to wreck it! His ultimate aim is to take God's own creation and stomp on it in childlike glee until there is nothing left but shards and splinters. And then, the red-eyed devil will rule the frothing nothingness that remains, bloated and content.

What deep and dark fears scribe Stephen is playing with here through his universal antagonist. What is it we, as collective humanity, really fear most? We dread this thin world of order and reason we inhabit will suddenly unravel. The guideposts of existence will crumble and we'll be lost forever in a landscape of madness. We fear worldwide Armageddon; the disintegration of society; the breakdown of the family unit; the loss of our personal sanity.

The Crimson King thrives on all of that! He revels in the collapse and chaos. He doesn't desire subjects or worshippers. He craves the absolute annihilation of all that is.

And in this volume of stories presented here, he tries to draw the young gunslinger, Roland Deschain himself, into his deadly web and convince him of the inevitability of his cause. The Crimson King has had centuries to brood and scheme and acquire power. If he can just entice his cousin Roland to his side, this greatest defender of the Dark Tower, all hope for reality is lost. Just the tiniest weakness or faltering on Roland's part and the Crimson King will exploit it. He is as committed to his goal as any creature in history has ever been. But Roland is a descendant of the Line of Eld. His life's mission is to preserve, at all costs, this ultimate edifice that is the foundation of existence itself. He is the lone bulwark against this agent of dissolution.

Order and chaos—or the Random and the Purpose—as Stephen King calls them, have rarely had a larger canvas on which to paint. In the coming struggle for the soul of all that is we must choose sides. Don't be too sure the choice is obvious. Consider: It takes forever to build a beautiful and intricate sand castle at the beach. And the result is worth it, isn't it? But then, isn't it actually the most fun when we then smash that castle beyond recognition? Isn't there somehow a deeper, more resonant satisfaction in

destroying it? All that hard work for nothing. What a shame.

I imagine the Crimson King sitting on his throne at Le Casse Roi Russe in the depths of End-World and smiling, smiling just a little as he contemplates his coming day at the beach.

Ralph Macchio

Ralph Macchio

June 2008

IN A WORLD THAT HAS MOVED ON...

Roland Deschain was goaded by his father's enemies into facing his coming-of-age battle early, earning the title of Gunslinger at the unheard-of age of fourteen. His unexpected victory placed him at the very top of the "Good Man" John Farson's hit list. Roland was faced with a choice—either flee his home of Gilead immediately or be dead by the following nightfall.

With his two ka-tet mates, Cuthbert Allgood and Alain Johns, Roland sought sanctuary in the backwater barony of Mejis under a false identity. There, in the seaside town of Hambry, Roland fell in love with Susan Delgado, but he also discovered that the entire barony had secretly sold its soul to Farson and Farson's evil master, The Crimson King.

Now Susan is dead, and Roland and his friends must outrun the Hambry posse so that they can return to Gilead bearing Farson's prize, the evil seeing sphere known as Maerlyn's Grapefruit.

STEPHEN KING

THE DARK TOWER

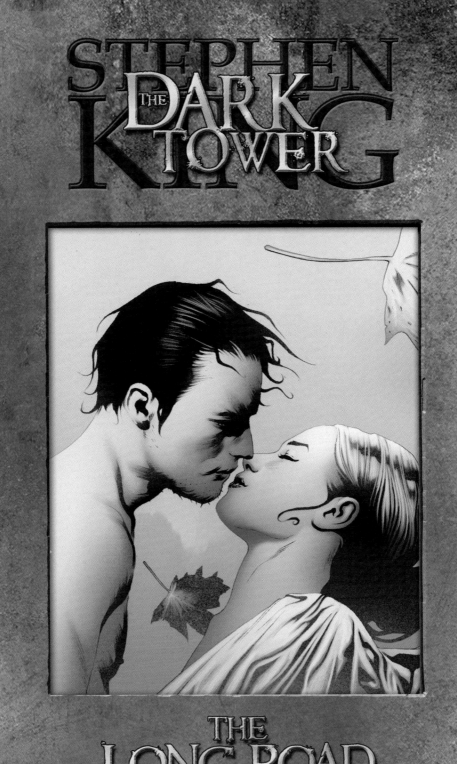

THE LONG ROAD HOME

CHAPTER ONE

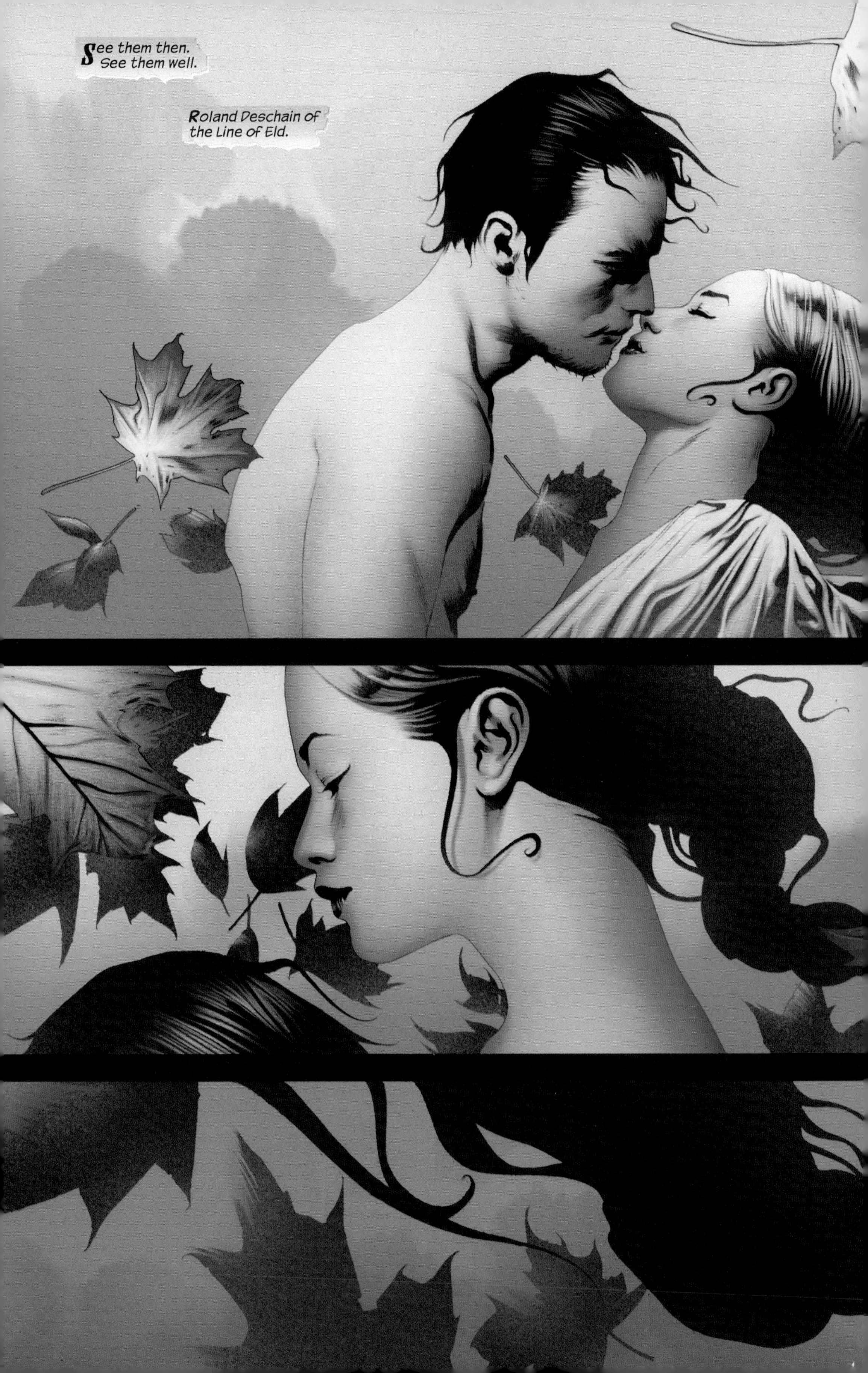
See them then. See them well.
Roland Deschain of the Line of Eld.

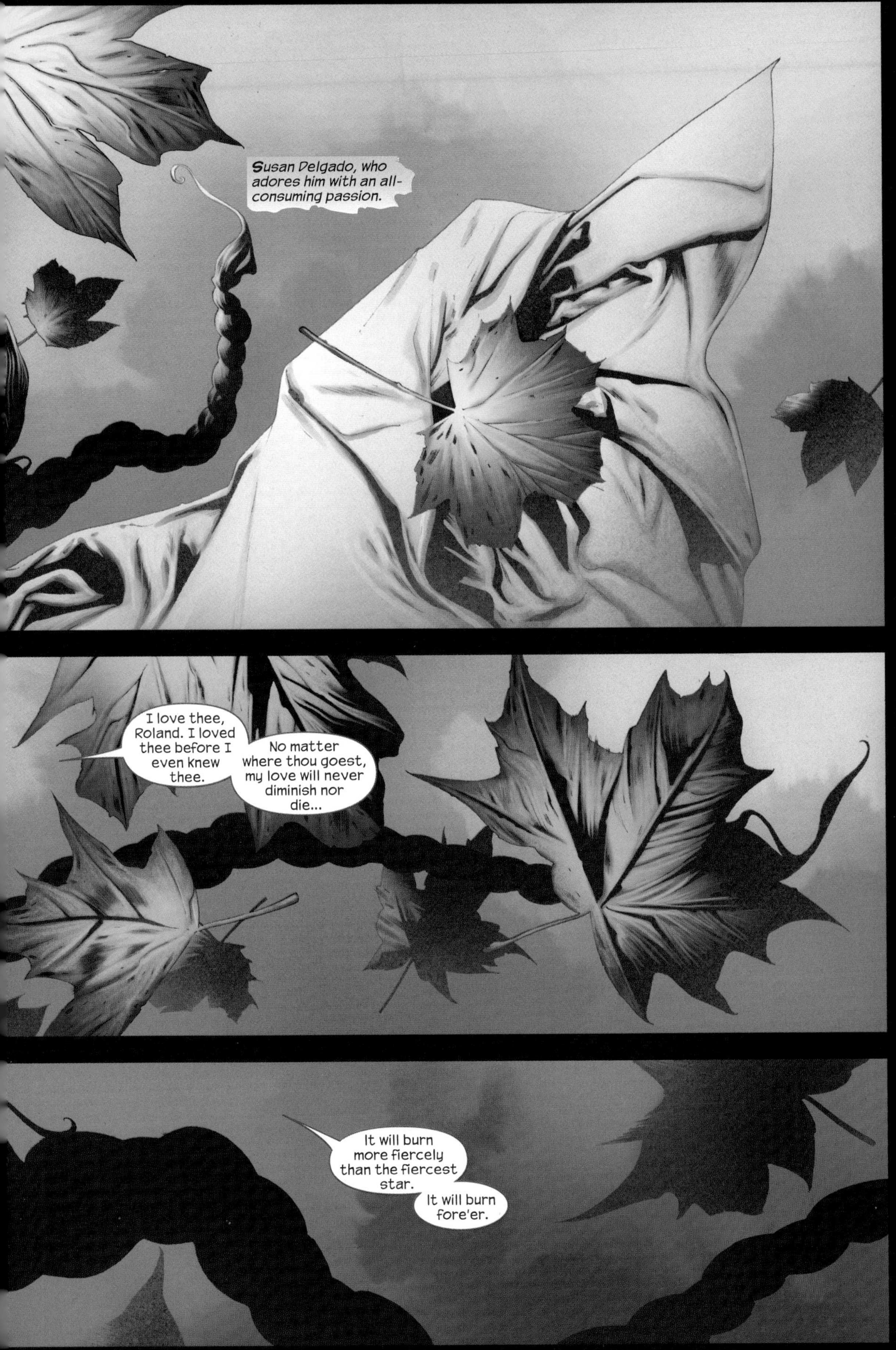
Susan Delgado, who adores him with an all-consuming passion.
I love thee, Roland. I loved thee before I even knew thee.
No matter where thou goest, my love will never diminish nor die...
It will burn more fiercely than the fiercest star.
It will burn fore'er.

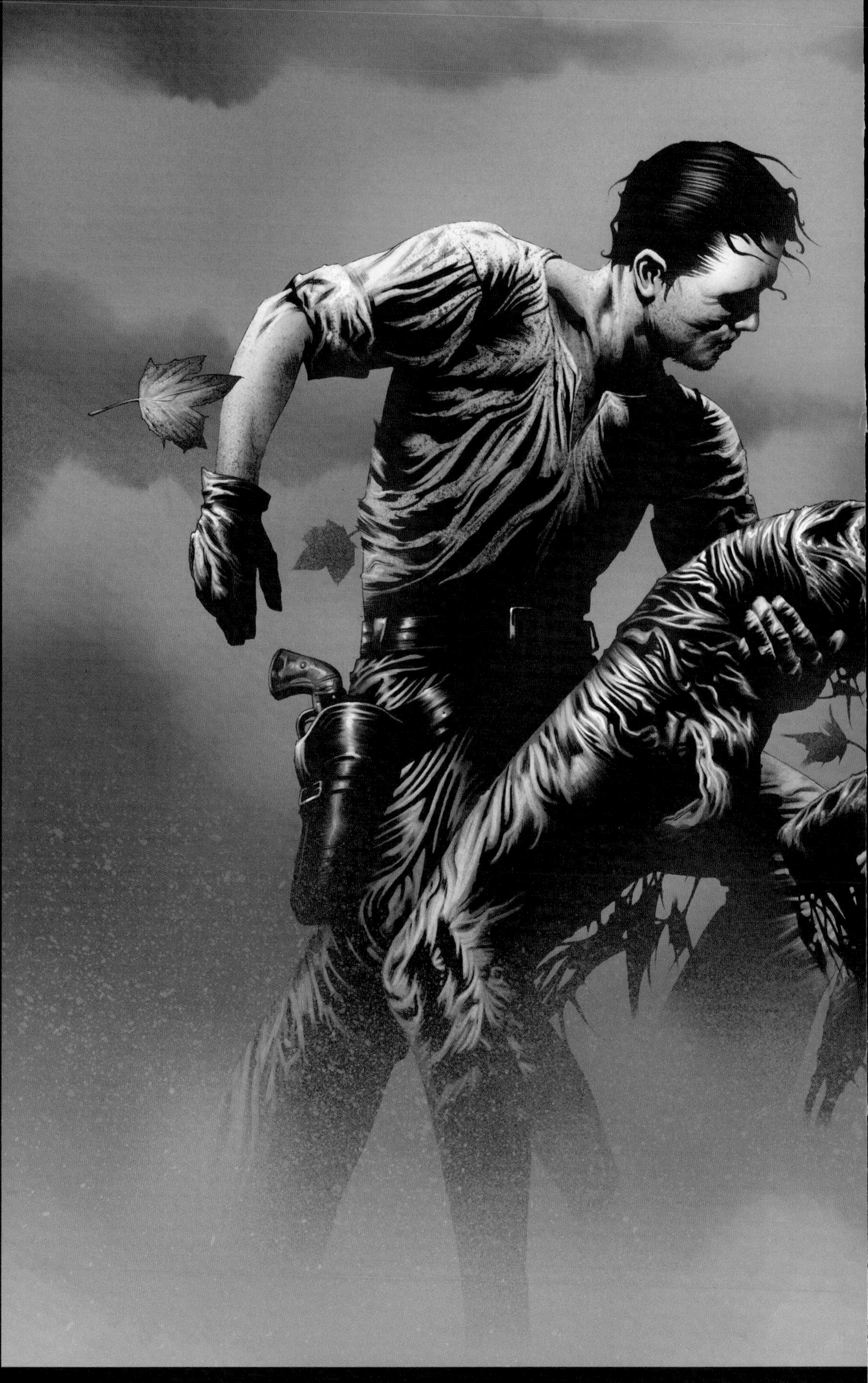

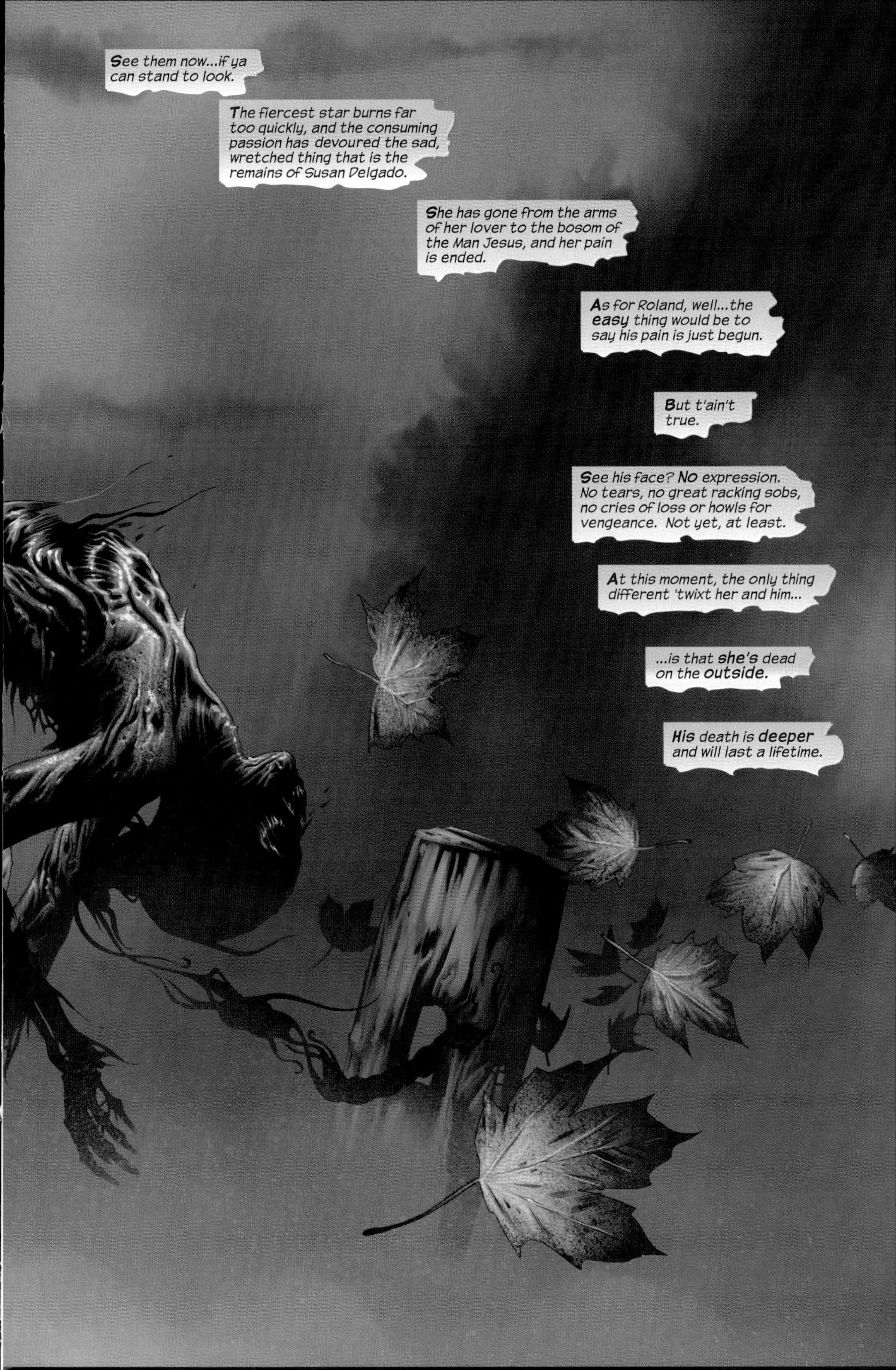
See them now...if ya can stand to look.
The fiercest star burns far too quickly, and the consuming passion has devoured the sad, wretched thing that is the remains of Susan Delgado.
She has gone from the arms of her lover to the bosom of the Man Jesus, and her pain is ended.
As for Roland, well...the easy thing would be to say his pain is just begun.
But t'ain't true.
See his face? No expression. No tears, no great racking sobs, no cries of loss or howls for vengeance. Not yet, at least.
At this moment, the only thing different 'twixt her and him...
...is that she's dead on the outside.
His death is deeper and will last a lifetime.

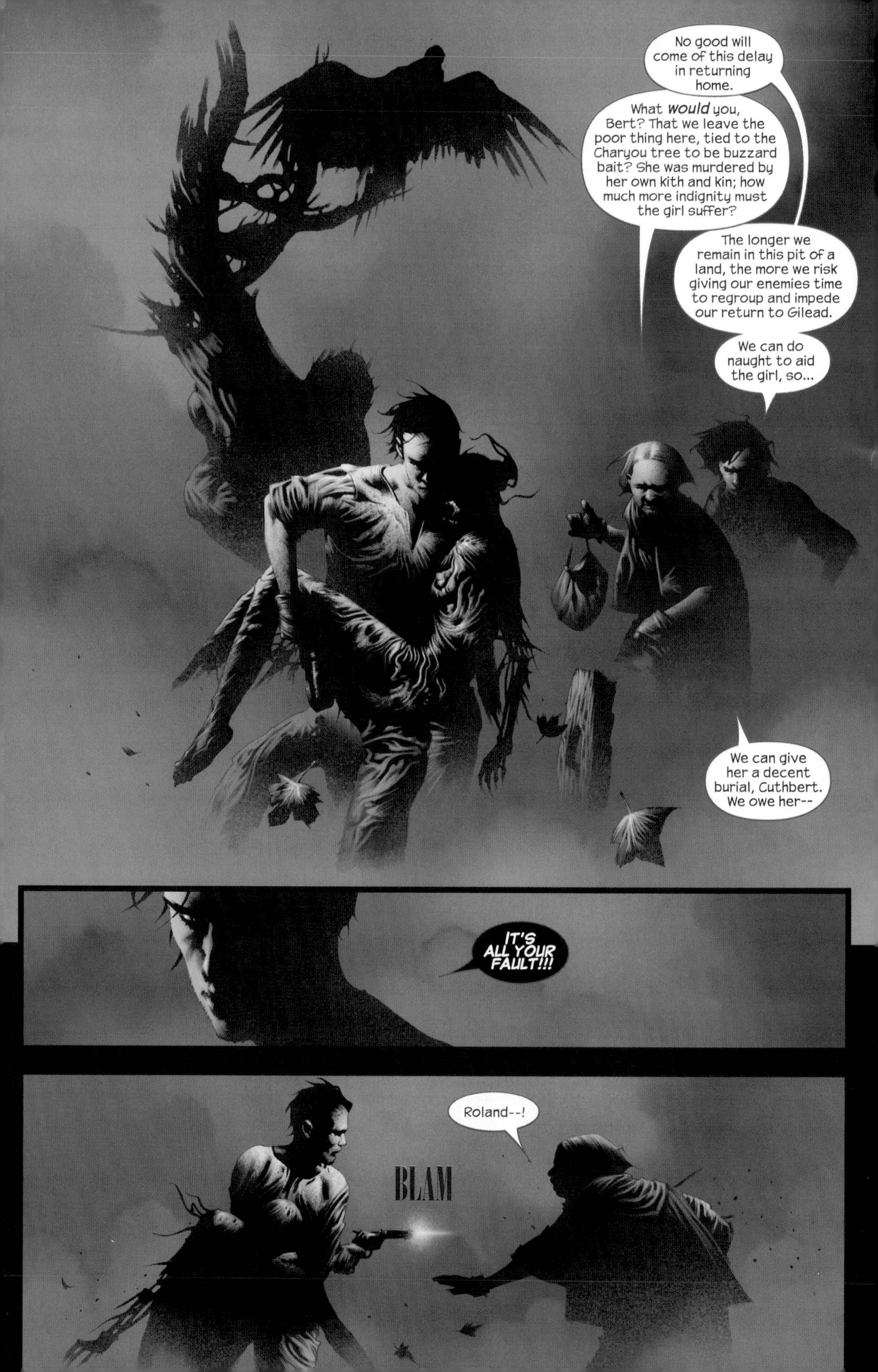
No good will come of this delay in returning home.
What *would* you, Bert? That we leave the poor thing here, tied to the Charyou tree to be buzzard bait? She was murdered by her own kith and kin; how much more indignity must the girl suffer?
The longer we remain in this pit of a land, the more we risk giving our enemies time to regroup and impede our return to Gilead.
We can do naught to aid the girl, so...
We can give her a decent burial, Cuthbert. We owe her--
IT'S ALL YOUR FAULT!!!
Roland--!
BLAM

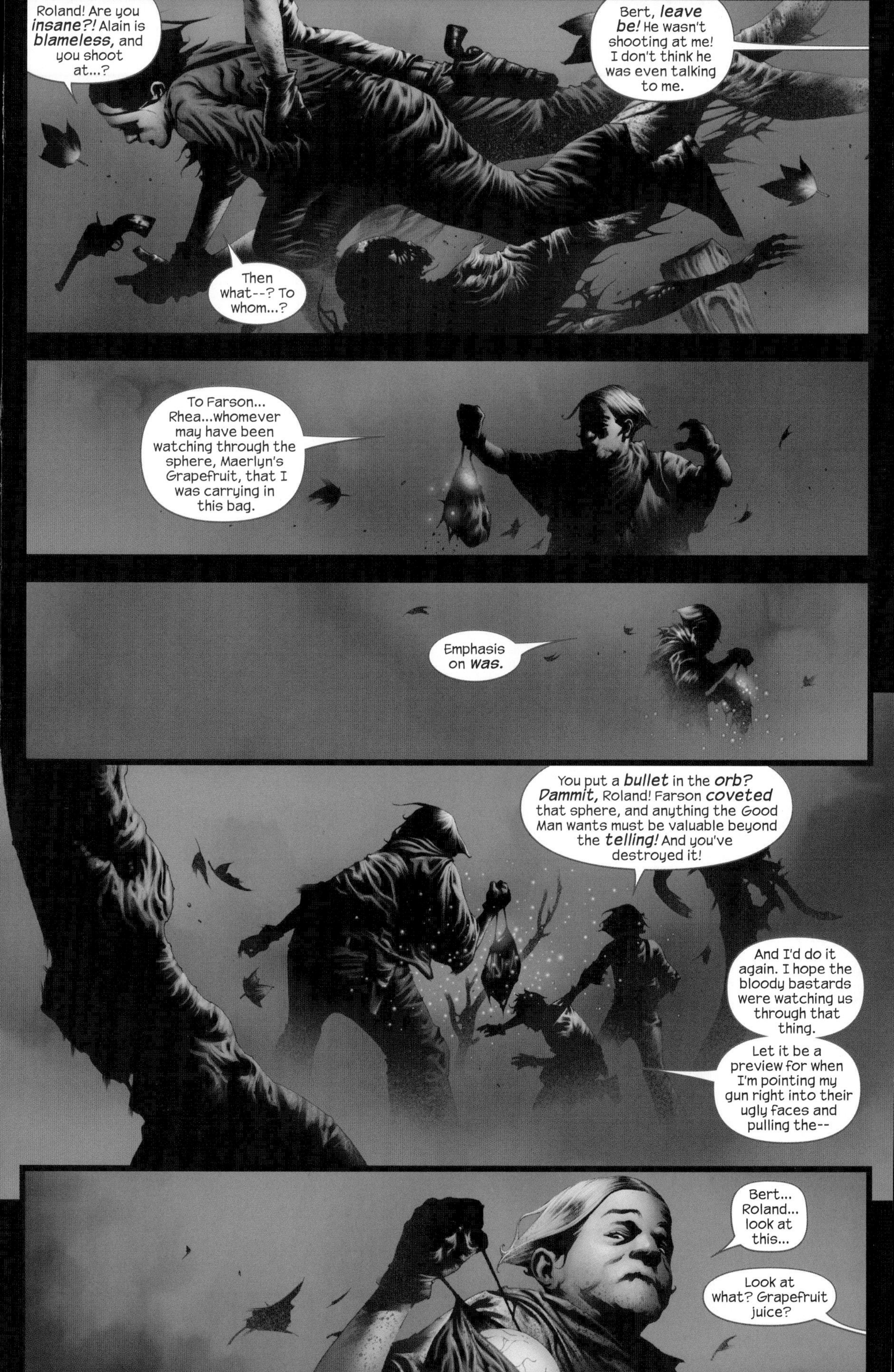

Roland! Are you *insane?!* Alain is *blameless,* and you shoot at...?
Bert, *leave be!* He wasn't shooting at me! I don't think he was even talking to me.
Then what--? To whom...?
To Farson... Rhea...whomever may have been watching through the sphere, Maerlyn's Grapefruit, that I was carrying in this bag.
Emphasis on *was.*
You put a *bullet* in the *orb? Dammit,* Roland! Farson *coveted* that sphere, and anything the Good Man wants must be valuable beyond the *telling!* And you've destroyed it!
And I'd do it again. I hope the bloody bastards were watching us through that thing.
Let it be a preview for when I'm pointing my gun right into their ugly faces and pulling the--
Bert... Roland... look at this...
Look at what? Grapefruit juice?

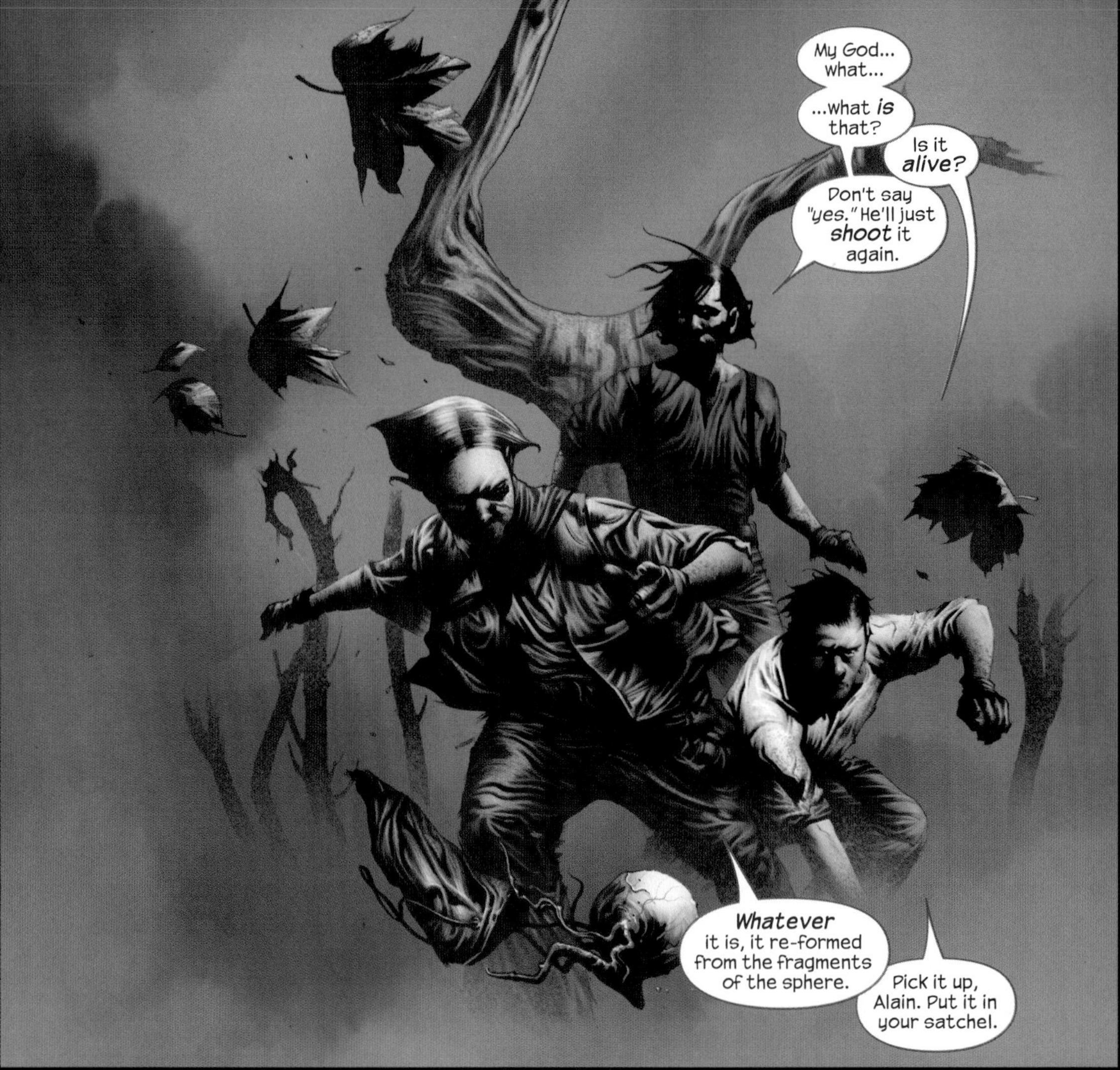
My God... what...
...what is that?
Is it alive?
Don't say "yes." He'll just shoot it again.
Whatever it is, it re-formed from the fragments of the sphere.
Pick it up, Alain. Put it in your satchel.

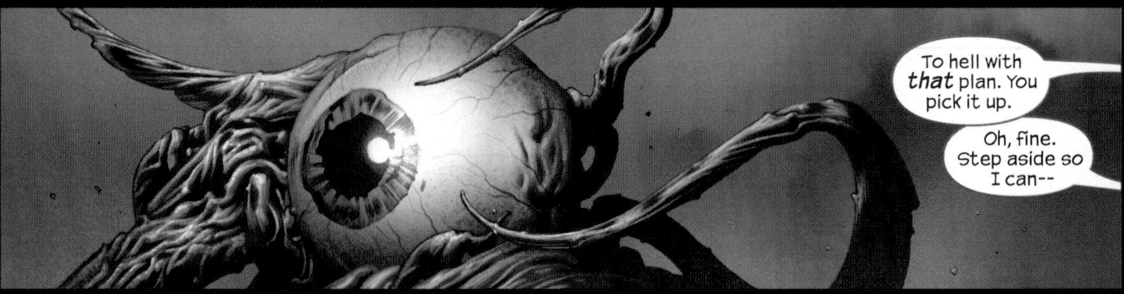
To hell with that plan. You pick it up.
Oh, fine. Step aside so I can--

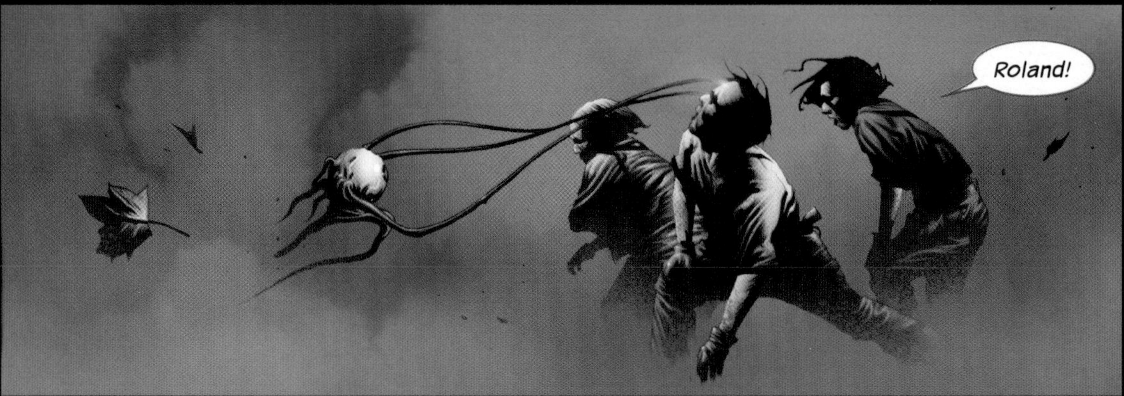
Roland!

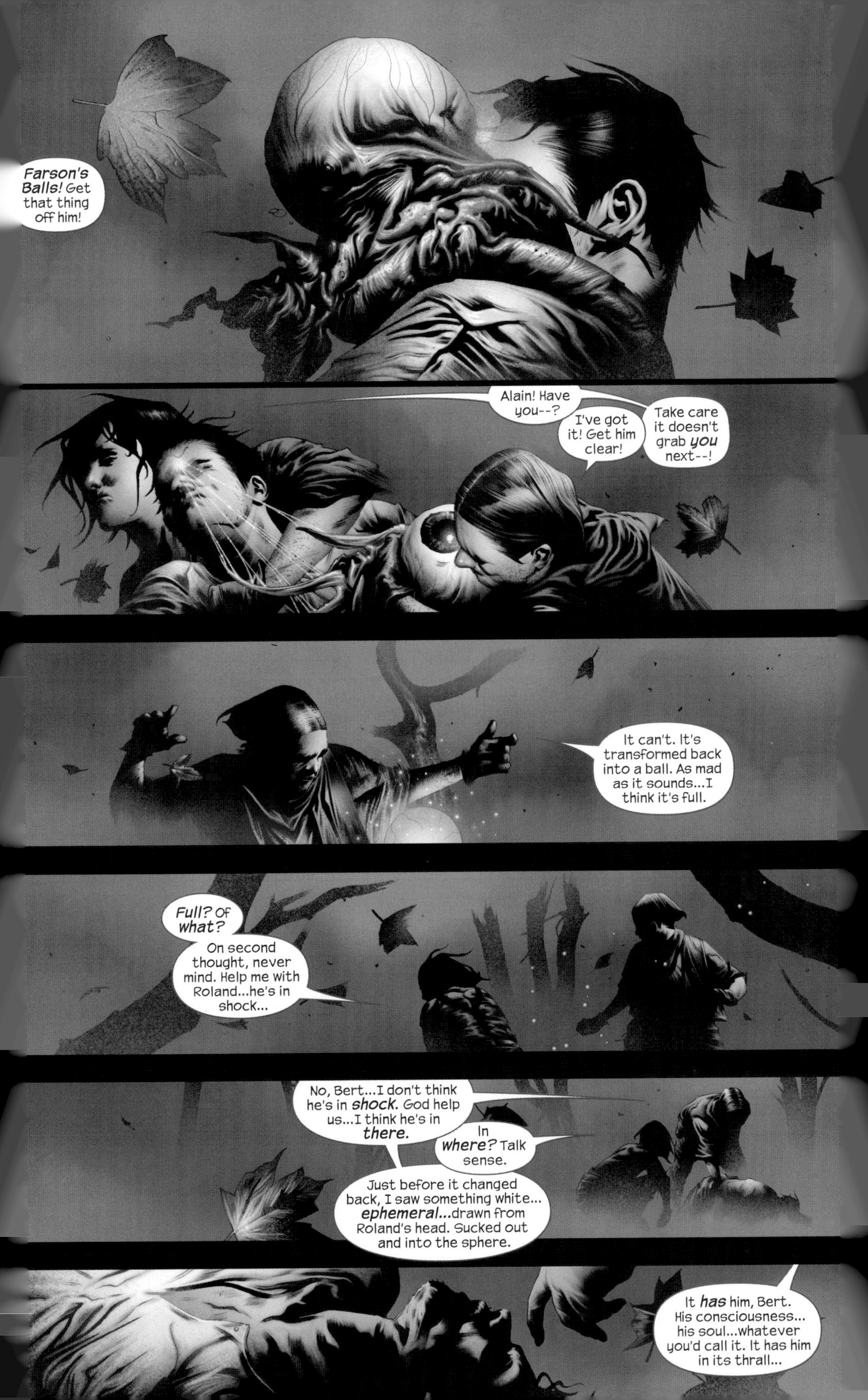
Farson's Balls! Get that thing off him!
Alain! Have you--?
I've got it! Get him clear!
Take care it doesn't grab you next--!
It can't. It's transformed back into a ball. As mad as it sounds...I think it's full.
Full? Of what?
On second thought, never mind. Help me with Roland...he's in shock...
No, Bert...I don't think he's in shock. God help us...I think he's in there.
In where? Talk sense.
Just before it changed back, I saw something white... ephemeral...drawn from Roland's head. Sucked out and into the sphere.
It has him, Bert. His consciousness... his soul...whatever you'd call it. It has him in its thrall...

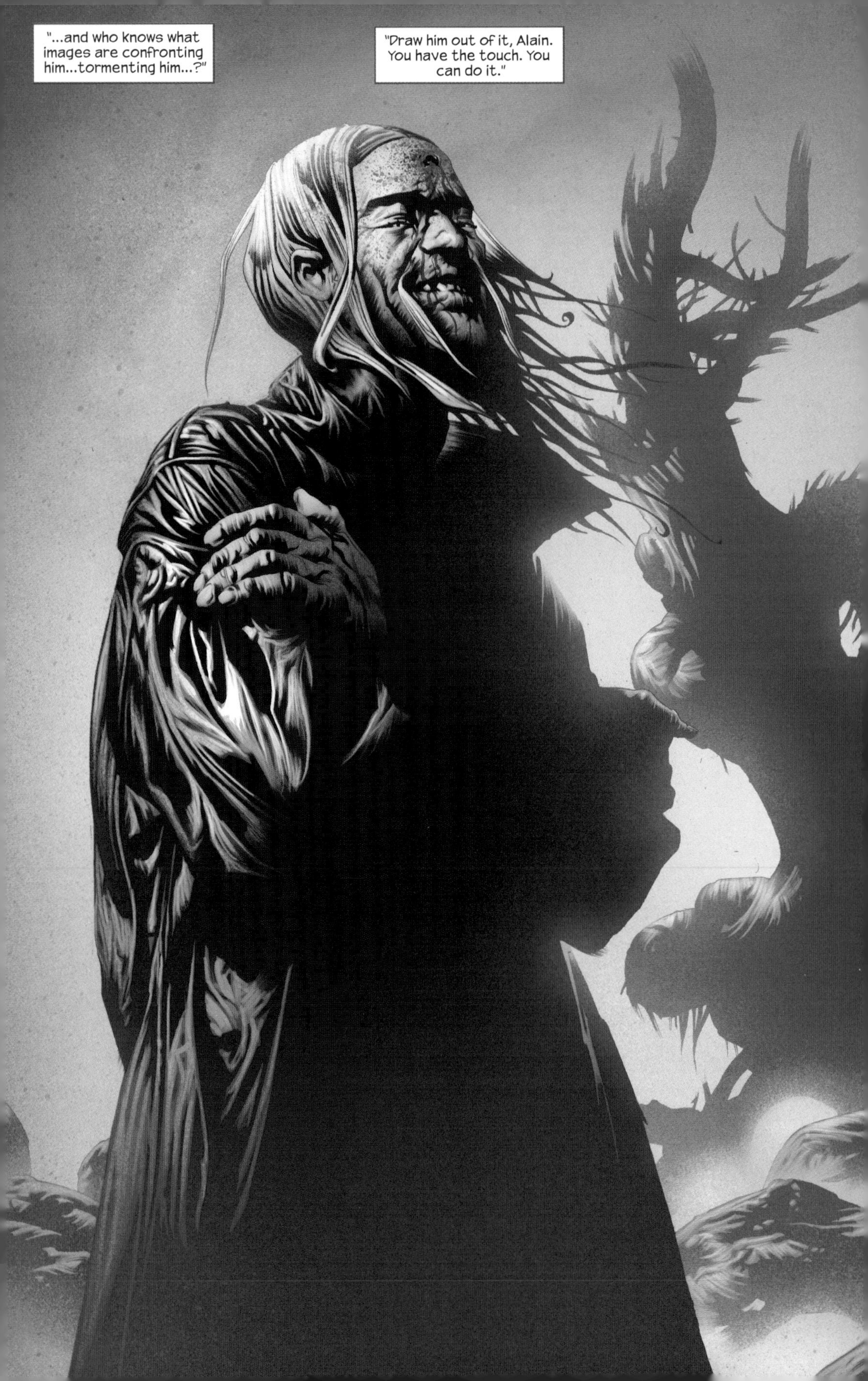
"...and who knows what images are confronting him...tormenting him...?"
"Draw him out of it, Alain. You have the touch. You can do it."

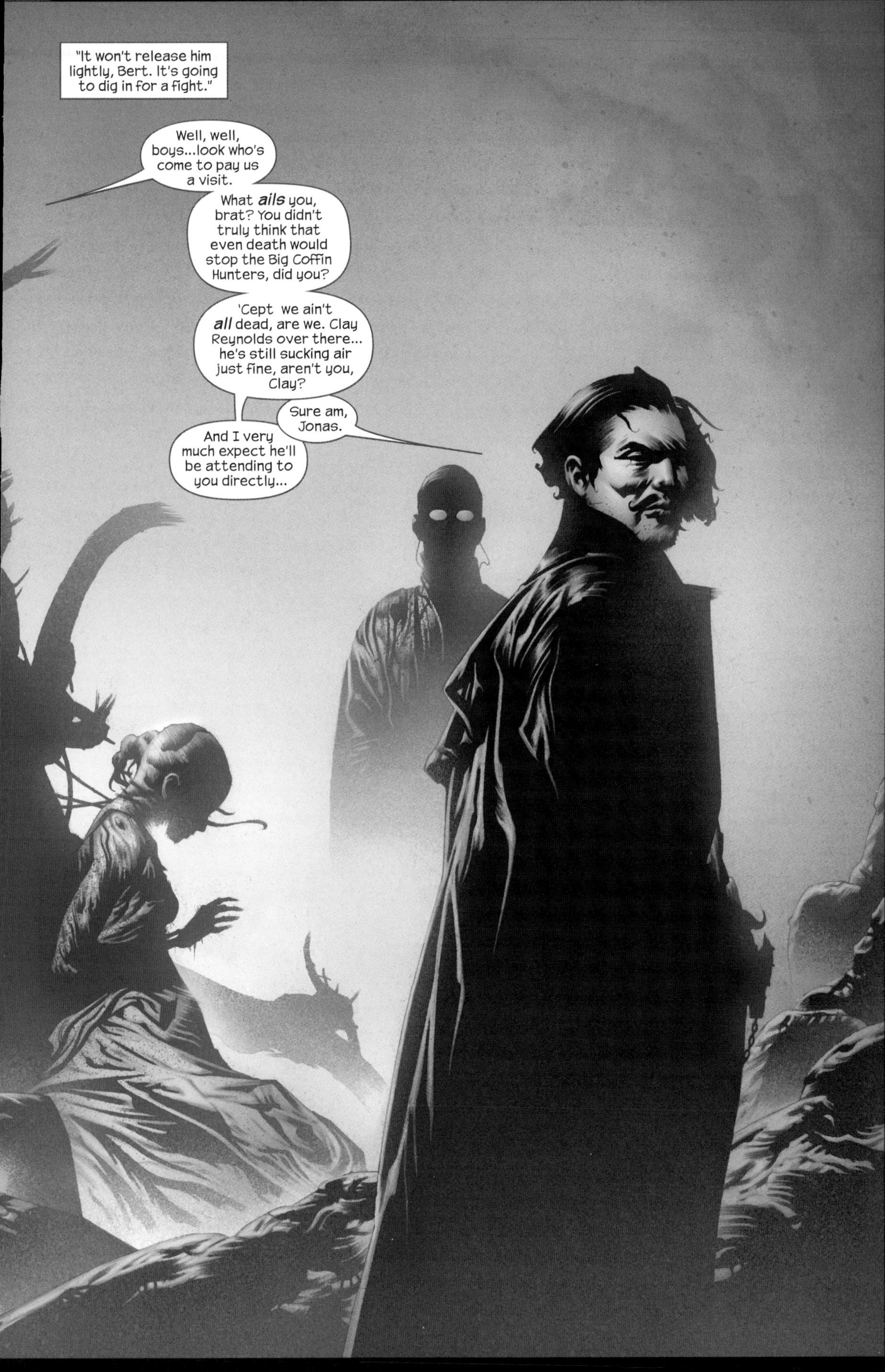
"It won't release him lightly, Bert. It's going to dig in for a fight."
Well, well, boys...look who's come to pay us a visit.
What *ails* you, brat? You didn't truly think that even death would stop the Big Coffin Hunters, did you?
'Cept we ain't *all* dead, are we. Clay Reynolds over there... he's still sucking air just fine, aren't you, Clay?
Sure am, Jonas.
And I very much expect he'll be attending to you directly...

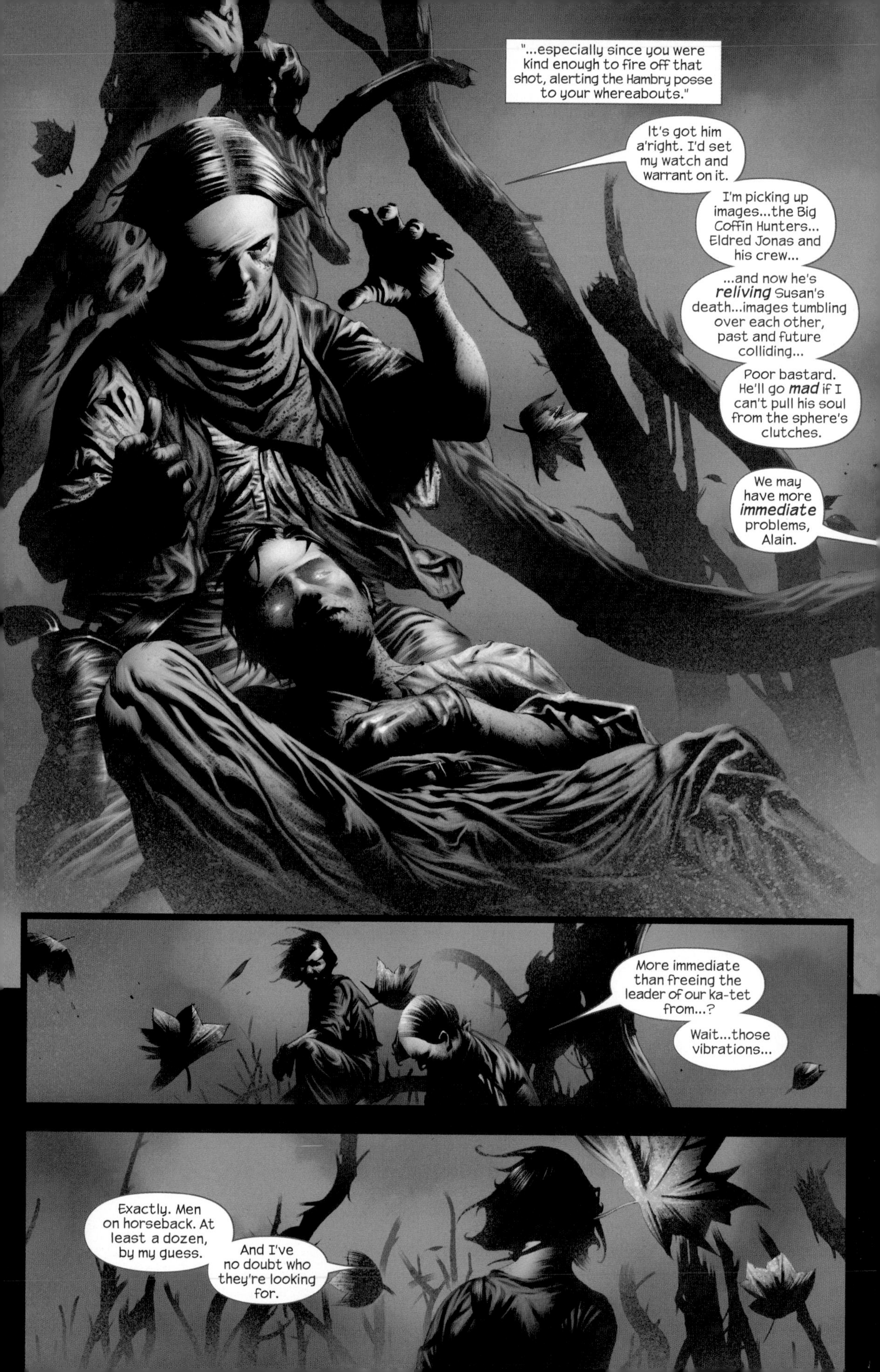
"...especially since you were kind enough to fire off that shot, alerting the Hambry posse to your whereabouts."
It's got him a'right. I'd set my watch and warrant on it.
I'm picking up images...the Big Coffin Hunters... Eldred Jonas and his crew...
...and now he's *reliving* Susan's death...images tumbling over each other, past and future colliding...
Poor bastard. He'll go *mad* if I can't pull his soul from the sphere's clutches.
We may have more *immediate* problems, Alain.
More immediate than freeing the leader of our ka-tet from...?
Wait...those vibrations...
Exactly. Men on horseback. At least a dozen, by my guess.
And I've no doubt who they're looking for.

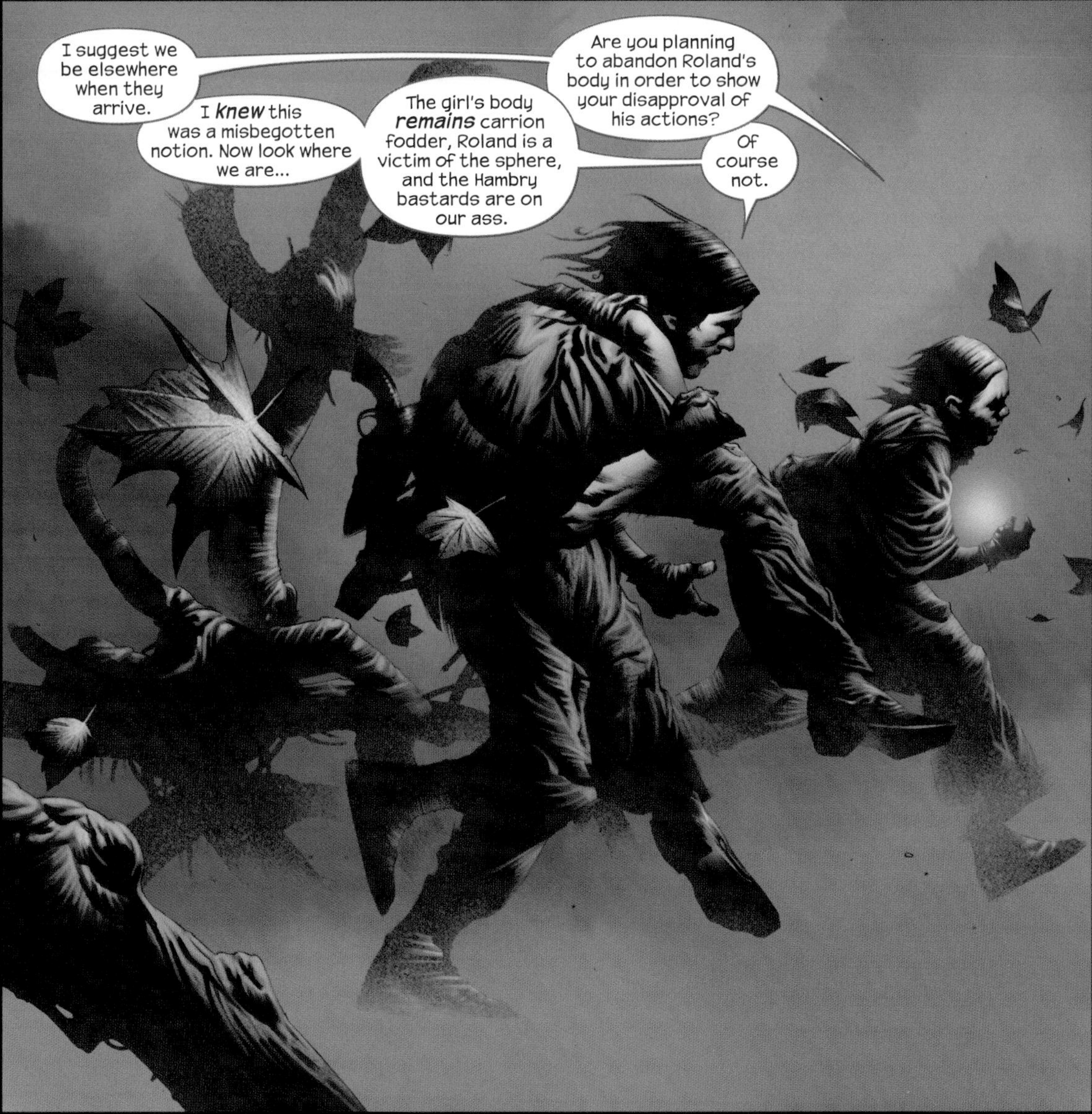
I suggest we be elsewhere when they arrive.
I knew this was a misbegotten notion. Now look where we are...
The girl's body remains carrion fodder, Roland is a victim of the sphere, and the Hambry bastards are on our ass.
Are you planning to abandon Roland's body in order to show your disapproval of his actions?
Of course not.

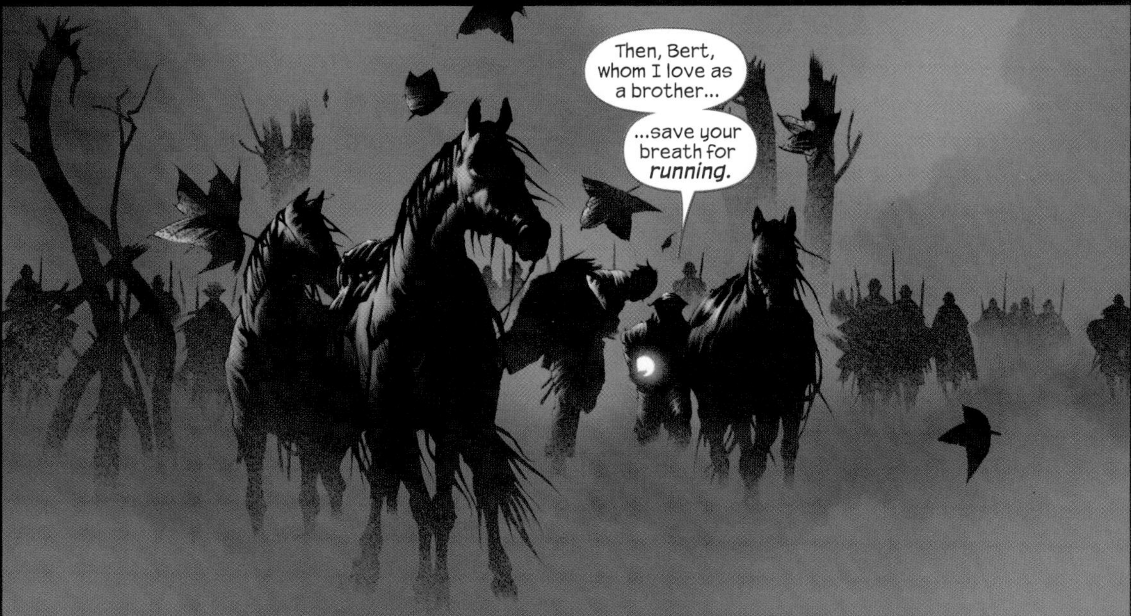
Then, Bert, whom I love as a brother...
...save your breath for running.

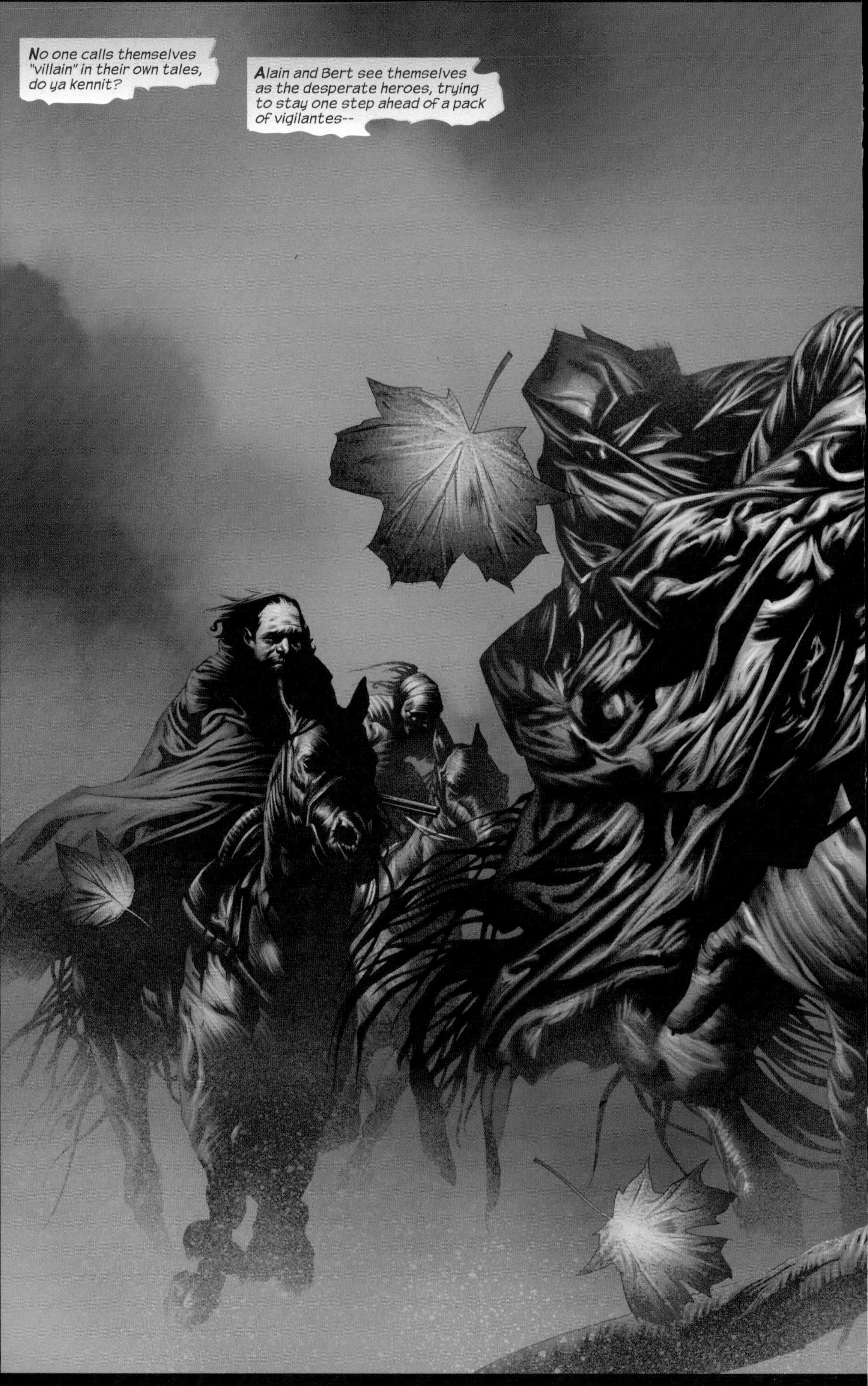
No one calls themselves "villain" in their own tales, do ya kennit?
Alain and Bert see themselves as the desperate heroes, trying to stay one step ahead of a pack of vigilantes--

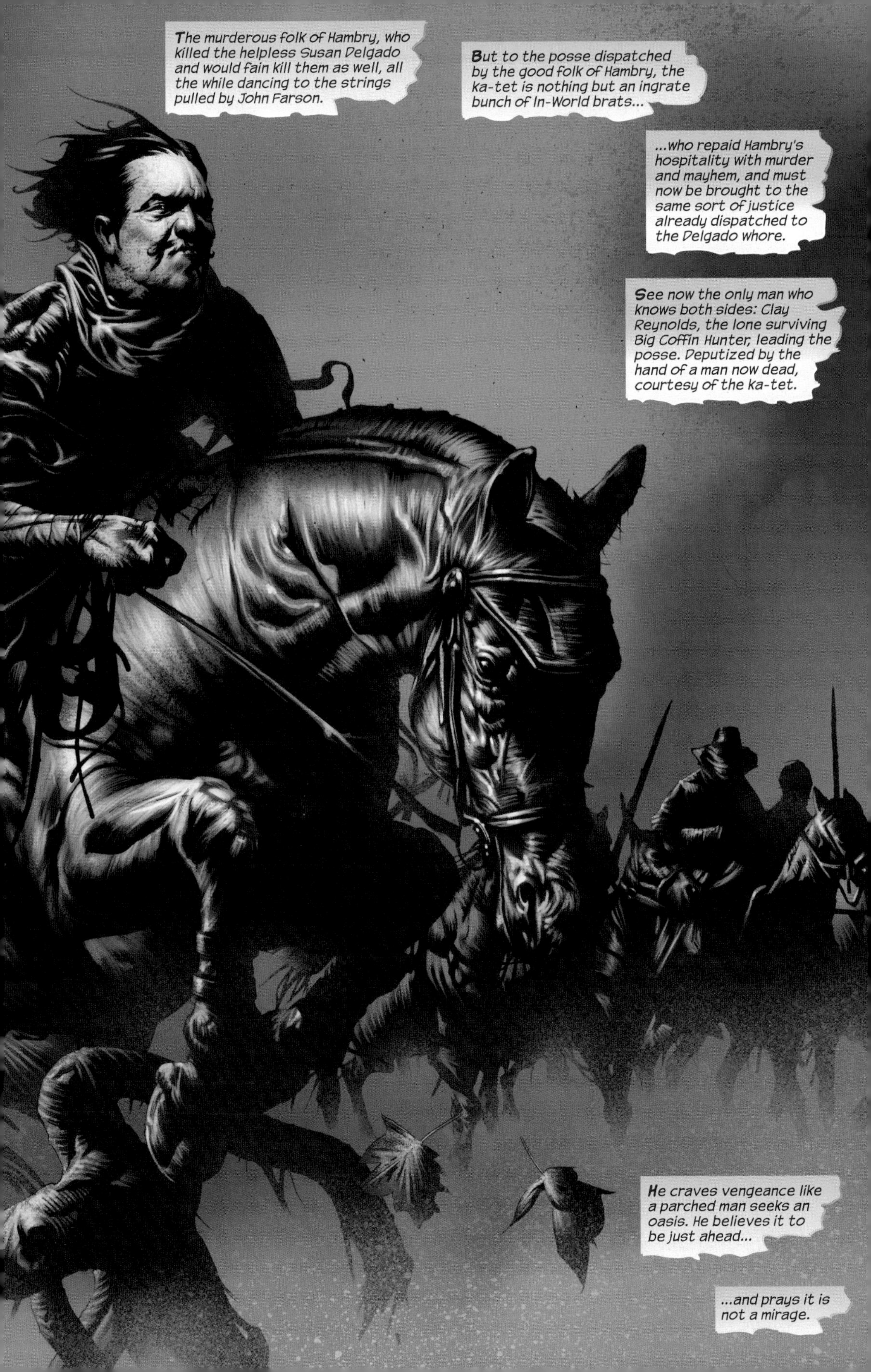
The murderous folk of Hambry, who killed the helpless Susan Delgado and would fain kill them as well, all the while dancing to the strings pulled by John Farson.
But to the posse dispatched by the good folk of Hambry, the ka-tet is nothing but an ingrate bunch of In-World brats...
...who repaid Hambry's hospitality with murder and mayhem, and must now be brought to the same sort of justice already dispatched to the Delgado whore.
See now the only man who knows both sides: Clay Reynolds, the lone surviving Big Coffin Hunter, leading the posse. Deputized by the hand of a man now dead, courtesy of the ka-tet.
He craves vengeance like a parched man seeks an oasis. He believes it to be just ahead...
...and prays it is not a mirage.

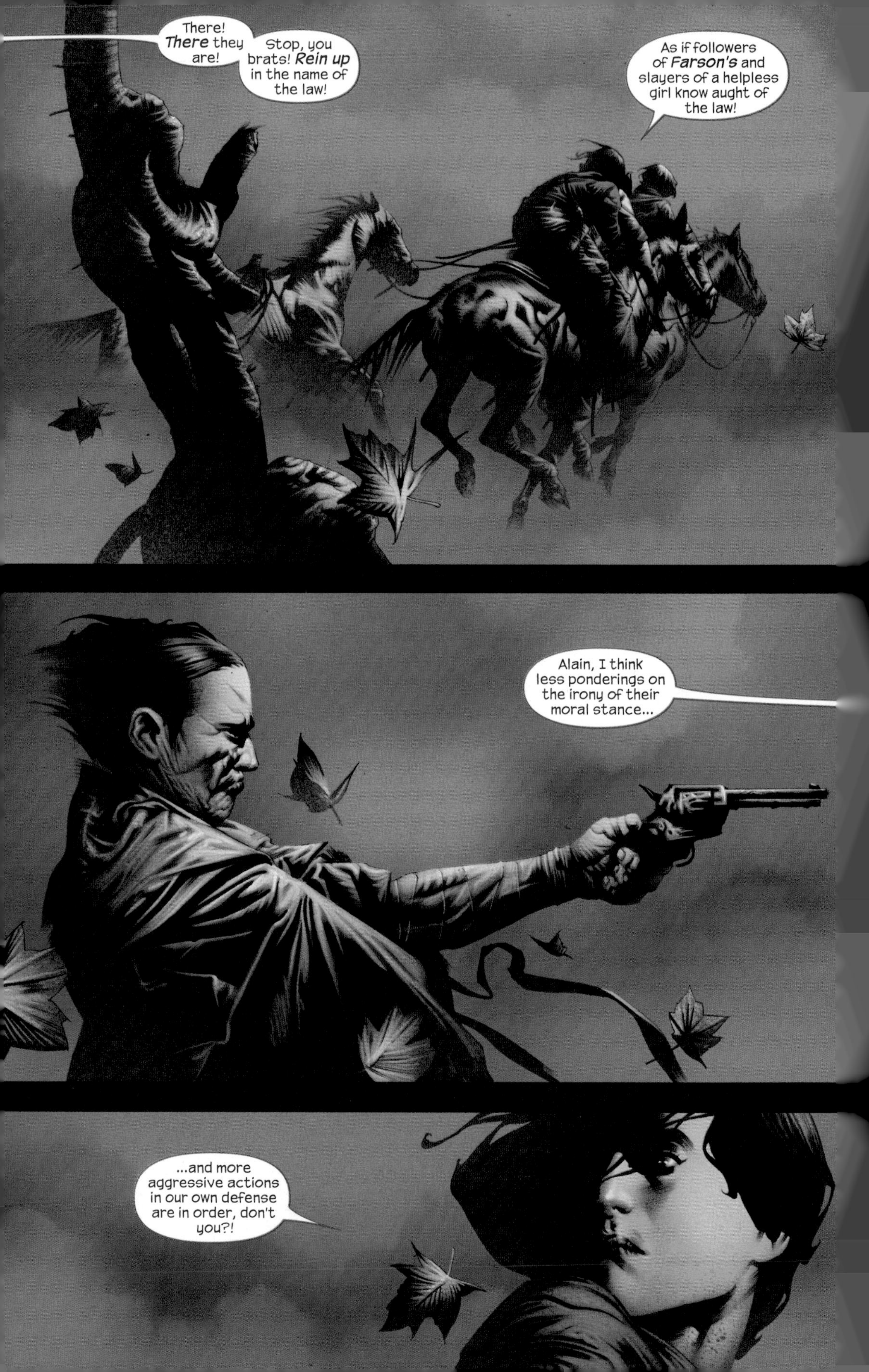
There! There they are!
Stop, you brats! Rein up in the name of the law!
As if followers of Farson's and slayers of a helpless girl know aught of the law!
Alain, I think less ponderings on the irony of their moral stance...
...and more aggressive actions in our own defense are in order, don't you?!

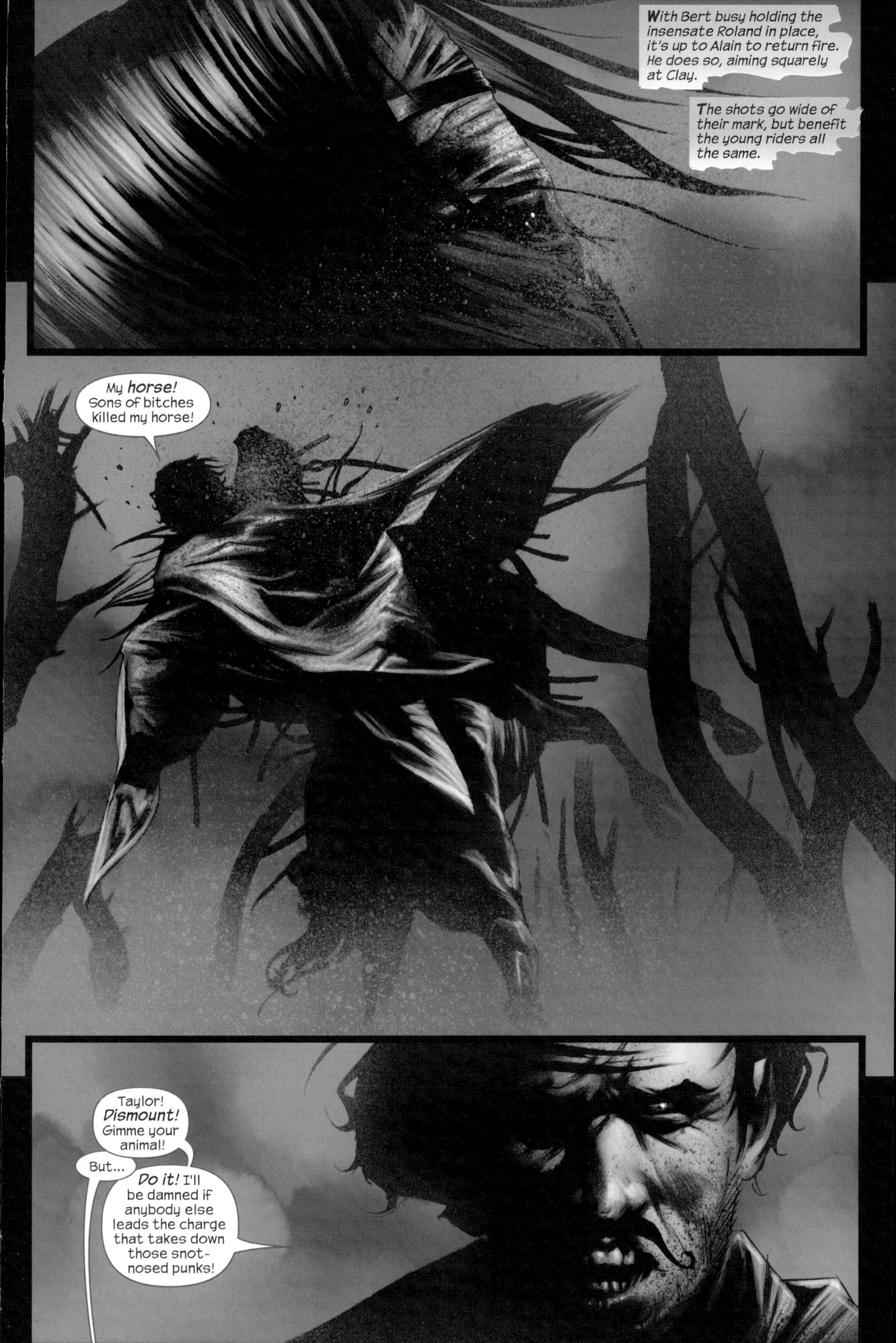
With Bert busy holding the insensate Roland in place, it's up to Alain to return fire. He does so, aiming squarely at Clay.
The shots go wide of their mark, but benefit the young riders all the same.
My *horse!* Sons of bitches killed my horse!
Taylor! *Dismount!* Gimme your animal!
But...
Do it! I'll be damned if anybody else leads the charge that takes down those snot-nosed punks!

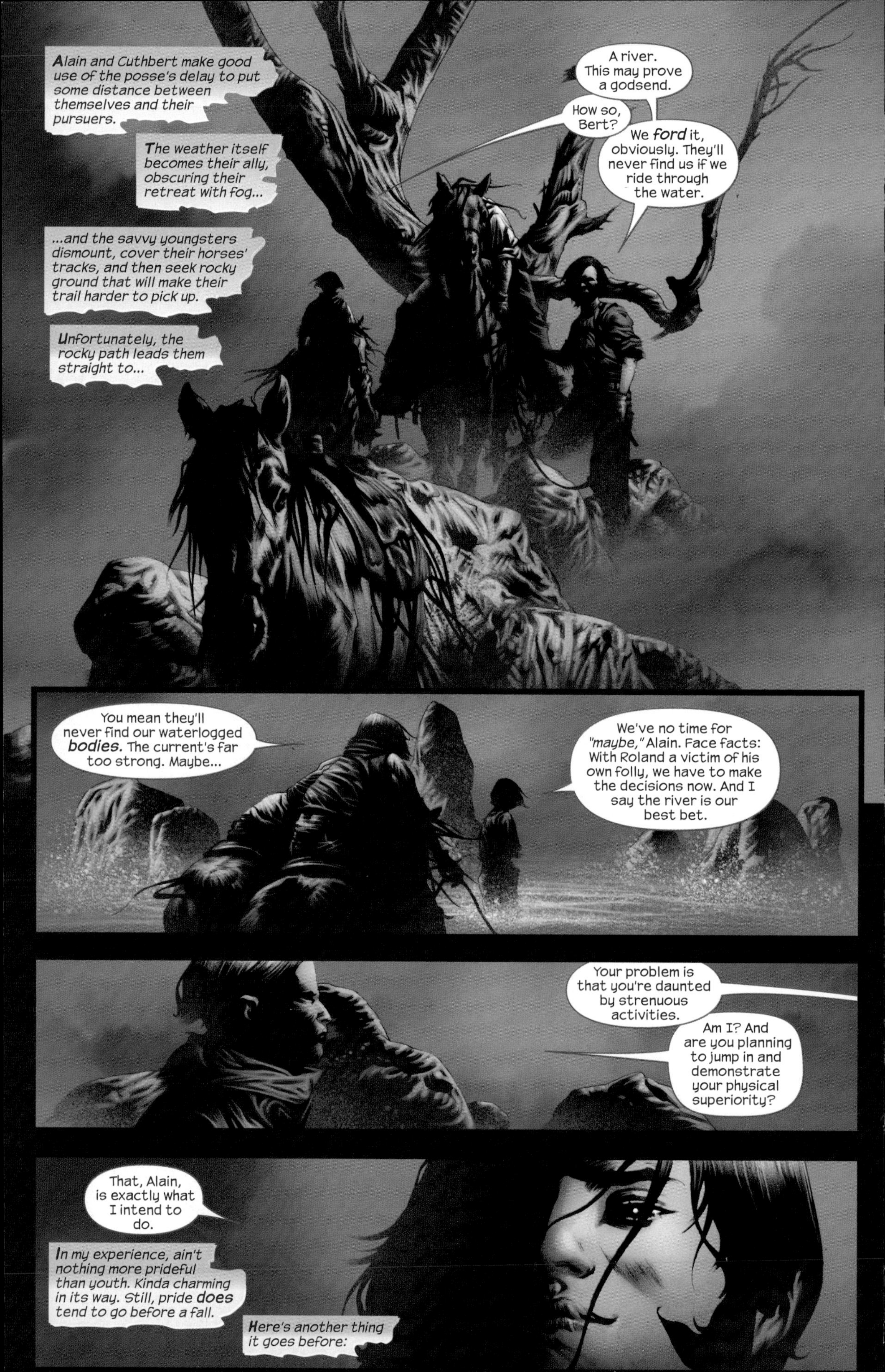
Alain and Cuthbert make good use of the posse's delay to put some distance between themselves and their pursuers.
The weather itself becomes their ally, obscuring their retreat with fog...
...and the savvy youngsters dismount, cover their horses' tracks, and then seek rocky ground that will make their trail harder to pick up.
Unfortunately, the rocky path leads them straight to...
A river. This may prove a godsend.
How so, Bert?
We ford it, obviously. They'll never find us if we ride through the water.
You mean they'll never find our waterlogged bodies. The current's far too strong. Maybe...
We've no time for "maybe," Alain. Face facts: With Roland a victim of his own folly, we have to make the decisions now. And I say the river is our best bet.
Your problem is that you're daunted by strenuous activities.
Am I? And are you planning to jump in and demonstrate your physical superiority?
That, Alain, is exactly what I intend to do.
In my experience, ain't nothing more prideful than youth. Kinda charming in its way. Still, pride does tend to go before a fall.
Here's another thing it goes before:

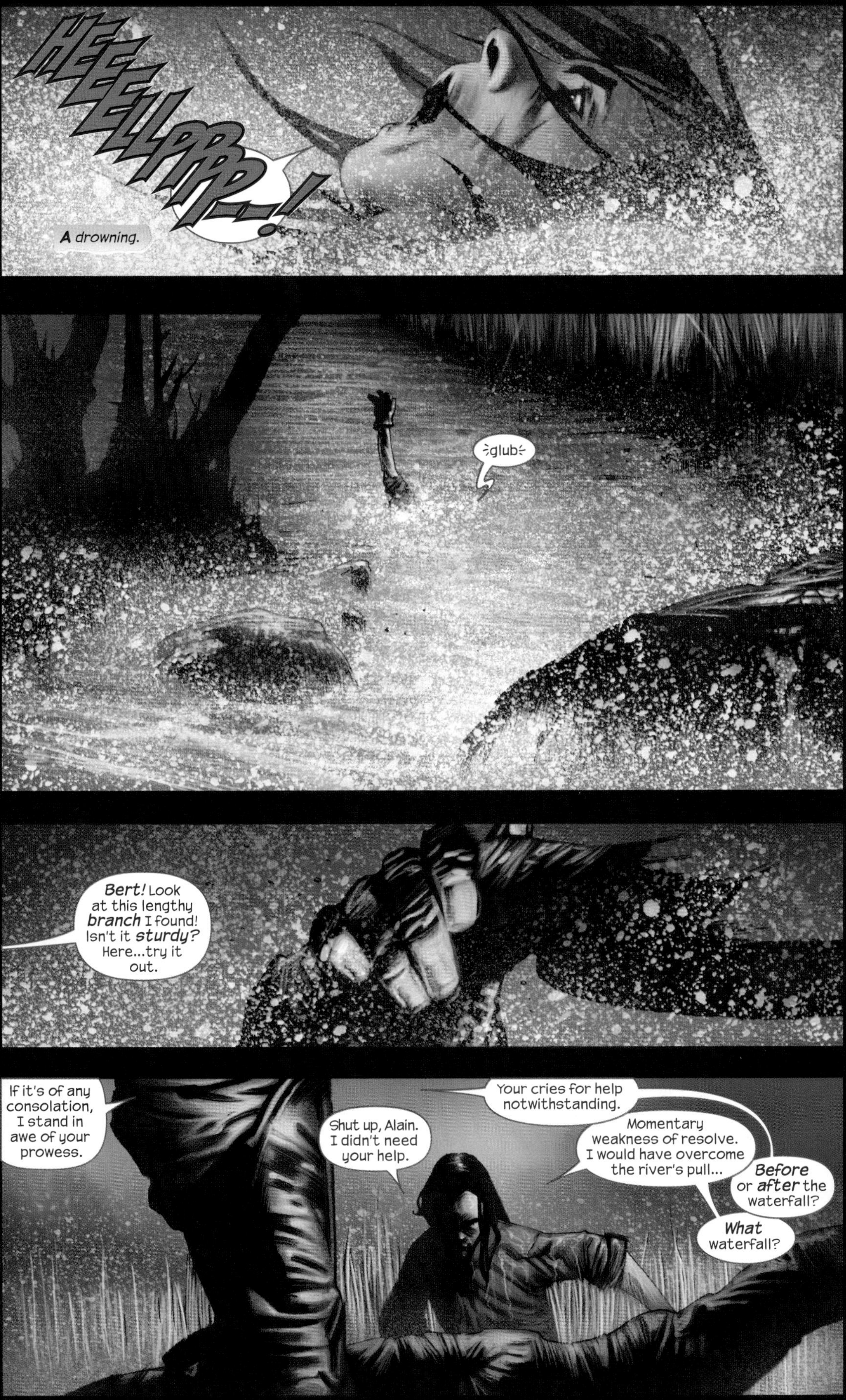
HEEELLPPP--!
A drowning.
glub
Bert! Look at this lengthy branch I found! Isn't it sturdy? Here...try it out.
If it's of any consolation, I stand in awe of your prowess.
Shut up, Alain. I didn't need your help.
Your cries for help notwithstanding.
Momentary weakness of resolve. I would have overcome the river's pull...
Before or after the waterfall?
What waterfall?

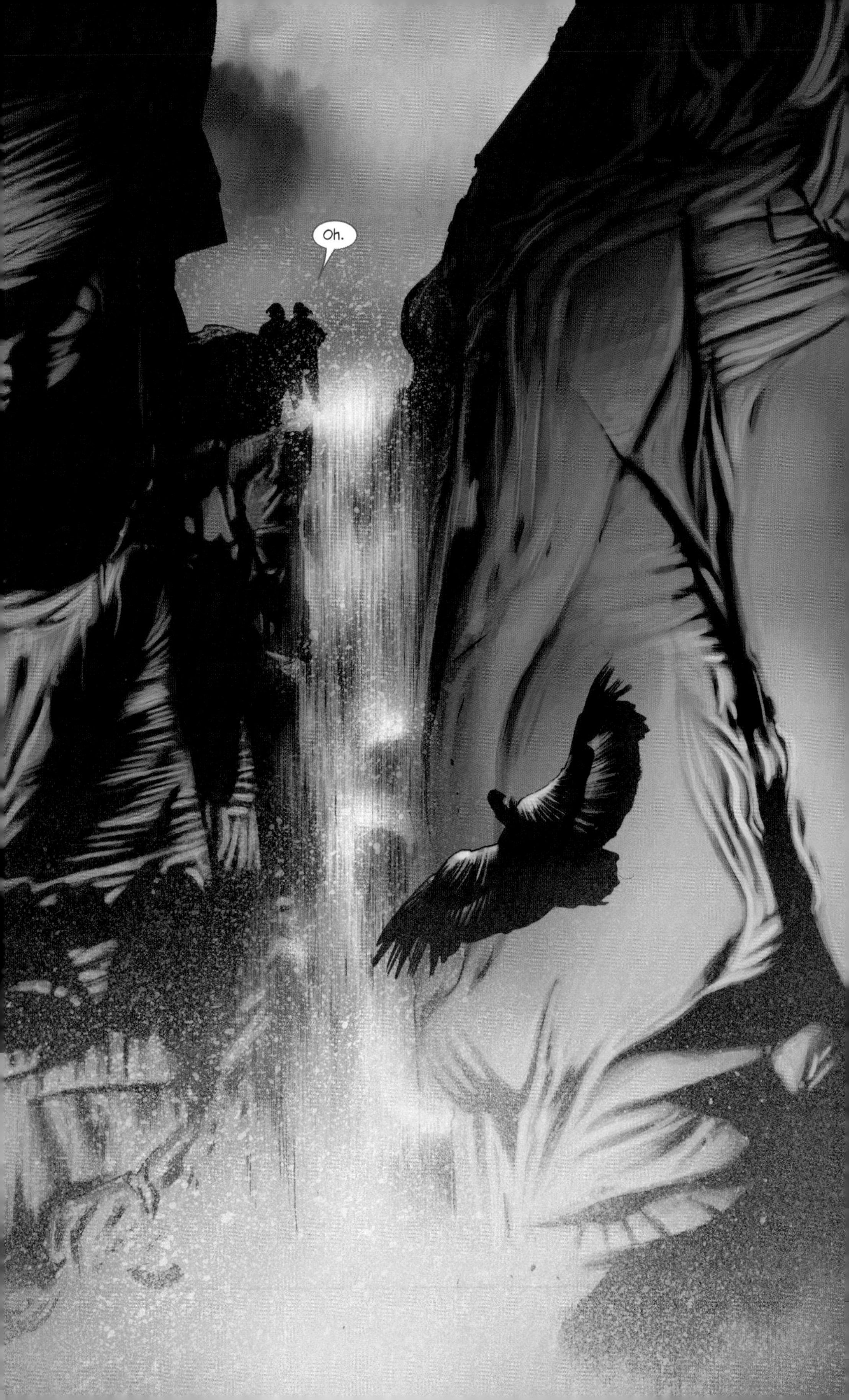
Oh.

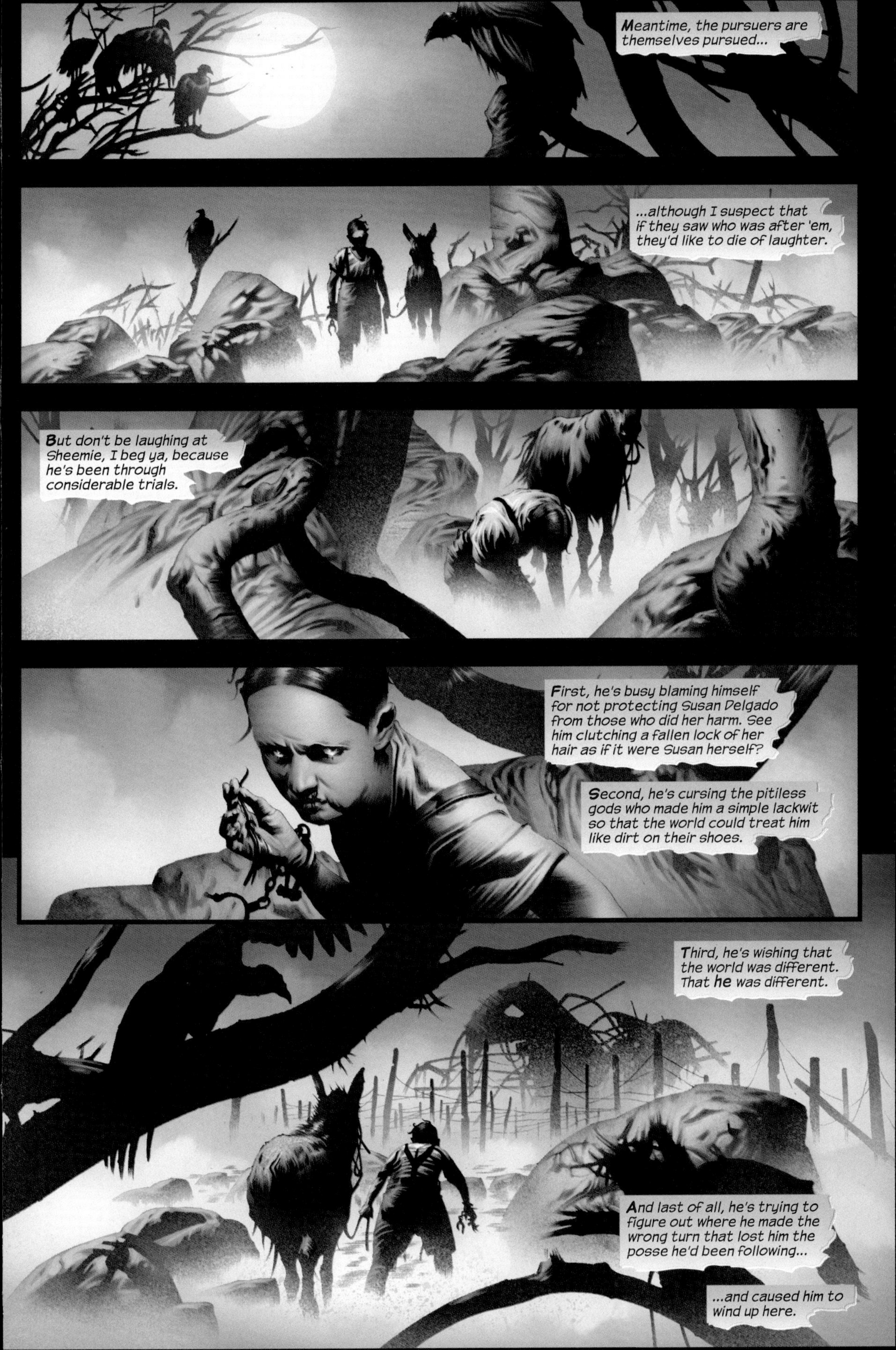
Meantime, the pursuers are themselves pursued...
...although I suspect that if they saw who was after 'em, they'd like to die of laughter.
But don't be laughing at Sheemie, I beg ya, because he's been through considerable trials.
First, he's busy blaming himself for not protecting Susan Delgado from those who did her harm. See him clutching a fallen lock of her hair as if it were Susan herself?
Second, he's cursing the pitiless gods who made him a simple lackwit so that the world could treat him like dirt on their shoes.
Third, he's wishing that the world was different. That he was different.
And last of all, he's trying to figure out where he made the wrong turn that lost him the posse he'd been following...
...and caused him to wind up here.

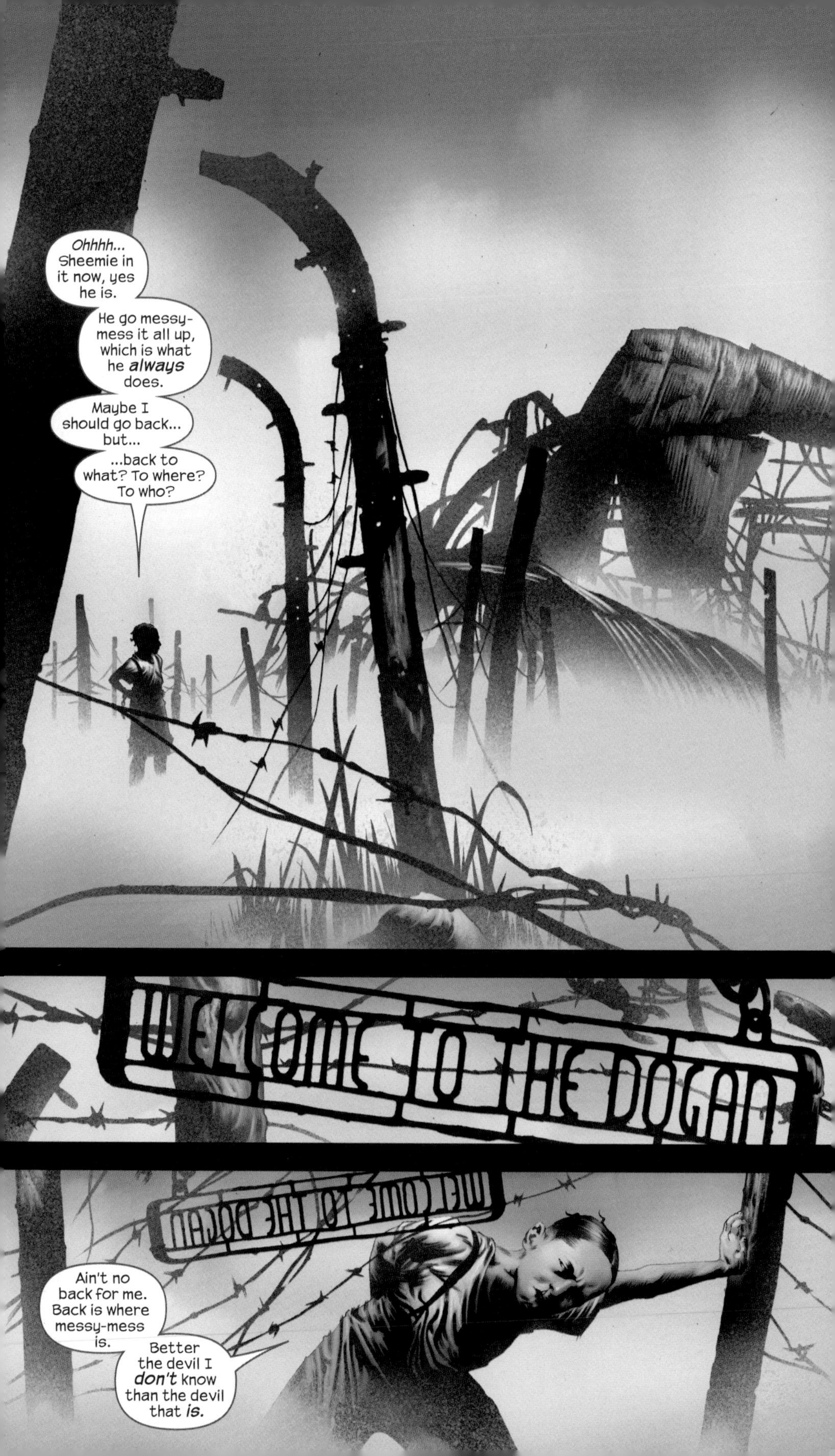

Ohhhh... Sheemie in it now, yes he is.
He go messy-mess it all up, which is what he *always* does.
Maybe I should go back... but...
...back to what? To where? To who?
WELCOME TO THE DOGAN
Ain't no back for me. Back is where messy-mess is.
Better the devil I *don't* know than the devil that *is.*

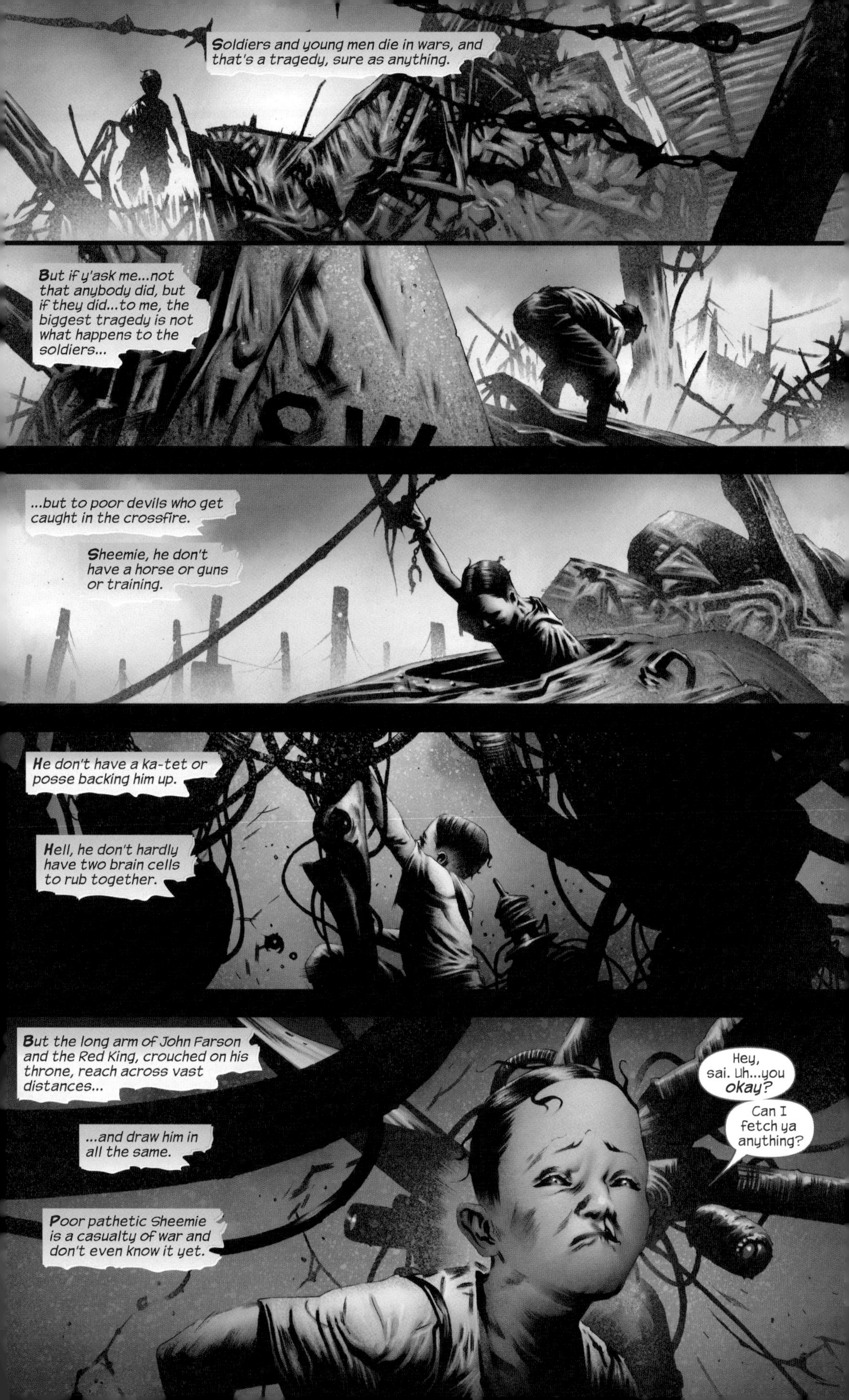
Soldiers and young men die in wars, and that's a tragedy, sure as anything.
But if y'ask me...not that anybody did, but if they did...to me, the biggest tragedy is not what happens to the soldiers...
...but to poor devils who get caught in the crossfire.
Sheemie, he don't have a horse or guns or training.
He don't have a ka-tet or posse backing him up.
Hell, he don't hardly have two brain cells to rub together.
But the long arm of John Farson and the Red King, crouched on his throne, reach across vast distances...
...and draw him in all the same.
Poor pathetic Sheemie is a casualty of war and don't even know it yet.
Hey, sai. Uh...you okay?
Can I fetch ya anything?

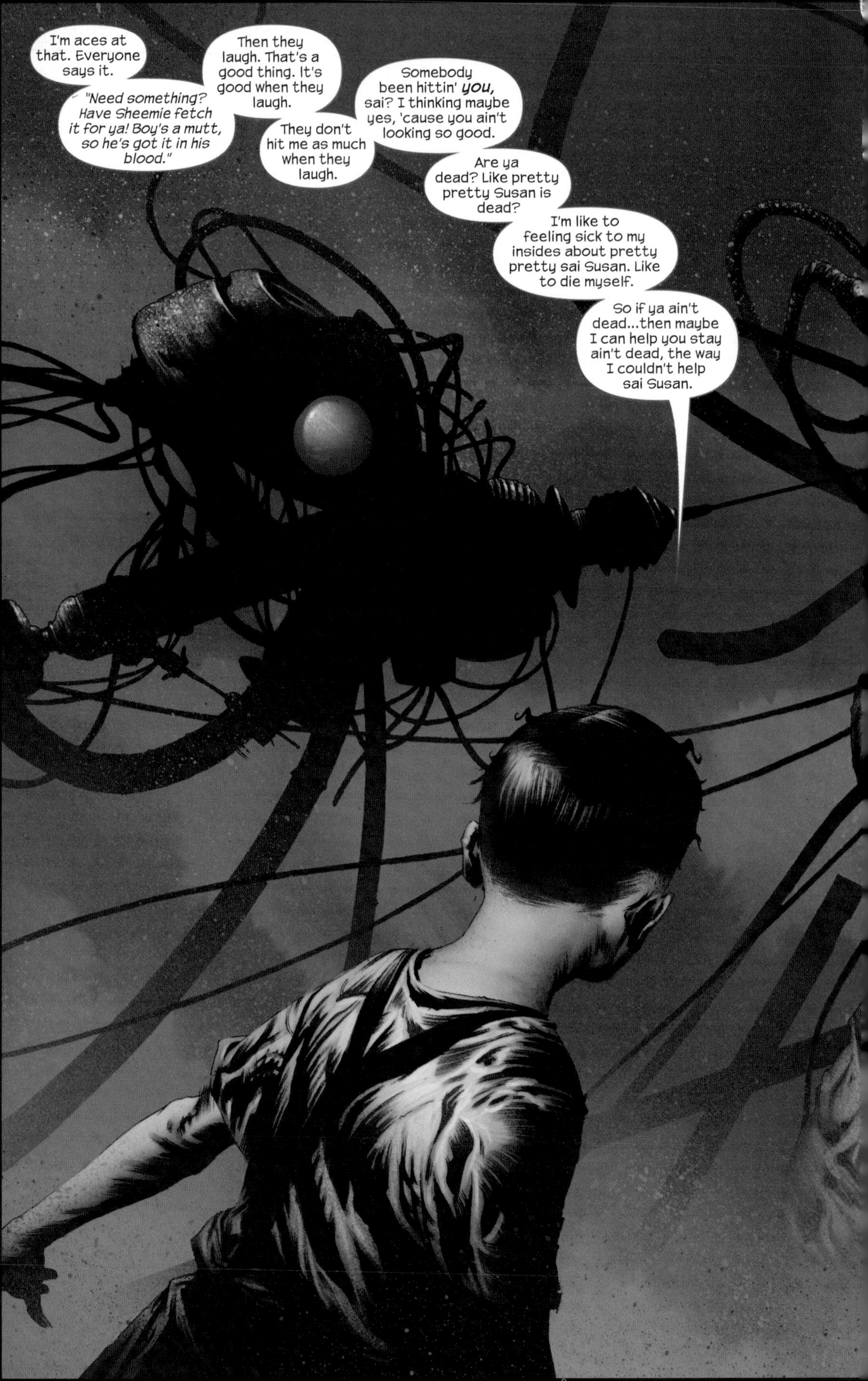
I'm aces at that. Everyone says it.
"Need something? Have Sheemie fetch it for ya! Boy's a mutt, so he's got it in his blood."
Then they laugh. That's a good thing. It's good when they laugh.
They don't hit me as much when they laugh.
Somebody been hittin' *you,* sai? I thinking maybe yes, 'cause you ain't looking so good.
Are ya dead? Like pretty pretty Susan is dead?
I'm like to feeling sick to my insides about pretty pretty sai Susan. Like to die myself.
So if ya ain't dead...then maybe I can help you stay ain't dead, the way I couldn't help sai Susan.

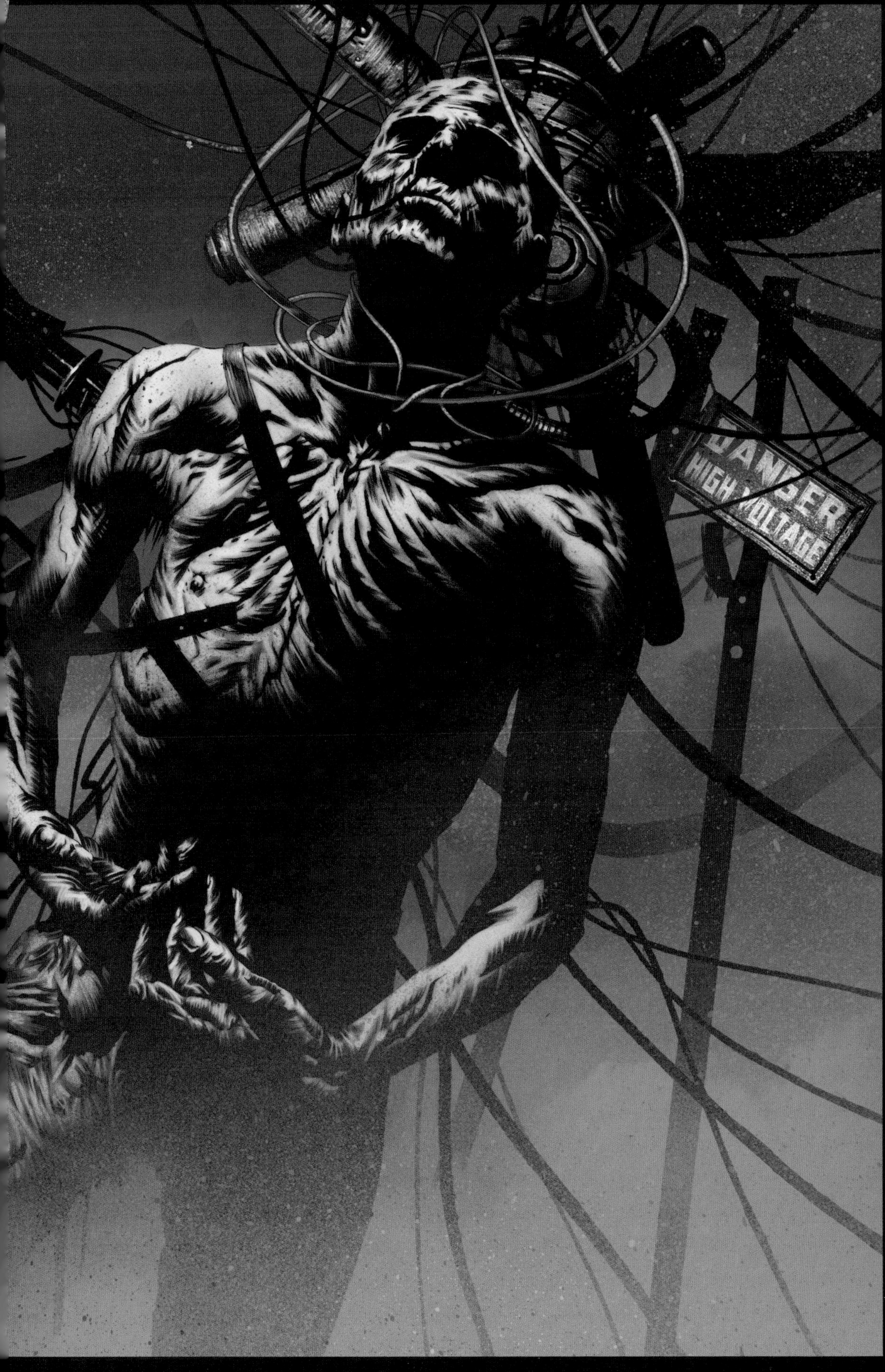
DANGER
HIGH VOLTAGE

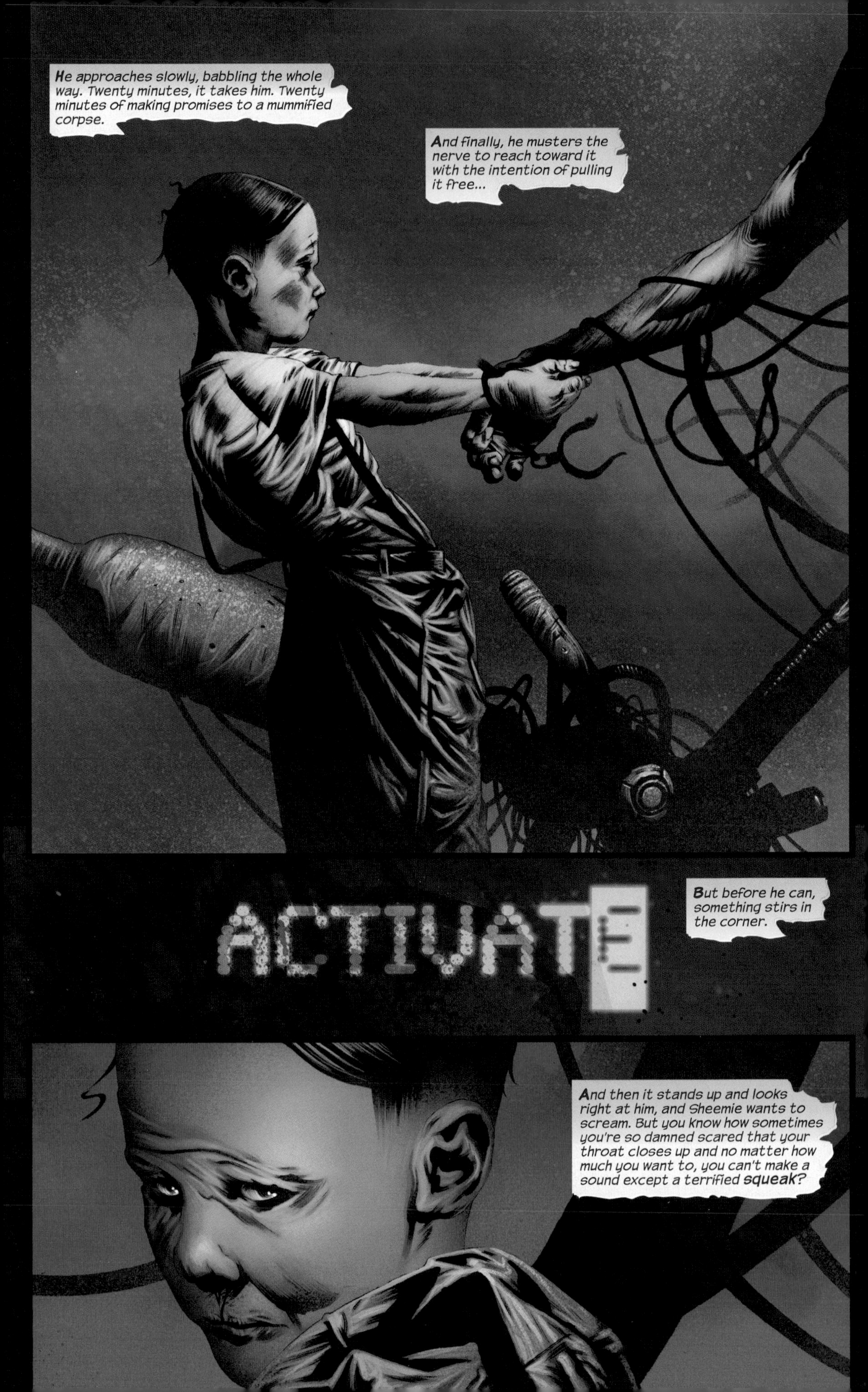
He approaches slowly, babbling the whole way. Twenty minutes, it takes him. Twenty minutes of making promises to a mummified corpse.
And finally, he musters the nerve to reach toward it with the intention of pulling it free...
ACTIVATE
But before he can, something stirs in the corner.
And then it stands up and looks right at him, and Sheemie wants to scream. But you know how sometimes you're so damned scared that your throat closes up and no matter how much you want to, you can't make a sound except a terrified squeak?

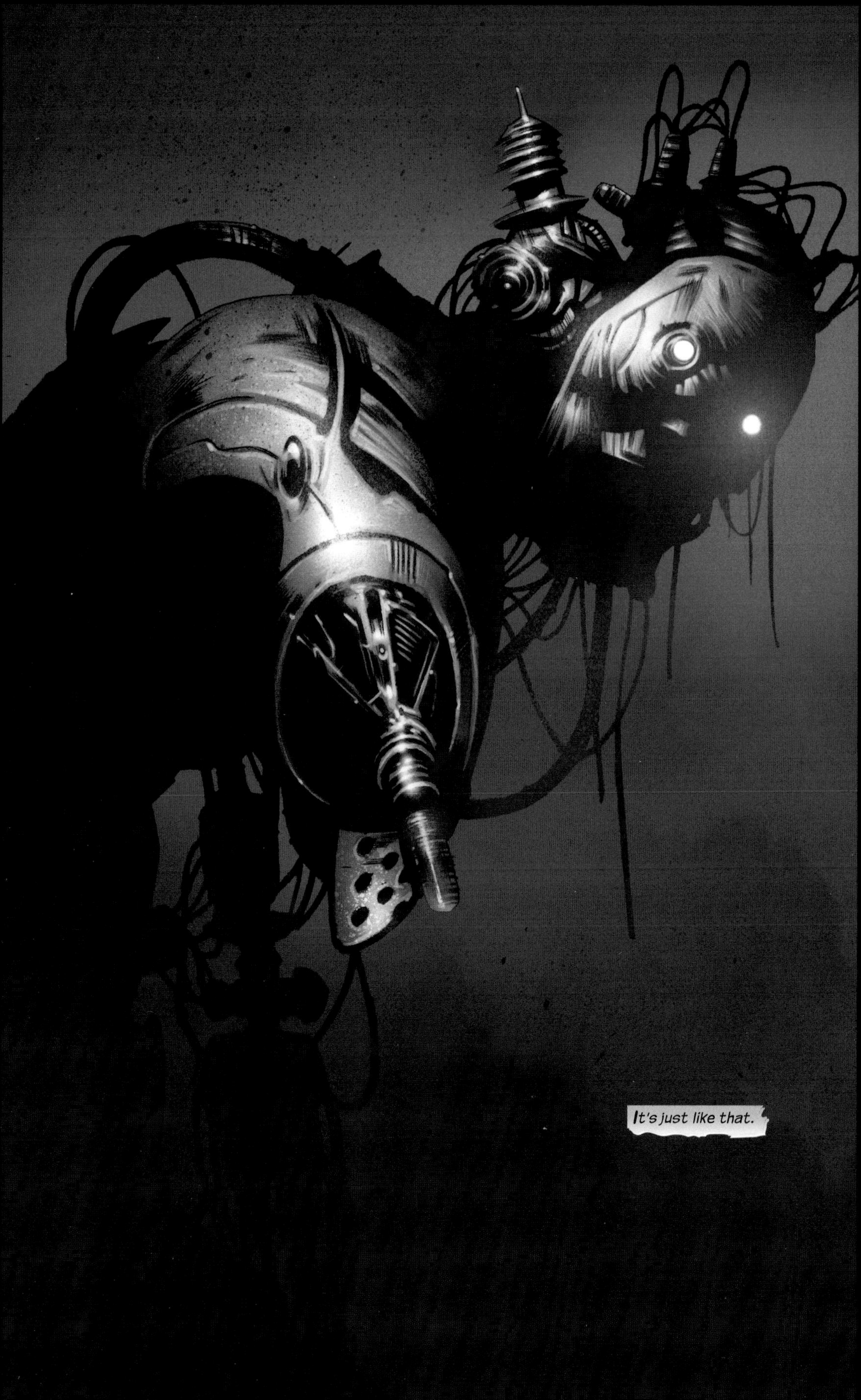
It's just like that.

STEPHEN KING

THE DARK TOWER

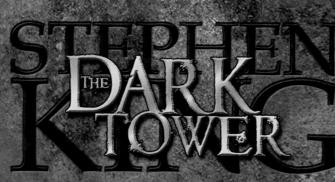

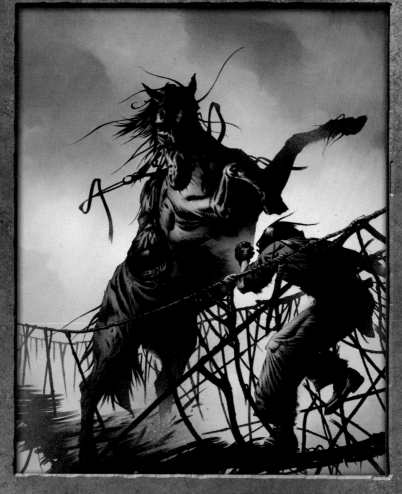

THE LONG ROAD HOME

CHAPTER TWO

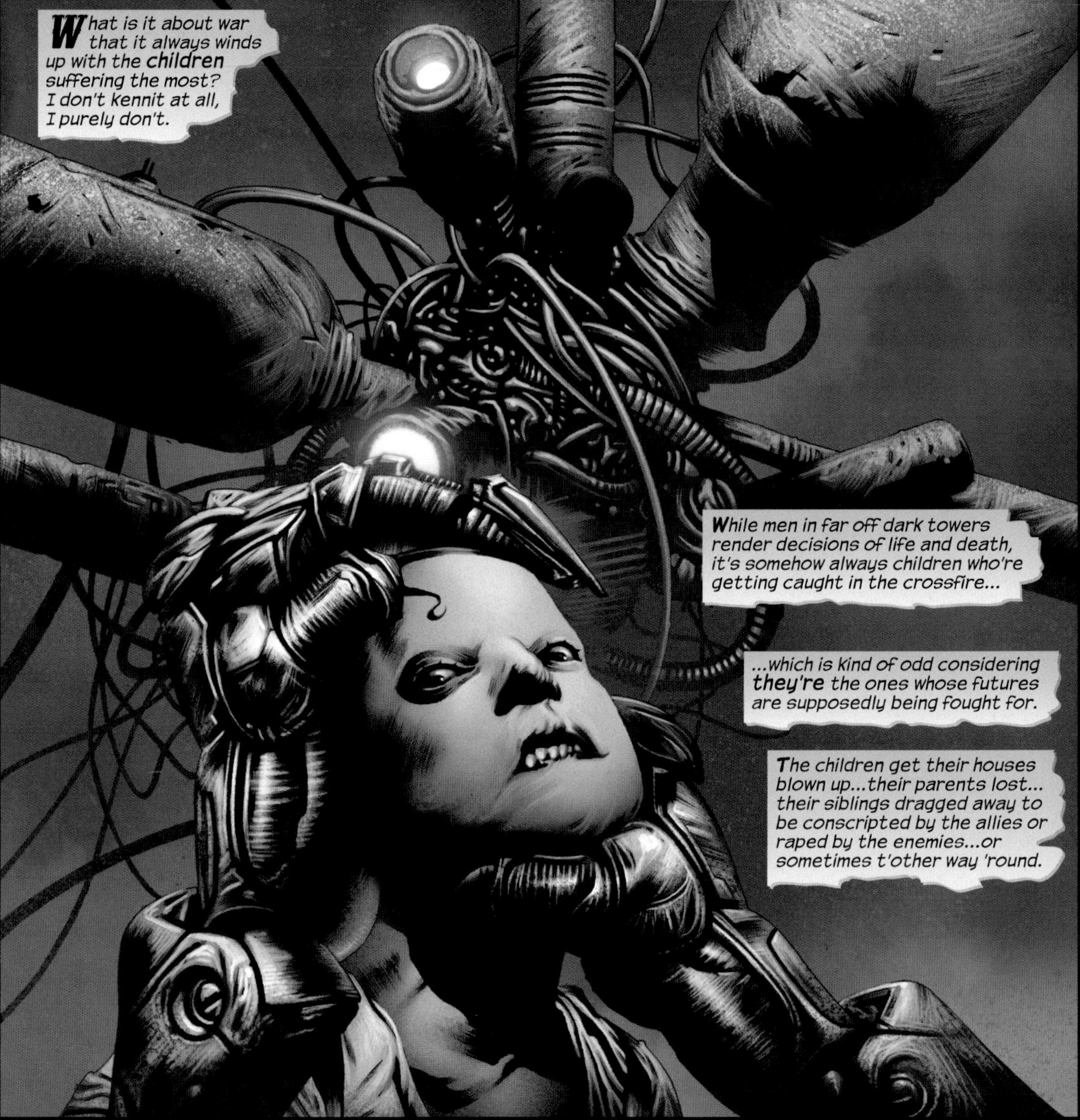
What is it about war that it always winds up with the children suffering the most? I don't kennit at all, I purely don't.
While men in far off dark towers render decisions of life and death, it's somehow always children who're getting caught in the crossfire...
...which is kind of odd considering they're the ones whose futures are supposedly being fought for.
The children get their houses blown up...their parents lost... their siblings dragged away to be conscripted by the allies or raped by the enemies...or sometimes t'other way 'round.

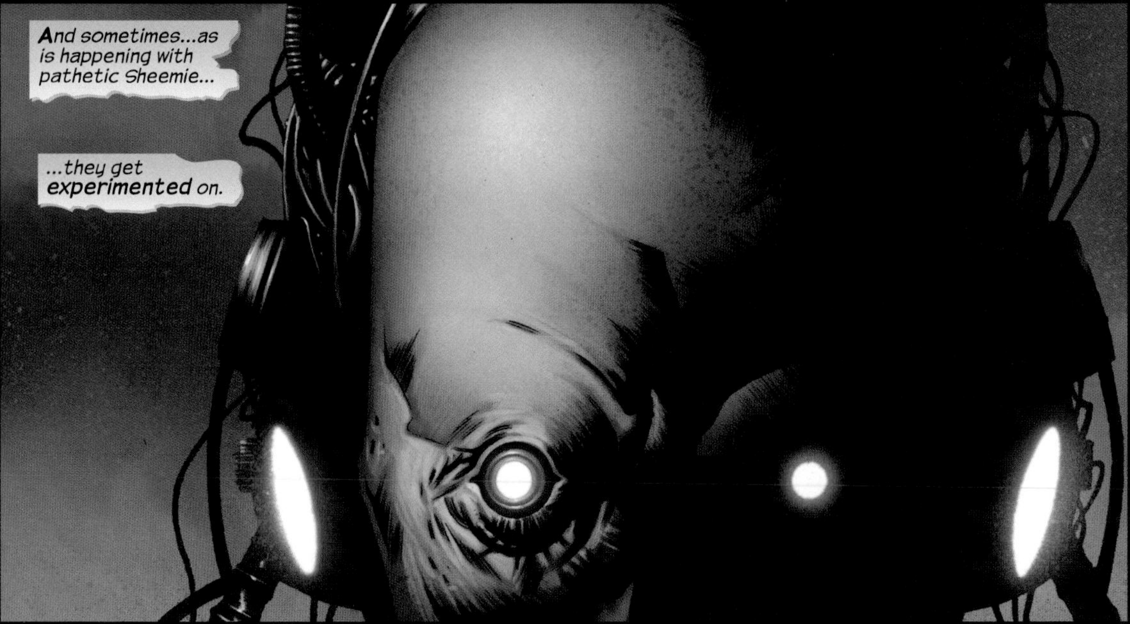
And sometimes...as is happening with pathetic Sheemie...
...they get experimented on.

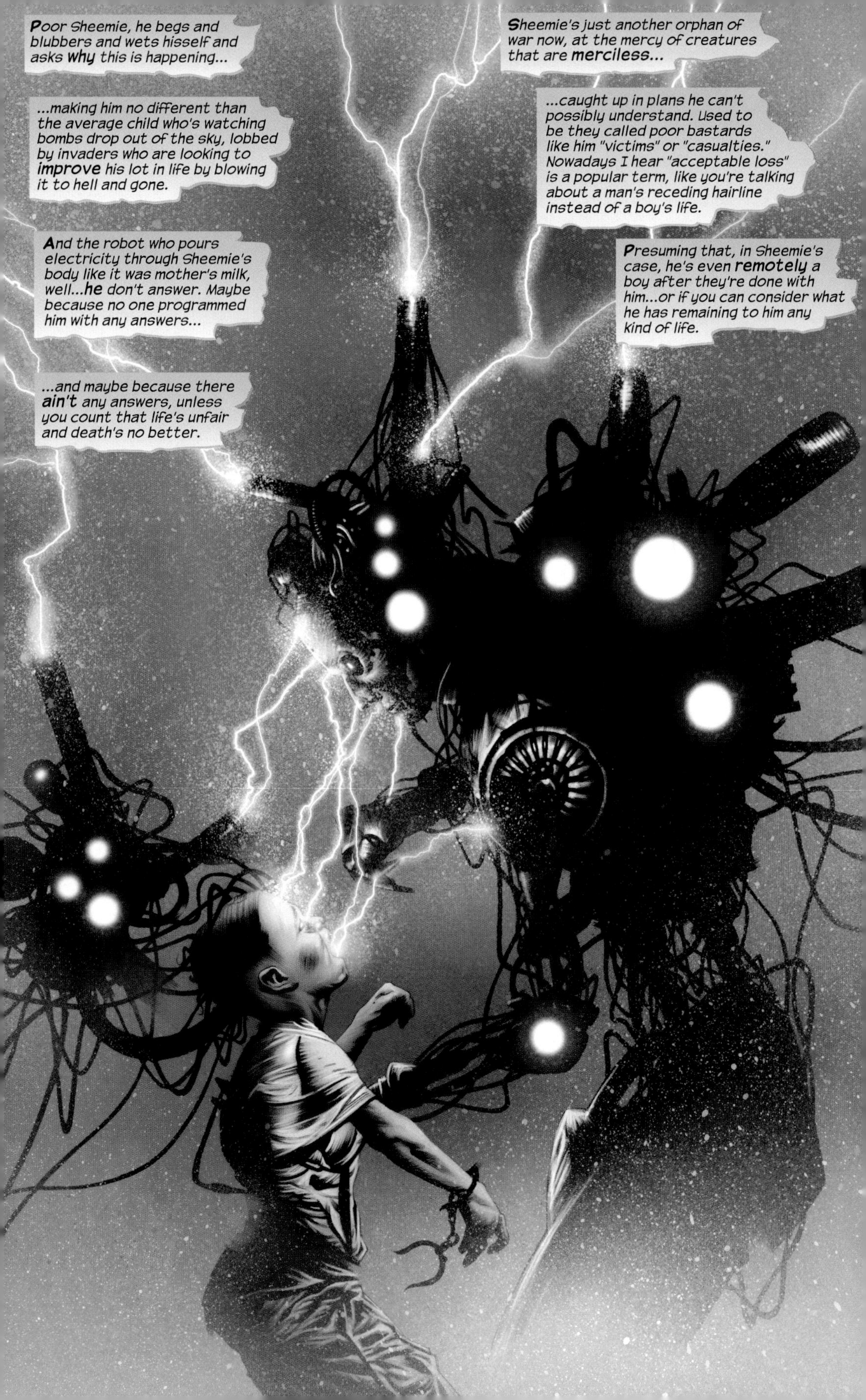
Poor Sheemie, he begs and blubbers and wets hisself and asks why this is happening...
...making him no different than the average child who's watching bombs drop out of the sky, lobbed by invaders who are looking to improve his lot in life by blowing it to hell and gone.
And the robot who pours electricity through Sheemie's body like it was mother's milk, well...he don't answer. Maybe because no one programmed him with any answers...
...and maybe because there ain't any answers, unless you count that life's unfair and death's no better.
Sheemie's just another orphan of war now, at the mercy of creatures that are merciless...
...caught up in plans he can't possibly understand. Used to be they called poor bastards like him "victims" or "casualties." Nowadays I hear "acceptable loss" is a popular term, like you're talking about a man's receding hairline instead of a boy's life.
Presuming that, in Sheemie's case, he's even remotely a boy after they're done with him...or if you can consider what he has remaining to him any kind of life.

'Course, there's two kinds of children in war...the **victims** of it...
...and those who **wage** it. Children fighting the good fight and singing hosannahs as they march to their graves.

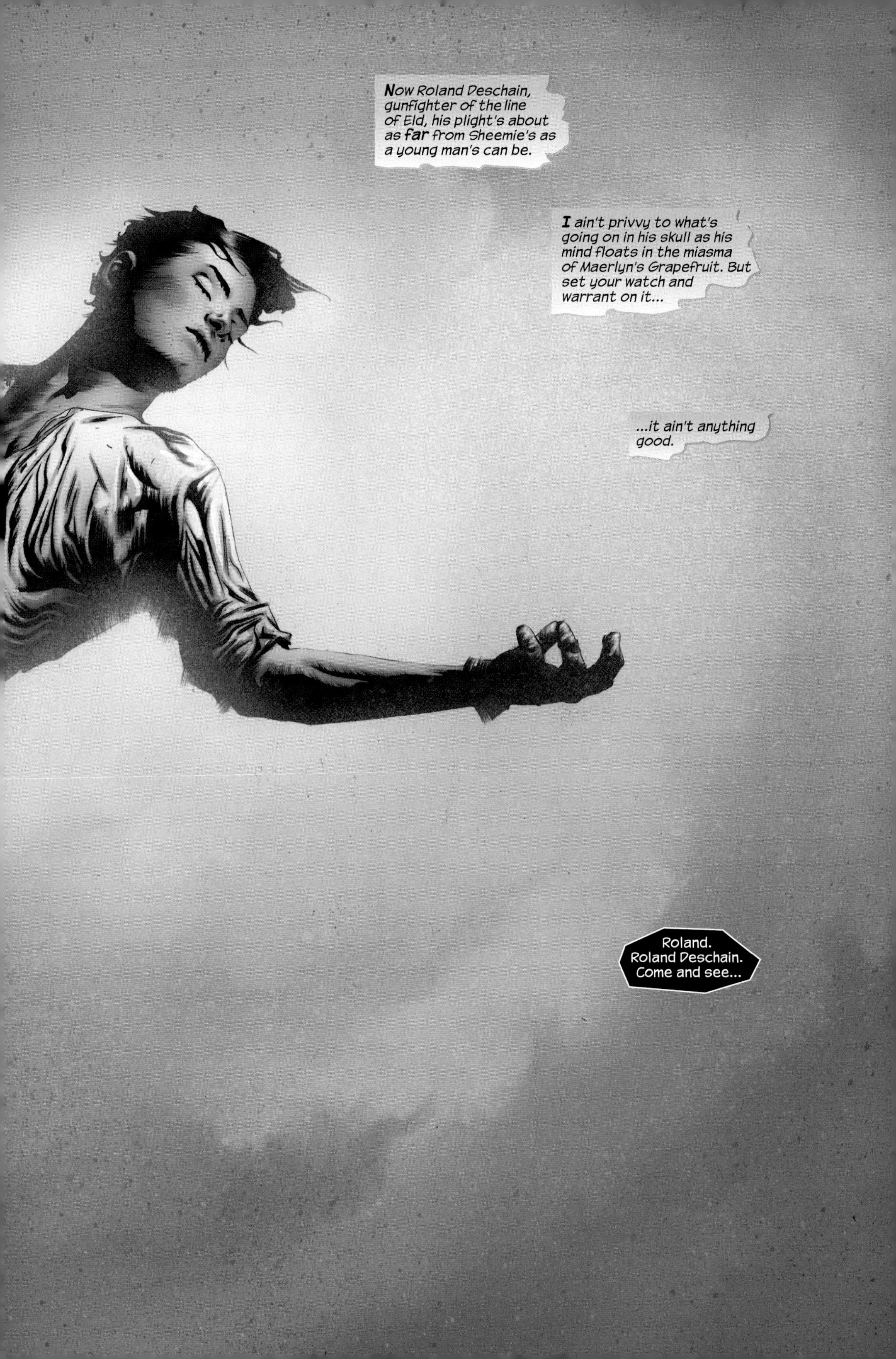
Now Roland Deschain, gunfighter of the line of Eld, his plight's about as **far** from Sheemie's as a young man's can be.
I ain't privvy to what's going on in his skull as his mind floats in the miasma of Maerlyn's Grapefruit. But set your watch and warrant on it...
...it ain't anything good.
Roland. Roland Deschain. Come and see...

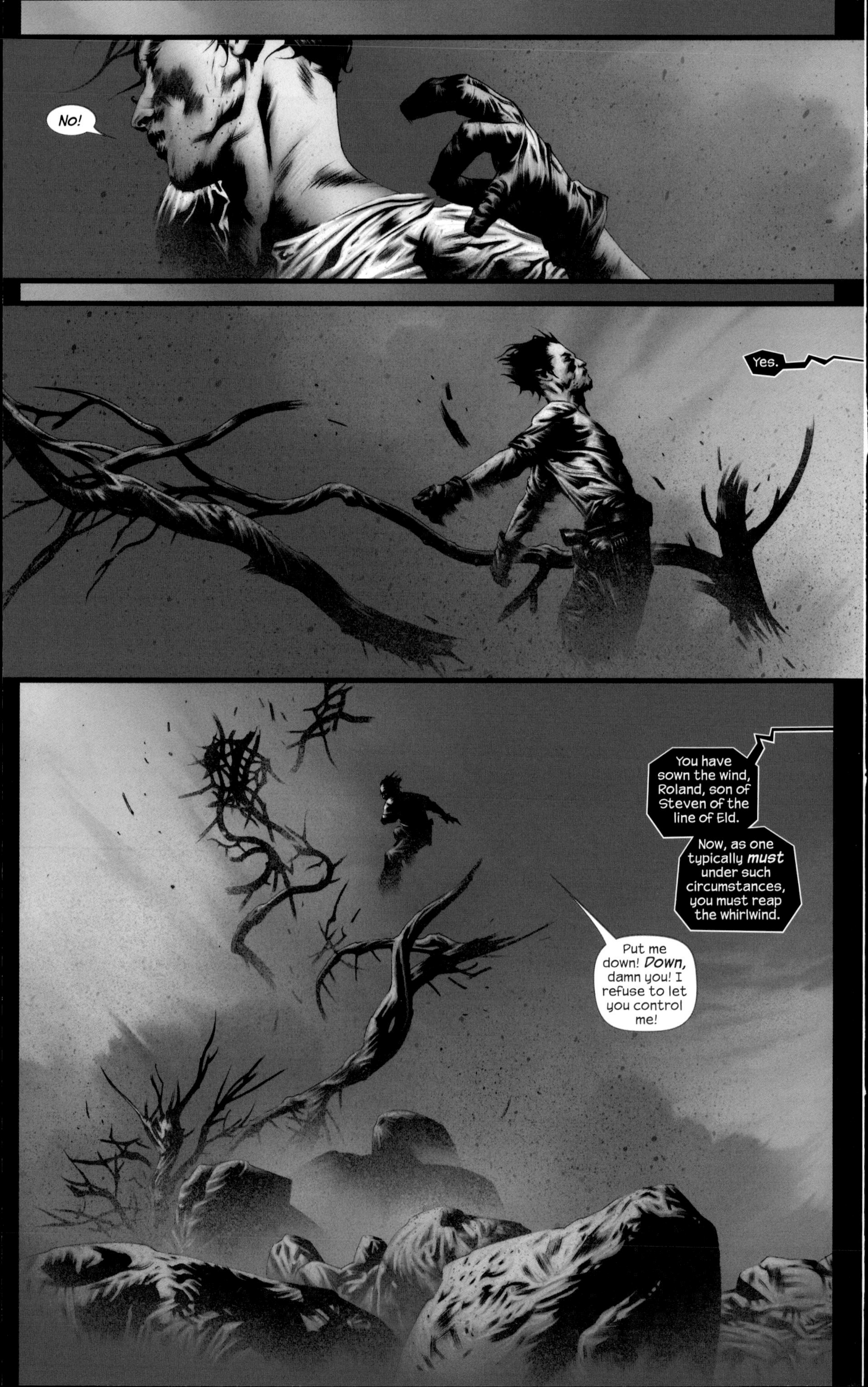
No!
Yes.
You have sown the wind, Roland, son of Steven of the line of Eld.
Now, as one typically *must* under such circumstances, you must reap the whirlwind.
Put me down! *Down,* damn you! I refuse to let you control me!

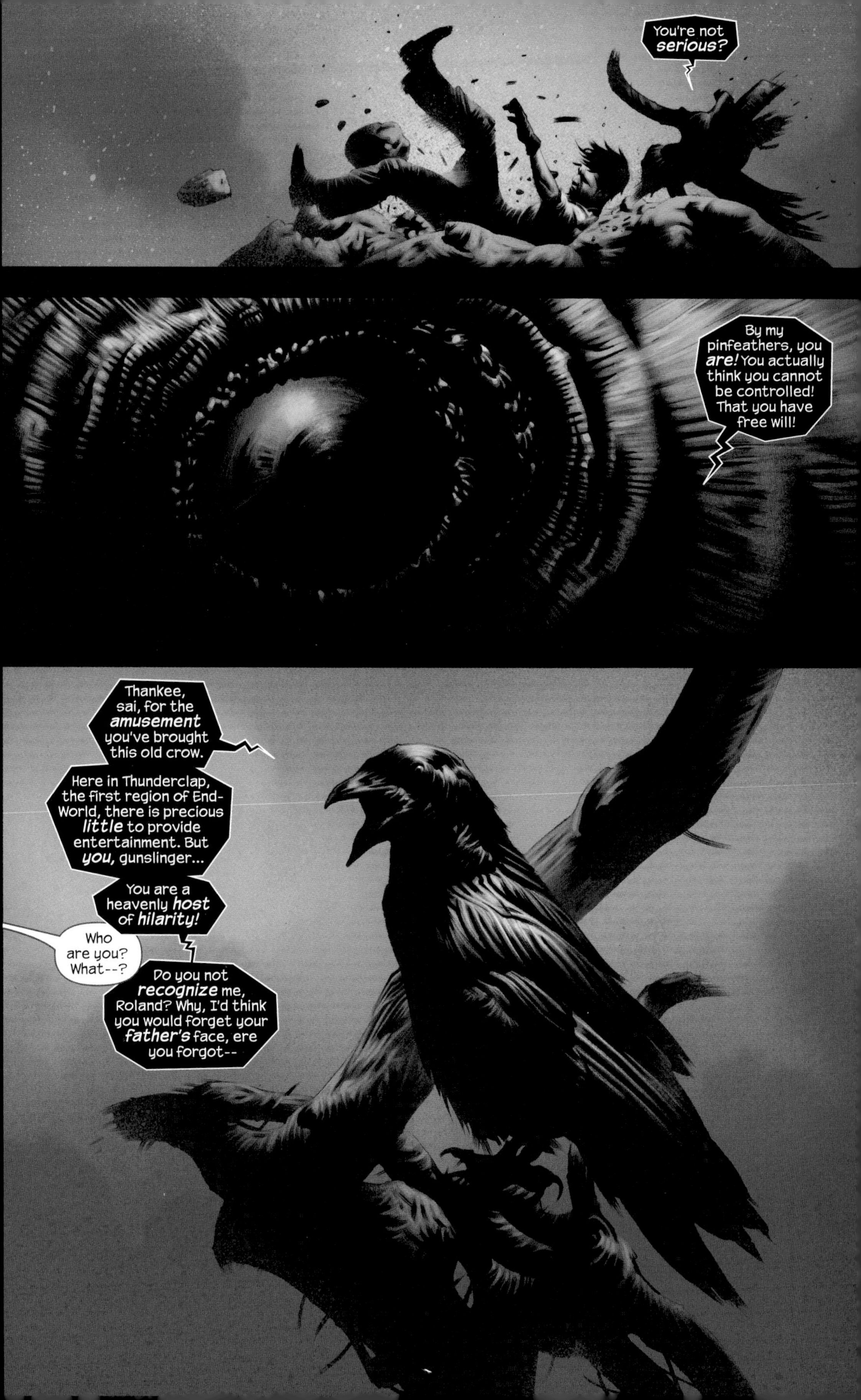

You're not *serious?*
By my pinfeathers, you *are!* You actually think you cannot be controlled! That you have free will!
Thankee, sai, for the *amusement* you've brought this old crow.
Here in Thunderclap, the first region of End-World, there is precious *little* to provide entertainment. But *you,* gunslinger...
You are a heavenly *host* of *hilarity!*
Who are you? What--?
Do you not *recognize* me, Roland? Why, I'd think you would forget your *father's* face, ere you forgot--

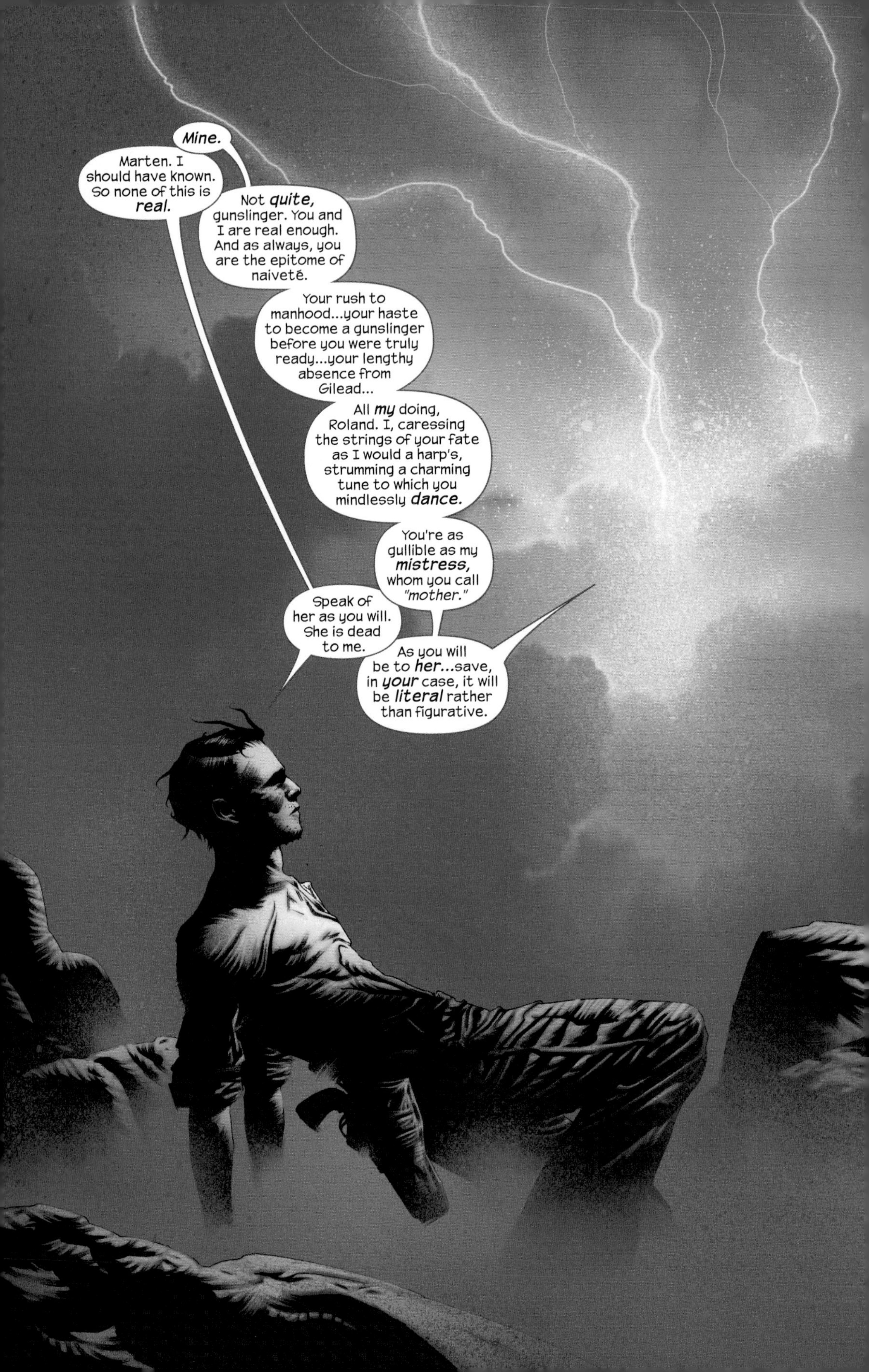
Mine.
Marten. I should have known. So none of this is *real.*
Not *quite,* gunslinger. You and I are real enough. And as always, you are the epitome of naiveté.
Your rush to manhood...your haste to become a gunslinger before you were truly ready...your lengthy absence from Gilead...
All *my* doing, Roland. I, caressing the strings of your fate as I would a harp's, strumming a charming tune to which you mindlessly *dance.*
You're as gullible as my *mistress,* whom you call *"mother."*
Speak of her as you will. She is dead to me.
As you will be to *her...*save, in *your* case, it will be *literal* rather than figurative.

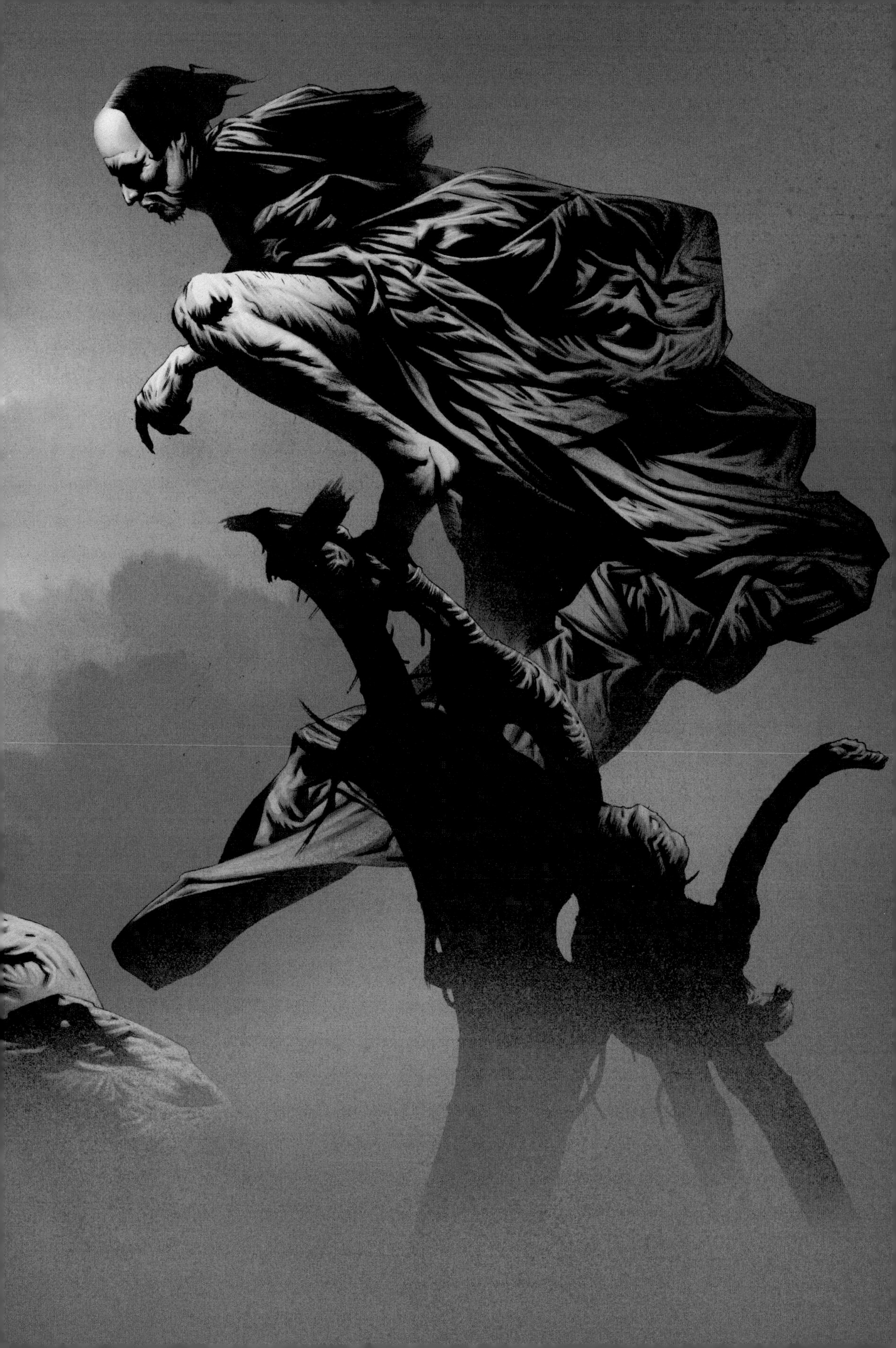

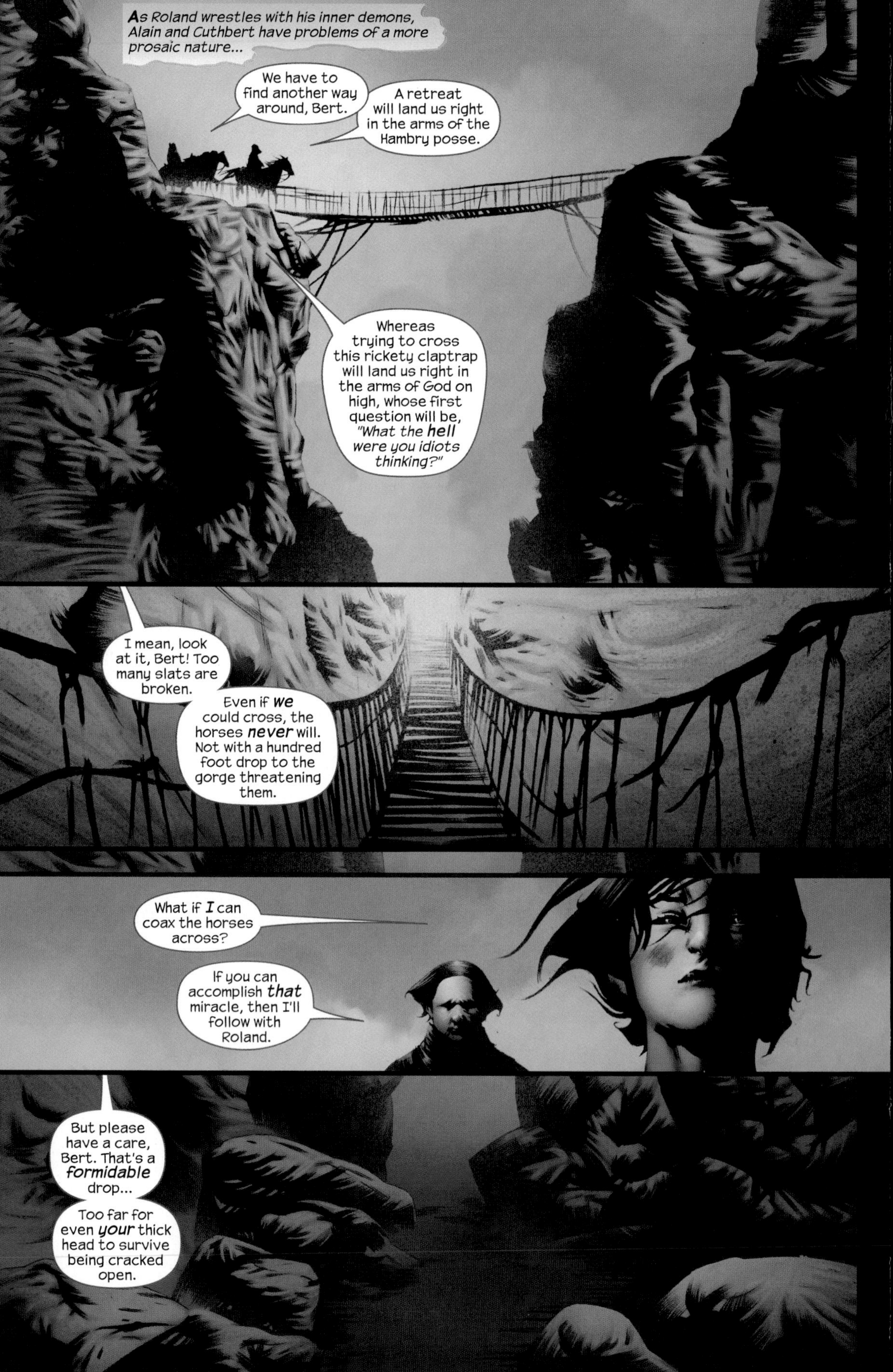

As Roland wrestles with his inner demons, Alain and Cuthbert have problems of a more prosaic nature...
We have to find another way around, Bert.
A retreat will land us right in the arms of the Hambry posse.
Whereas trying to cross this rickety claptrap will land us right in the arms of God on high, whose first question will be, "What the hell were you idiots thinking?"
I mean, look at it, Bert! Too many slats are broken.
Even if we could cross, the horses never will. Not with a hundred foot drop to the gorge threatening them.
What if I can coax the horses across?
If you can accomplish that miracle, then I'll follow with Roland.
But please have a care, Bert. That's a formidable drop...
Too far for even your thick head to survive being cracked open.

I'll be damned. He's actually managed to get two horses across already. But the third--his *own* mount--always *was* the most skittish of the three.
Roland, you were the *only* one who could ever talk sense into him, on those rare occasions *anyone* could.
A tragic time for you to be ensnared into a Grapefruit-induced coma, I must say.
Bert, please reconsider! I fear for you--!
Come now, Alain! Does it annoy you *that* much, seeing me accomplish what you swore I couldn't, that you have to make a last ditch effort to stop me? Why, this hardy beast isn't fazed in the slightest by--
Uh-oh.
Come now, girl...don't make a *liar* of me.

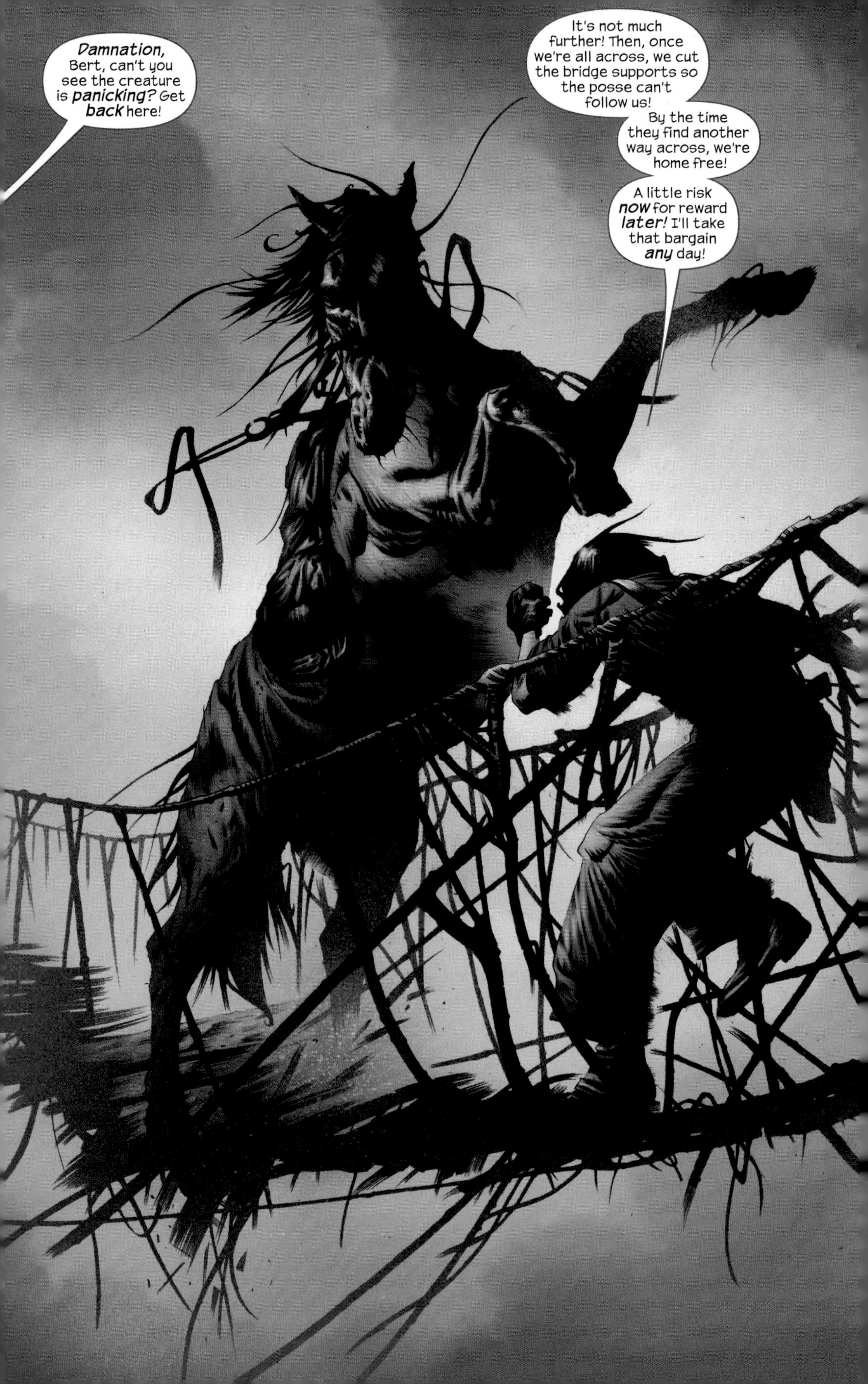
Damnation, Bert, can't you see the creature is panicking? Get back here!
It's not much further! Then, once we're all across, we cut the bridge supports so the posse can't follow us!
By the time they find another way across, we're home free!
A little risk now for reward later! I'll take that bargain any day!

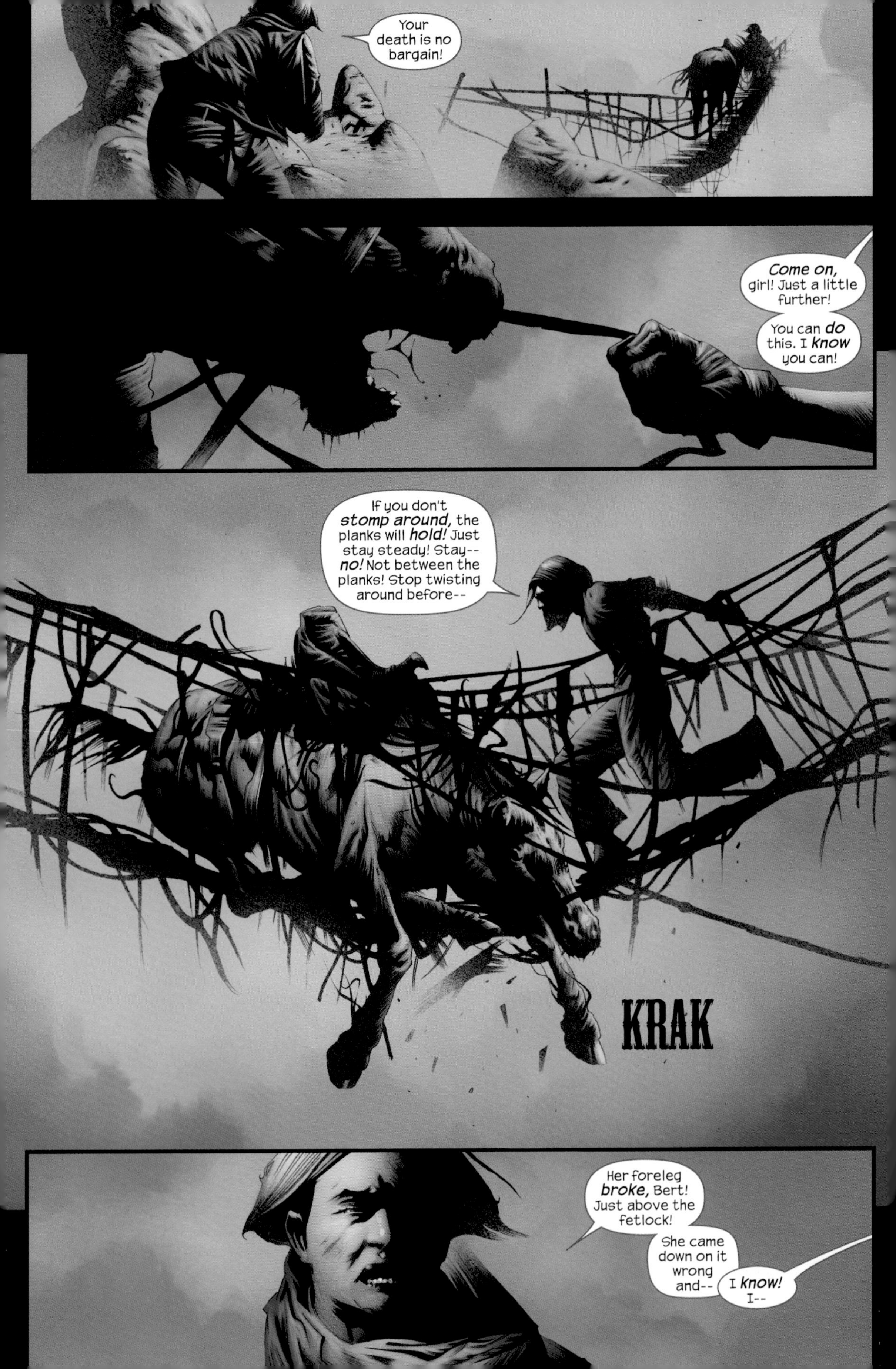
Your death is no bargain!
Come on, girl! Just a little further!
You can *do* this. I *know* you can!
If you don't *stomp around,* the planks will *hold!* Just stay steady! Stay-- *no!* Not between the planks! Stop twisting around before--
KRAK
Her foreleg *broke,* Bert! Just above the fetlock!
She came down on it wrong and--
I *know!* I--

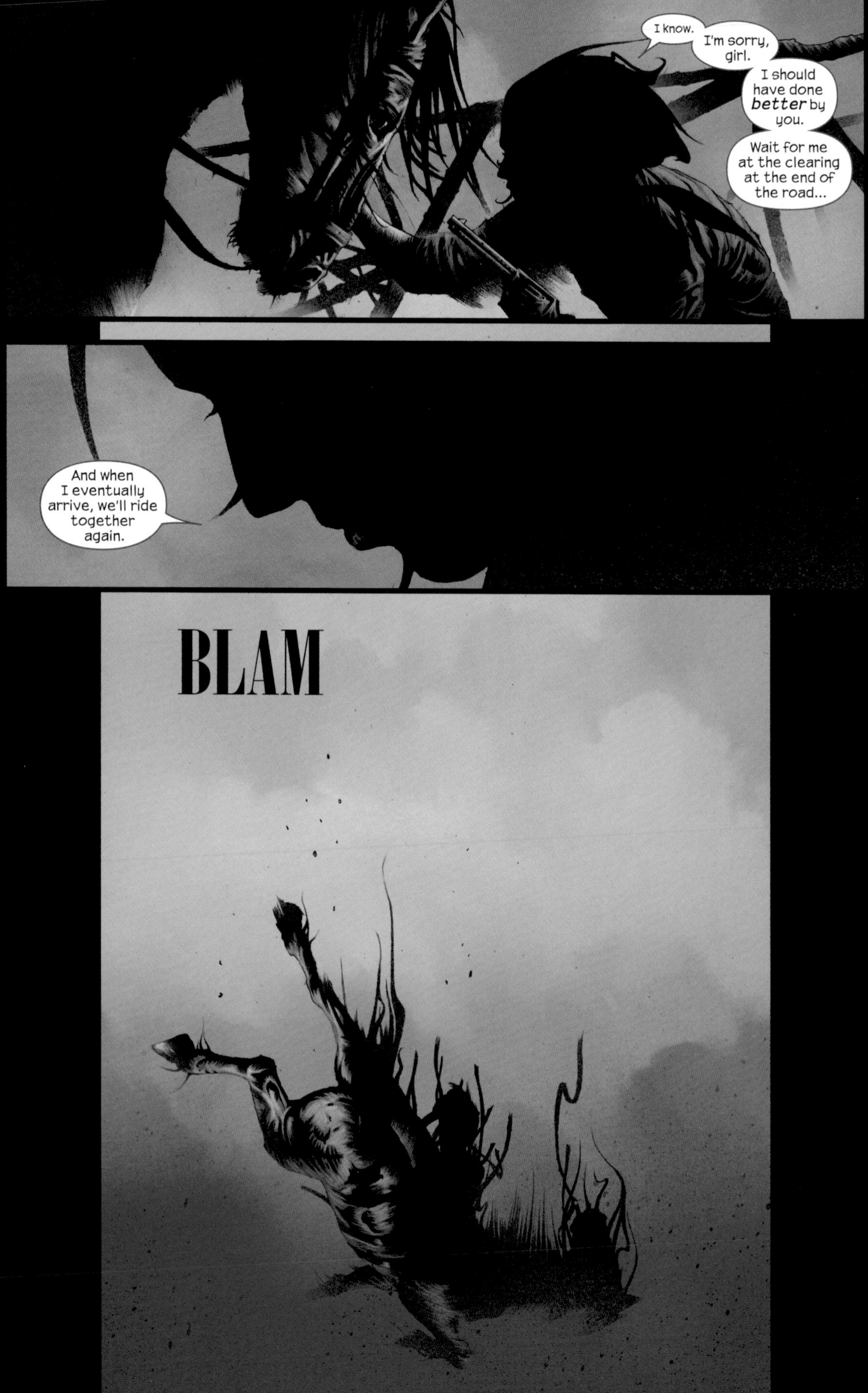
I know.
I'm sorry, girl.
I should have done better by you.
Wait for me at the clearing at the end of the road...
And when I eventually arrive, we'll ride together again.
BLAM

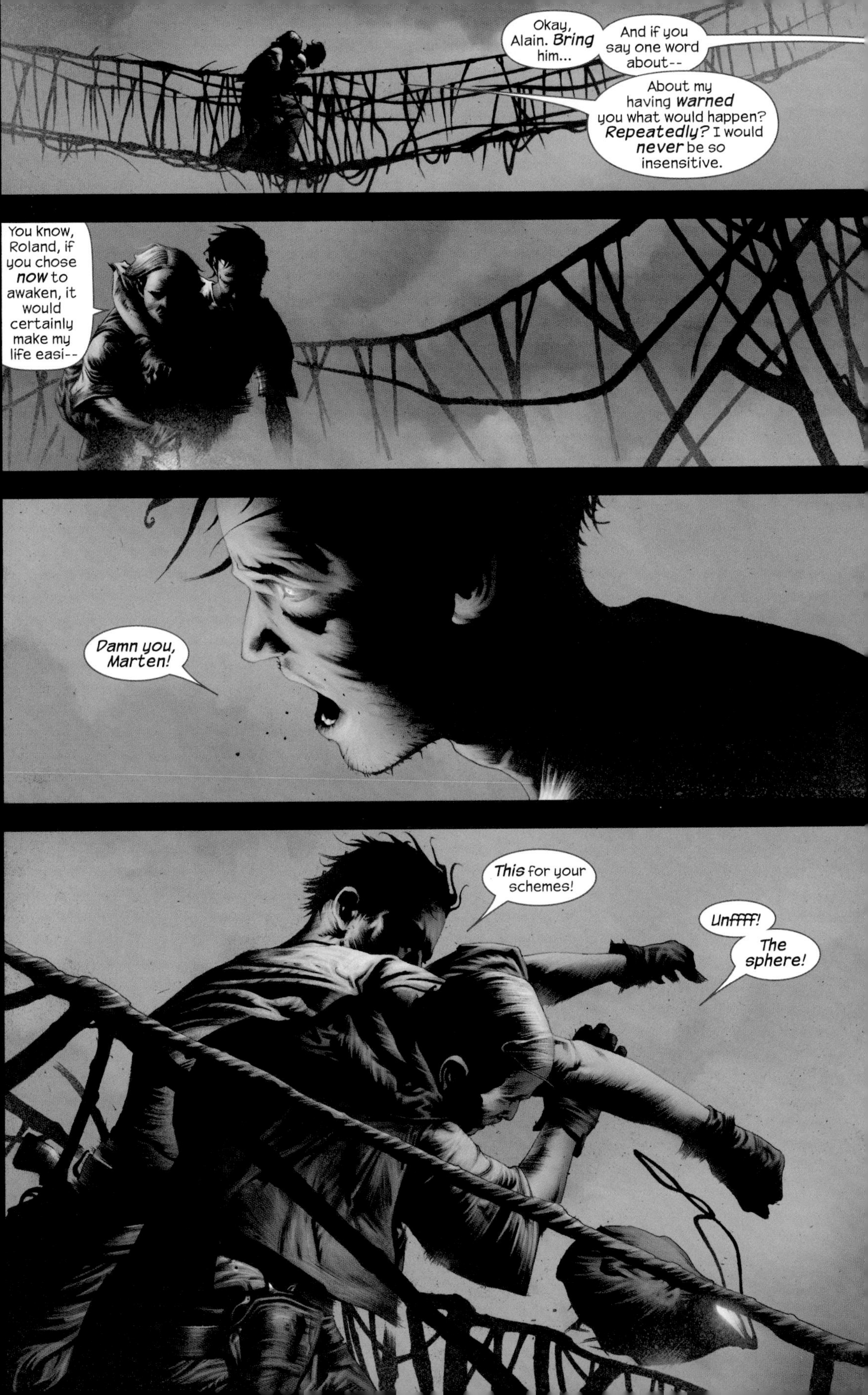
Okay, Alain. Bring him...
And if you say one word about--
About my having warned you what would happen? Repeatedly? I would never be so insensitive.
You know, Roland, if you chose now to awaken, it would certainly make my life easi--
Damn you, Marten!
This for your schemes!
Unffff!
The sphere!

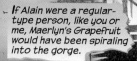 If Alain were a regular-type person, like you or me, Maerlyn's Grapefruit would have been spiraling into the gorge.

But gunslingers in general are a special breed, and Alain is no exception. Which is why, snake-quick, he catches that satchel and saves the precious globe.

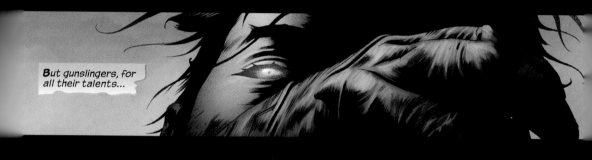

But gunslingers, for all their talents...

...still don't have the ability to be in two places at once.

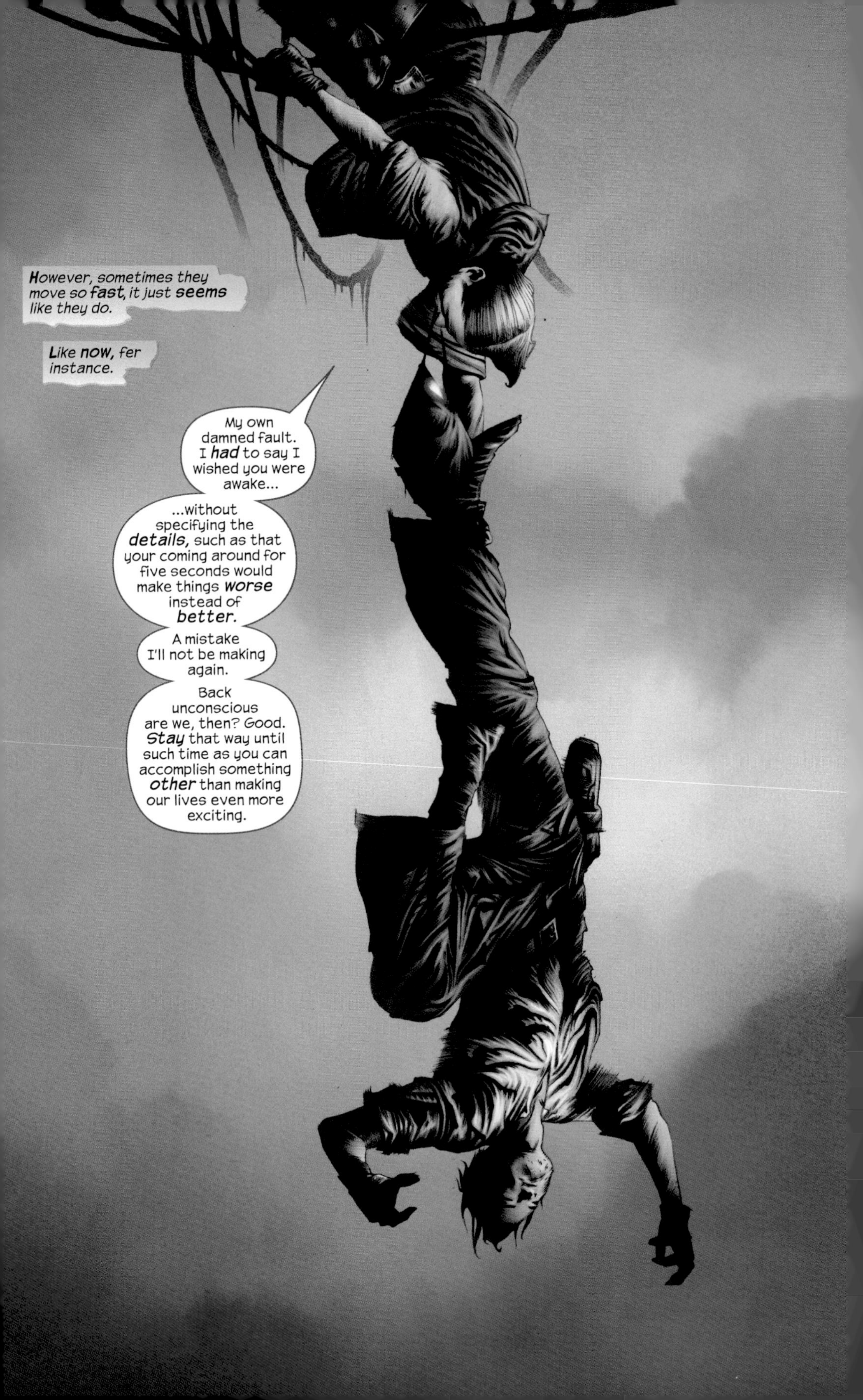
However, sometimes they move so fast, it just seems like they do.
Like now, fer instance.
My own damned fault. I had to say I wished you were awake...
...without specifying the details, such as that your coming around for five seconds would make things worse instead of better.
A mistake I'll not be making again.
Back unconscious are we, then? Good. Stay that way until such time as you can accomplish something other than making our lives even more exciting.

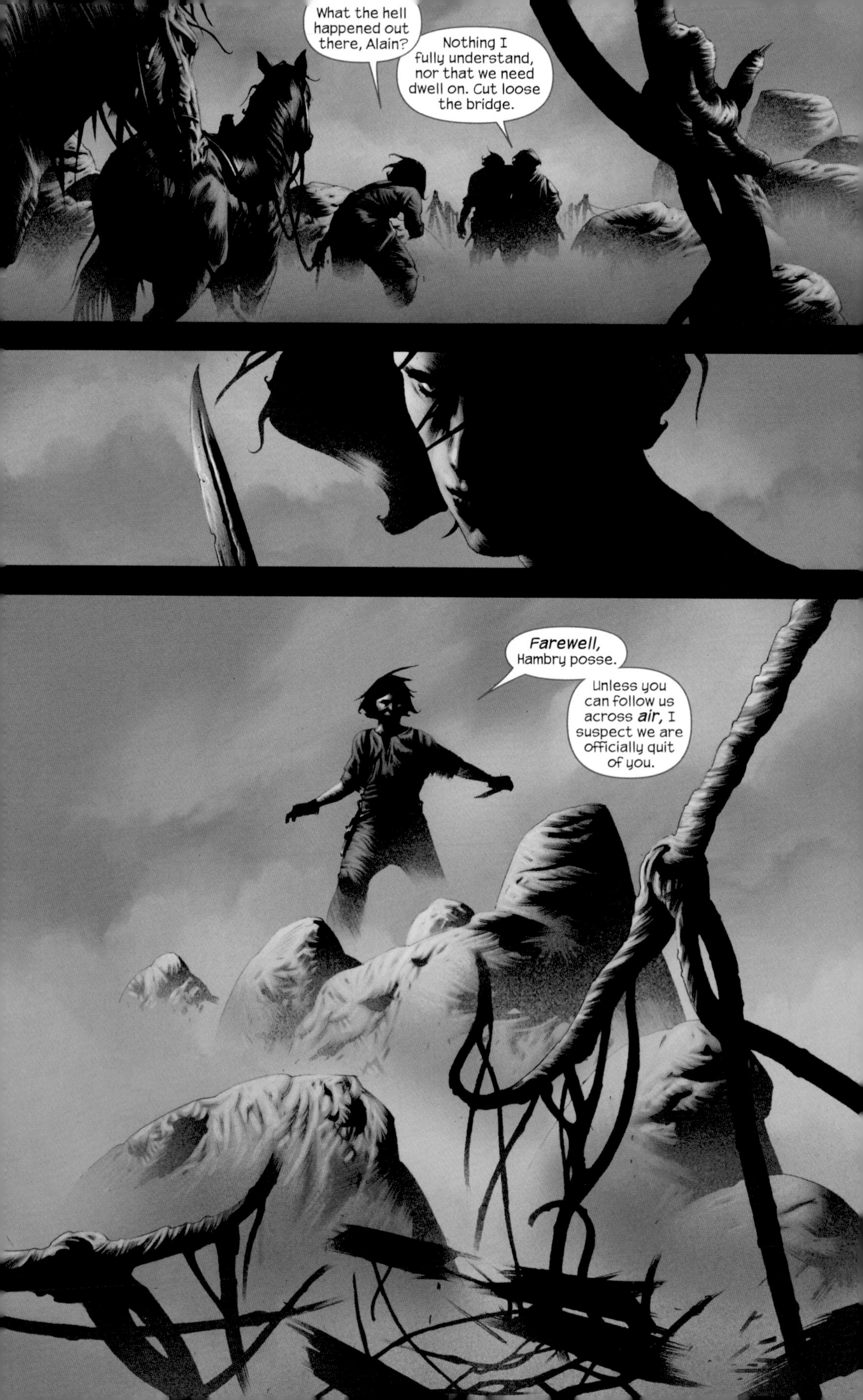
What the hell happened out there, Alain?
Nothing I fully understand, nor that we need dwell on. Cut loose the bridge.
Farewell, Hambry posse.
Unless you can follow us across air, I suspect we are officially quit of you.

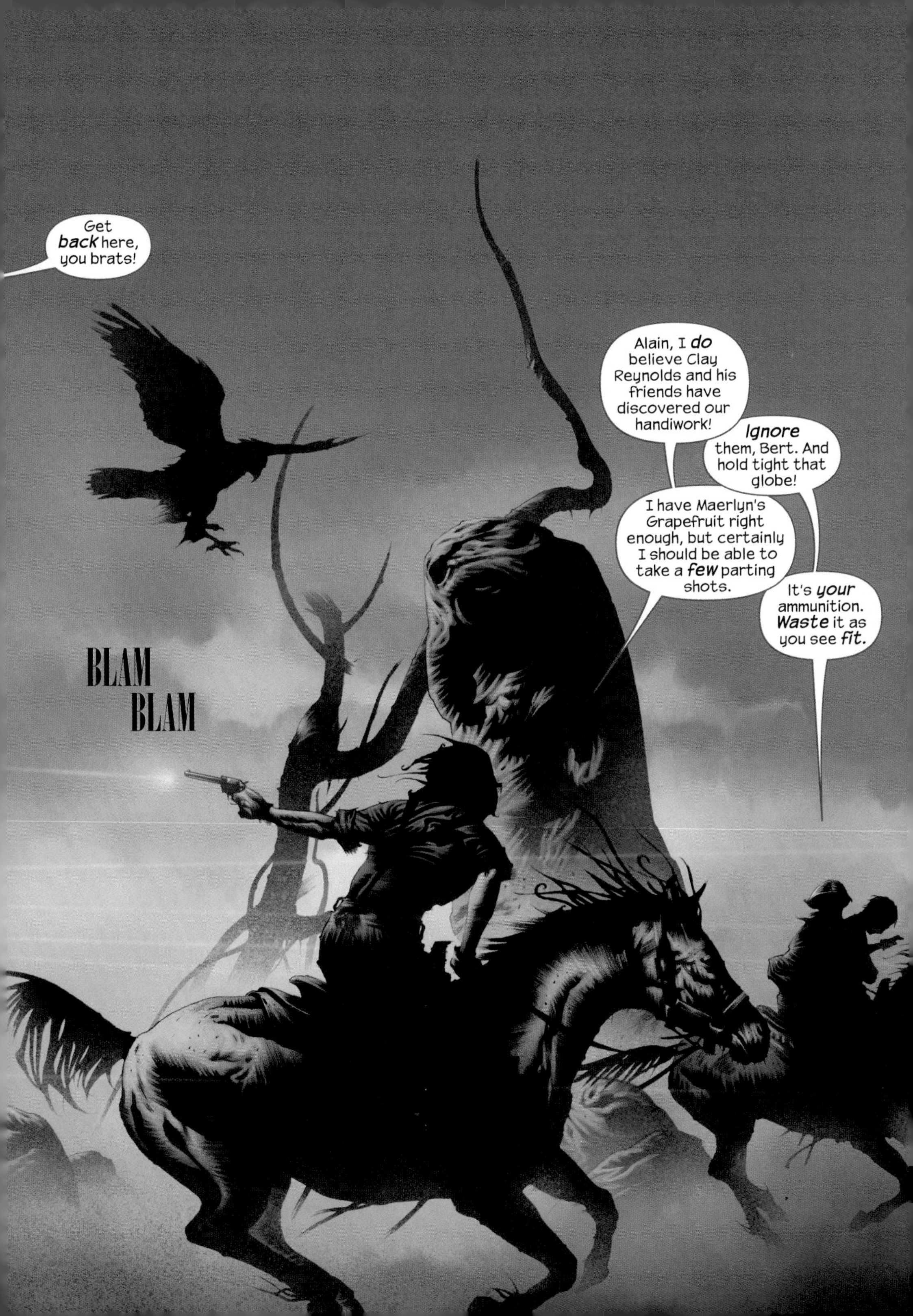
Get back here, you brats!
Alain, I do believe Clay Reynolds and his friends have discovered our handiwork!
Ignore them, Bert. And hold tight that globe!
I have Maerlyn's Grapefruit right enough, but certainly I should be able to take a few parting shots.
It's your ammunition. Waste it as you see fit.
BLAM
BLAM

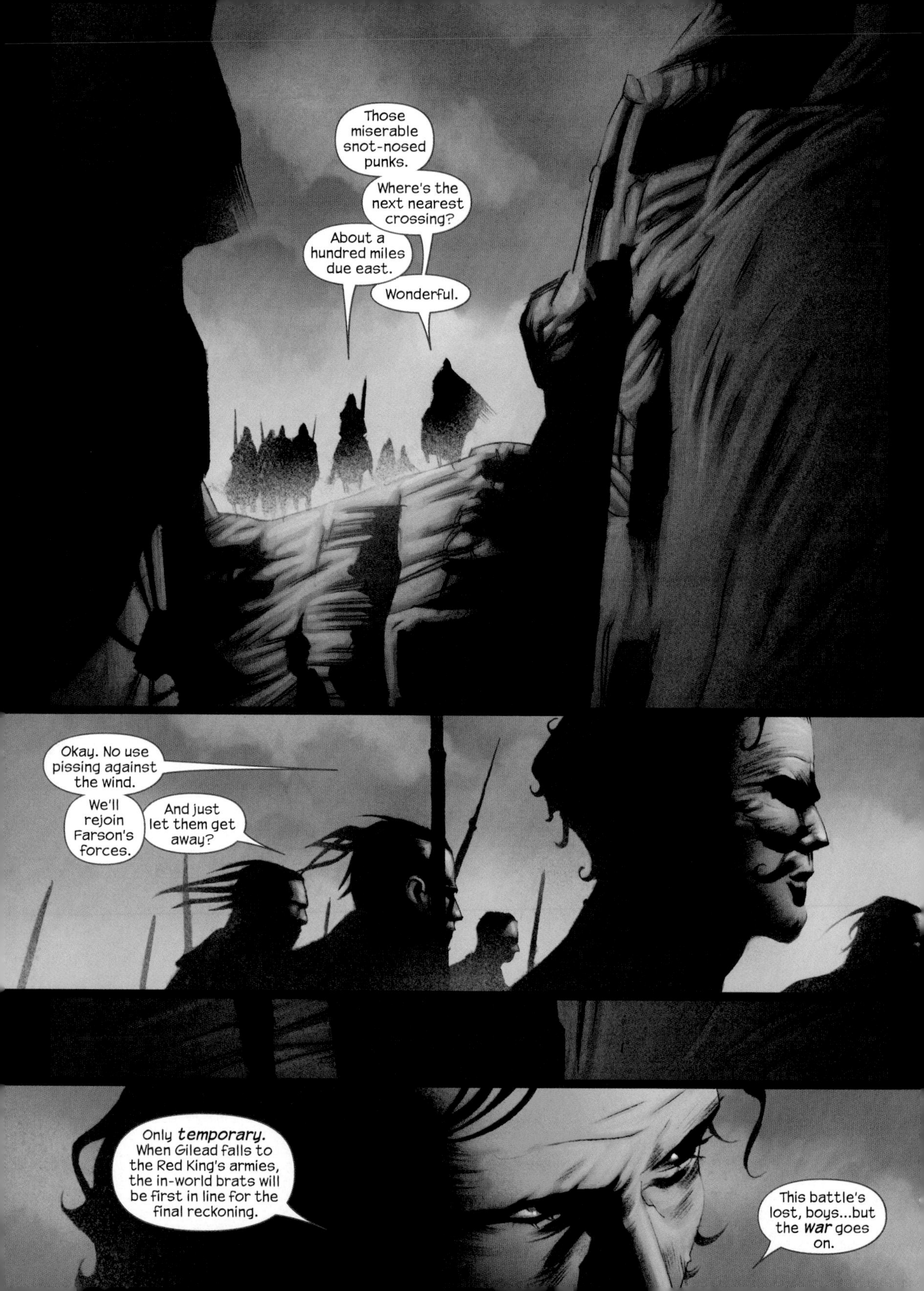
Those miserable snot-nosed punks.
Where's the next nearest crossing?
About a hundred miles due east.
Wonderful.
Okay. No use pissing against the wind.
We'll rejoin Farson's forces.
And just let them get away?
Only temporary. When Gilead falls to the Red King's armies, the in-world brats will be first in line for the final reckoning.
This battle's lost, boys...but the war goes on.

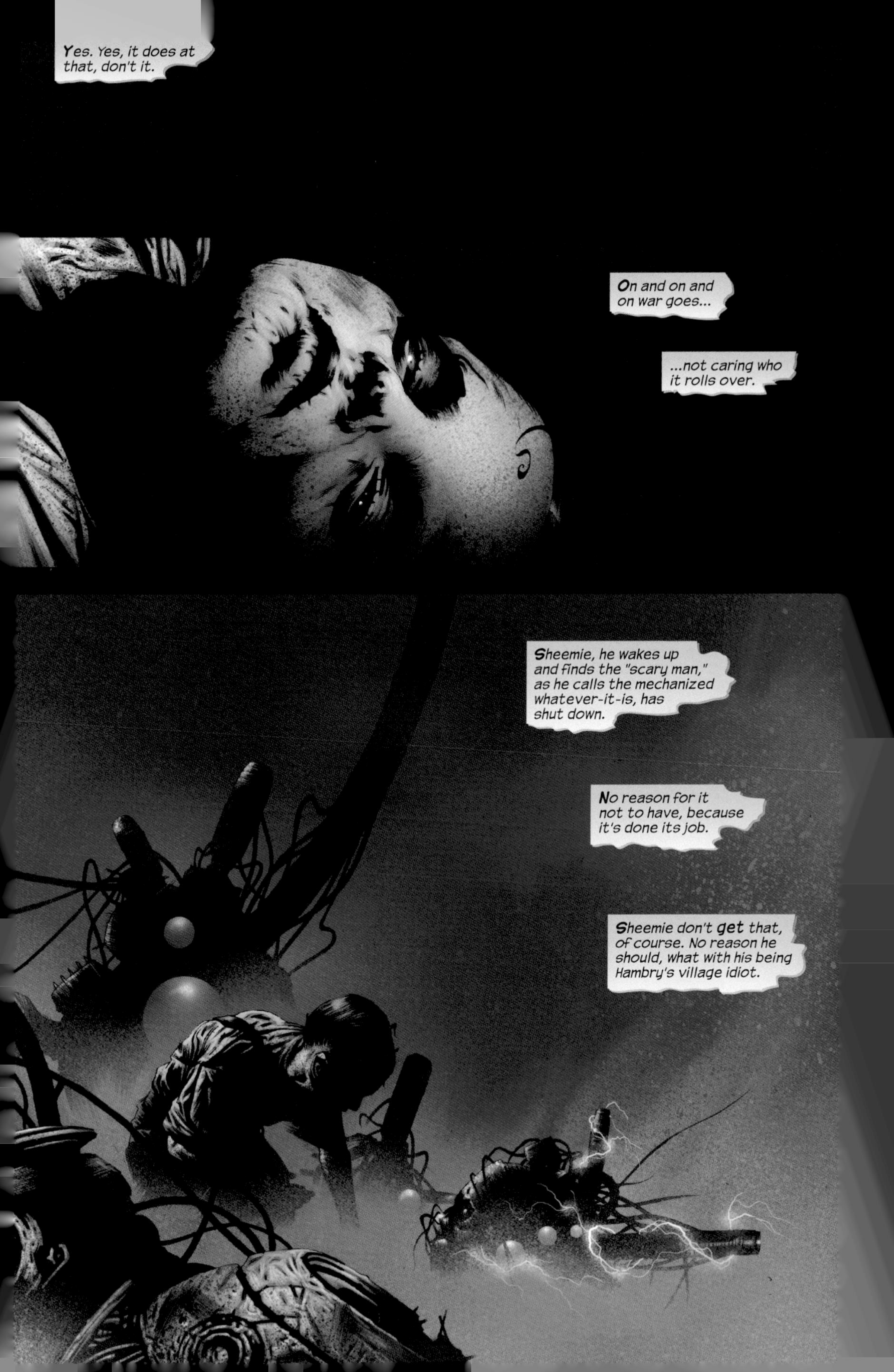
Yes. Yes, it does at that, don't it.
On and on and on war goes...
...not caring who it rolls over.
Sheemie, he wakes up and finds the "scary man," as he calls the mechanized whatever-it-is, has shut down.
No reason for it not to have, because it's done its job.
Sheemie don't get that, of course. No reason he should, what with his being Hambry's village idiot.

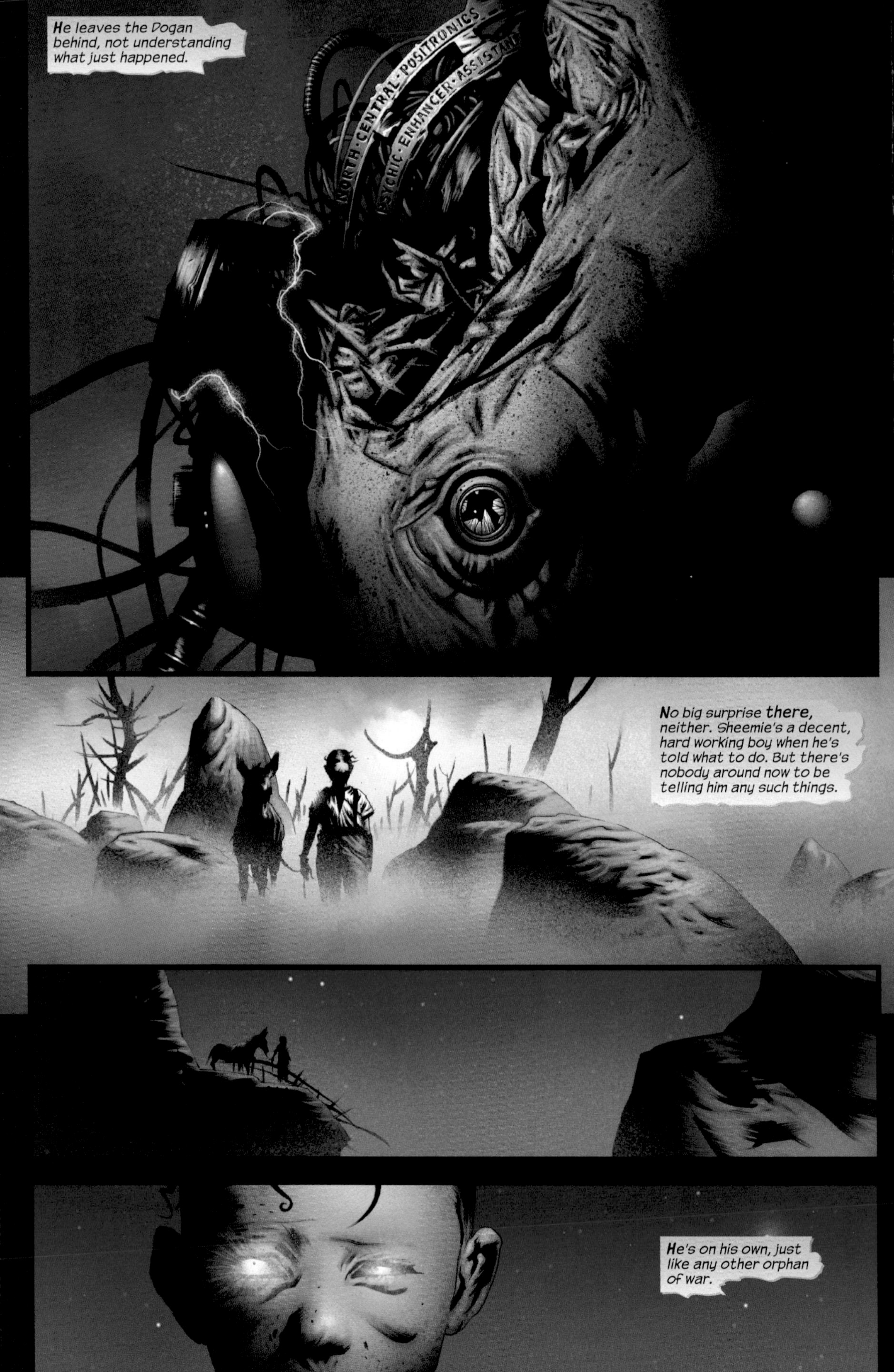
He leaves the Dogan behind, not understanding what just happened.
NORTH · CENTRAL · POSITRONICS
PSYCHIC · ENHANCER · ASSISTANT
No big surprise there, neither. Sheemie's a decent, hard working boy when he's told what to do. But there's nobody around now to be telling him any such things.
He's on his own, just like any other orphan of war.

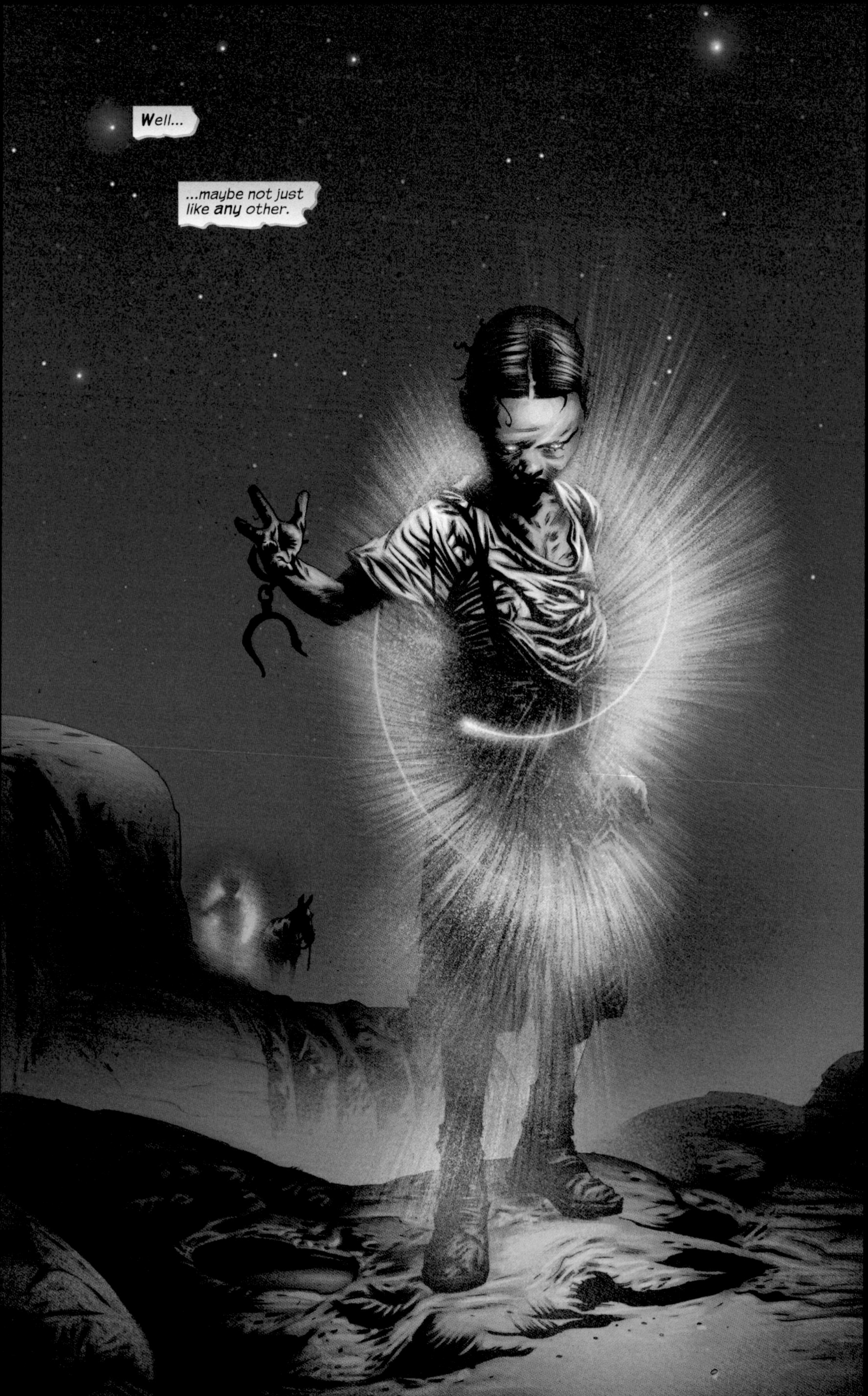
Well...
...maybe not just like any other.

STEPHEN KING

THE DARK TOWER

THE LONG ROAD HOME

CHAPTER THREE

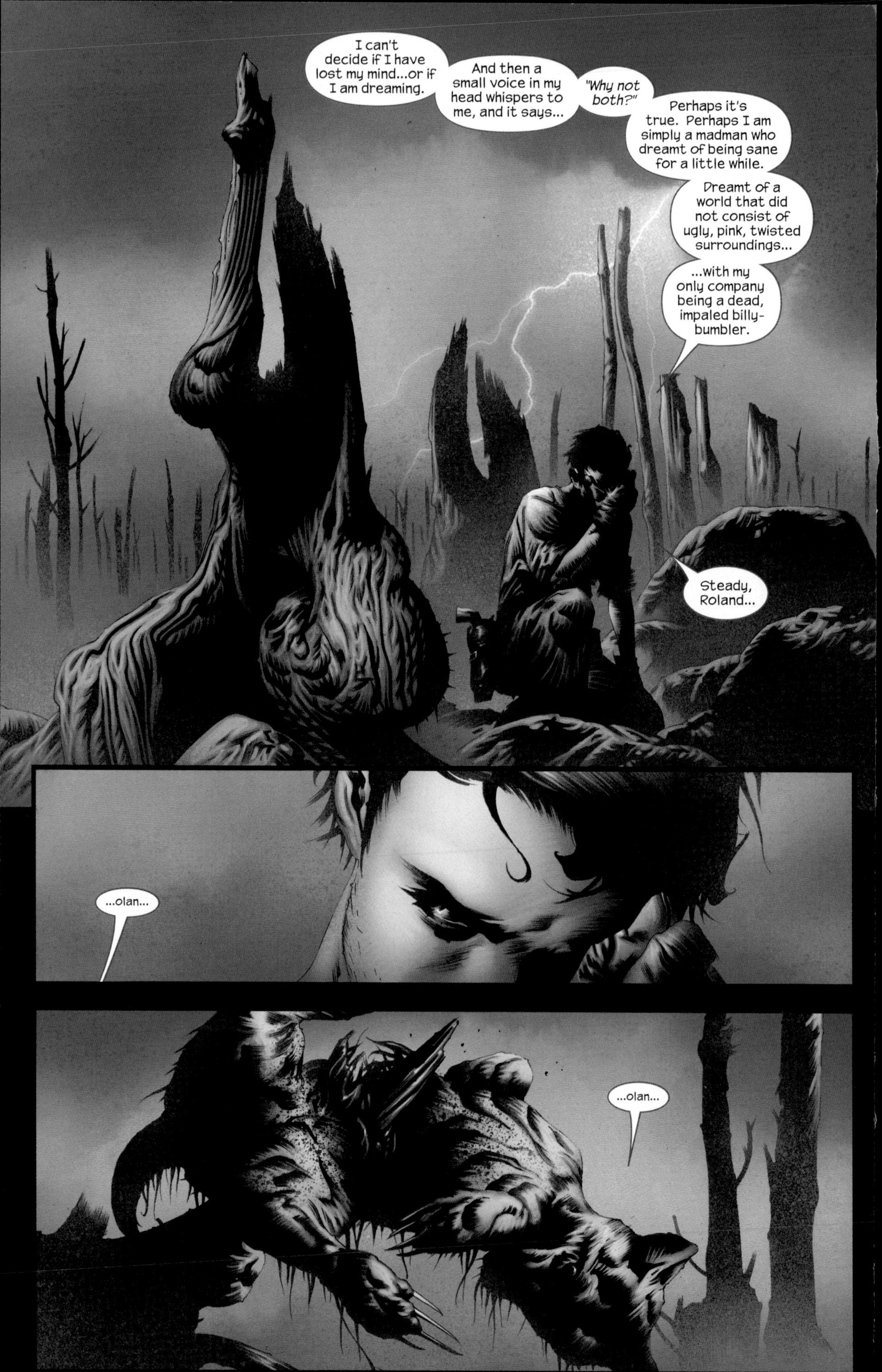
I can't decide if I have lost my mind...or if I am dreaming.
And then a small voice in my head whispers to me, and it says...
"Why not both?"
Perhaps it's true. Perhaps I am simply a madman who dreamt of being sane for a little while.
Dreamt of a world that did not consist of ugly, pink, twisted surroundings...
...with my only company being a dead, impaled billy-bumbler.
Steady, Roland...
...olan...
...olan...

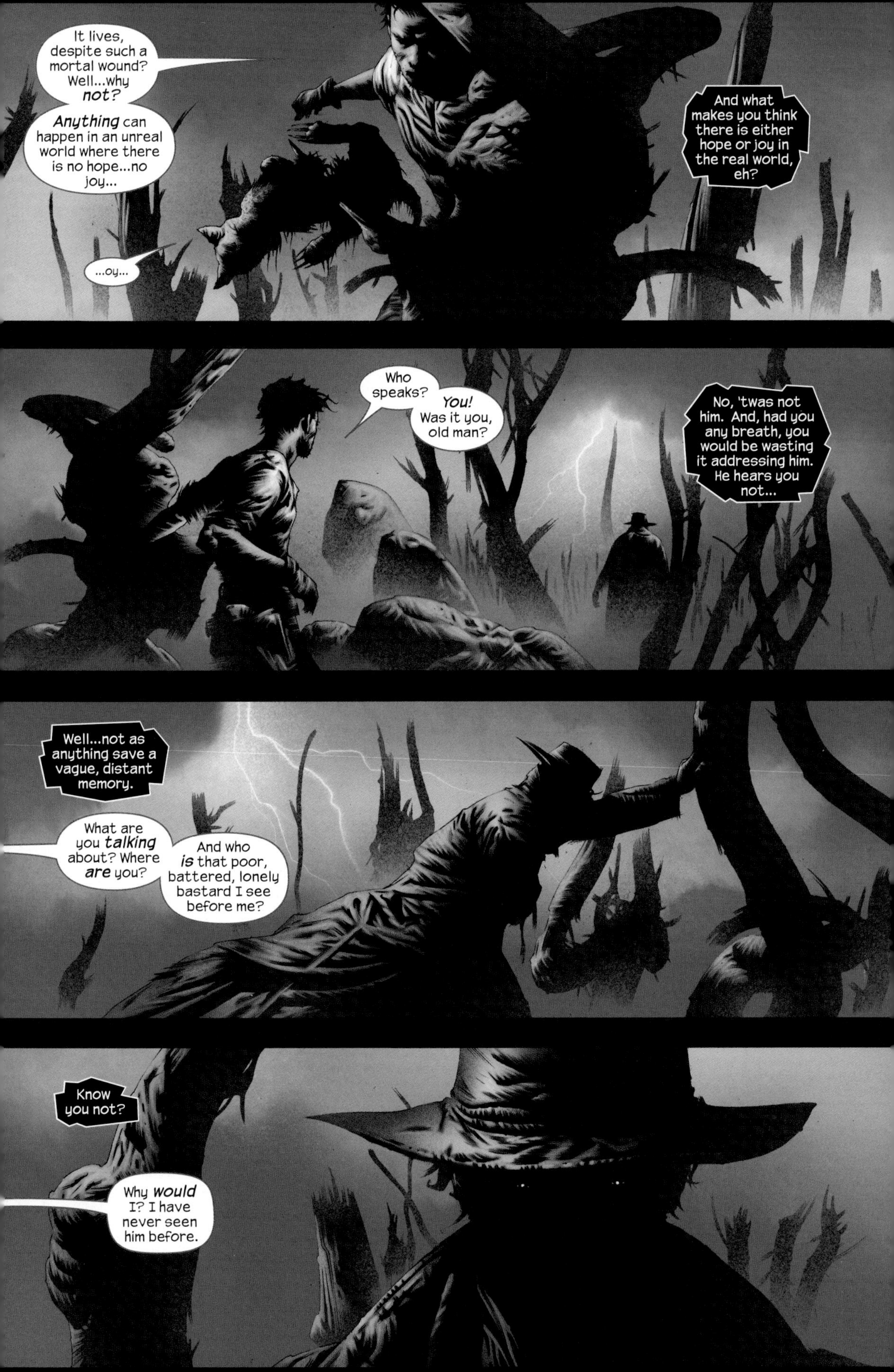
It lives, despite such a mortal wound? Well...why *not?*
Anything can happen in an unreal world where there is no hope...no joy...
...oy...
And what makes you think there is either hope or joy in the real world, eh?
Who speaks? *You!* Was it you, old man?
No, 'twas not him. And, had you any breath, you would be wasting it addressing him. He hears you not...
Well...not as anything save a vague, distant memory.
What are you *talking* about? Where *are* you?
And who *is* that poor, battered, lonely bastard I see before me?
Know you not?
Why *would* I? I have never seen him before.

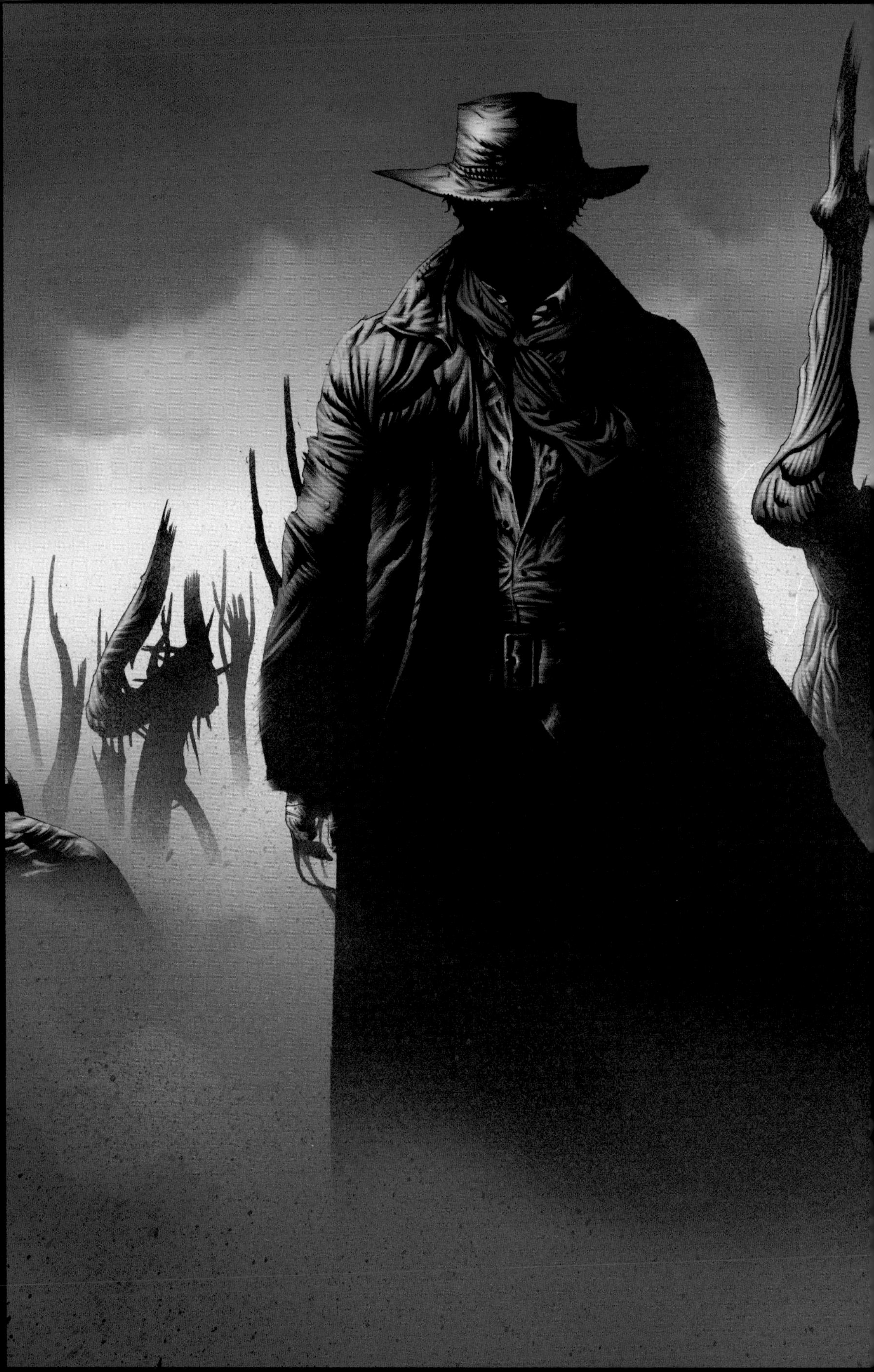

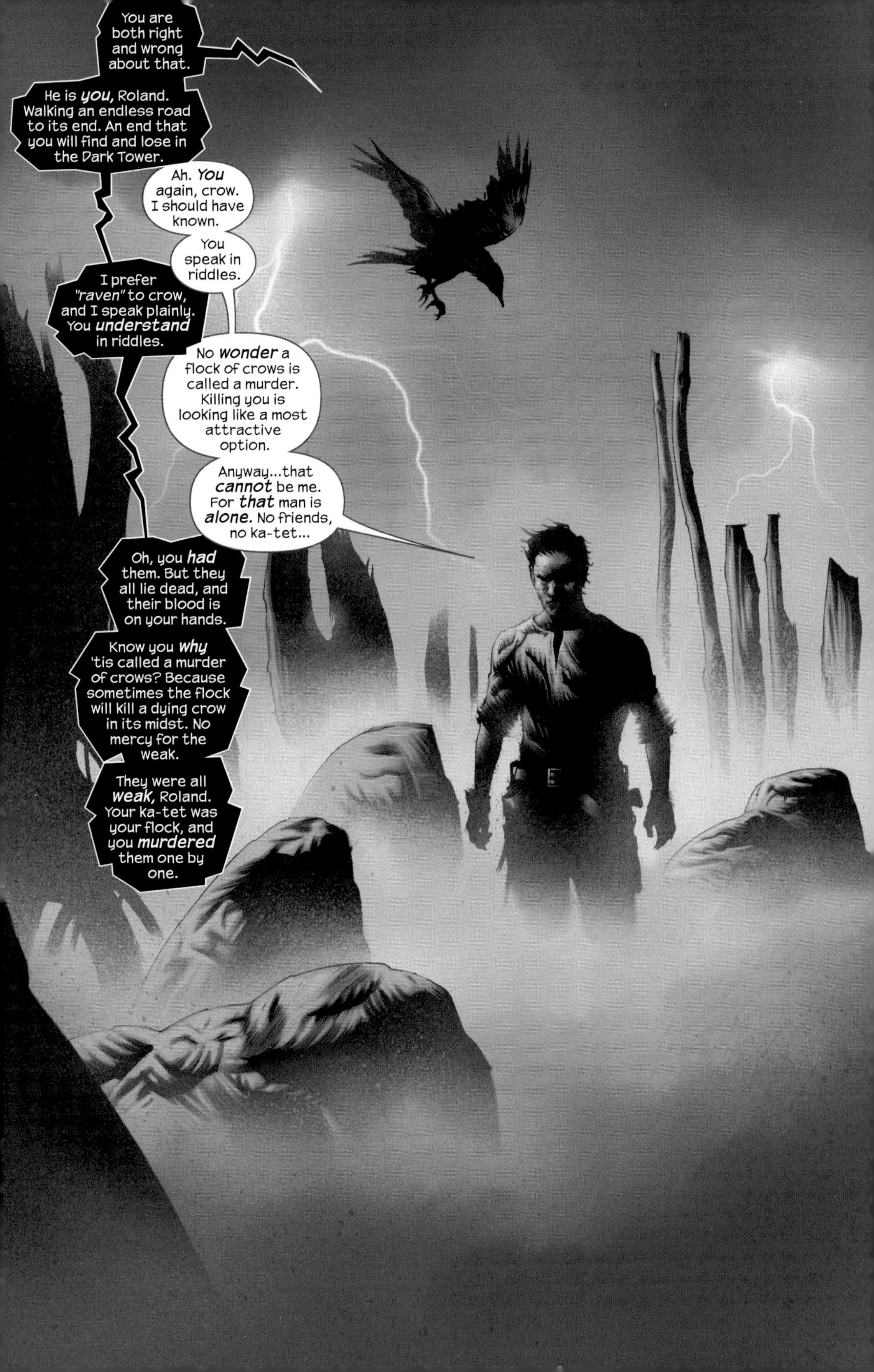

You are both right and wrong about that.
He is *you,* Roland. Walking an endless road to its end. An end that you will find and lose in the Dark Tower.
Ah. *You* again, crow. I should have known.
You speak in riddles.
I prefer *"raven"* to crow, and I speak plainly. You *understand* in riddles.
No *wonder* a flock of crows is called a murder. Killing you is looking like a most attractive option.
Anyway...that *cannot* be me. For *that* man is *alone.* No friends, no ka-tet...
Oh, you *had* them. But they all lie dead, and their blood is on your hands.
Know you *why* 'tis called a murder of crows? Because sometimes the flock will kill a dying crow in its midst. No mercy for the weak.
They were all *weak,* Roland. Your ka-tet was your flock, and you *murdered* them one by one.

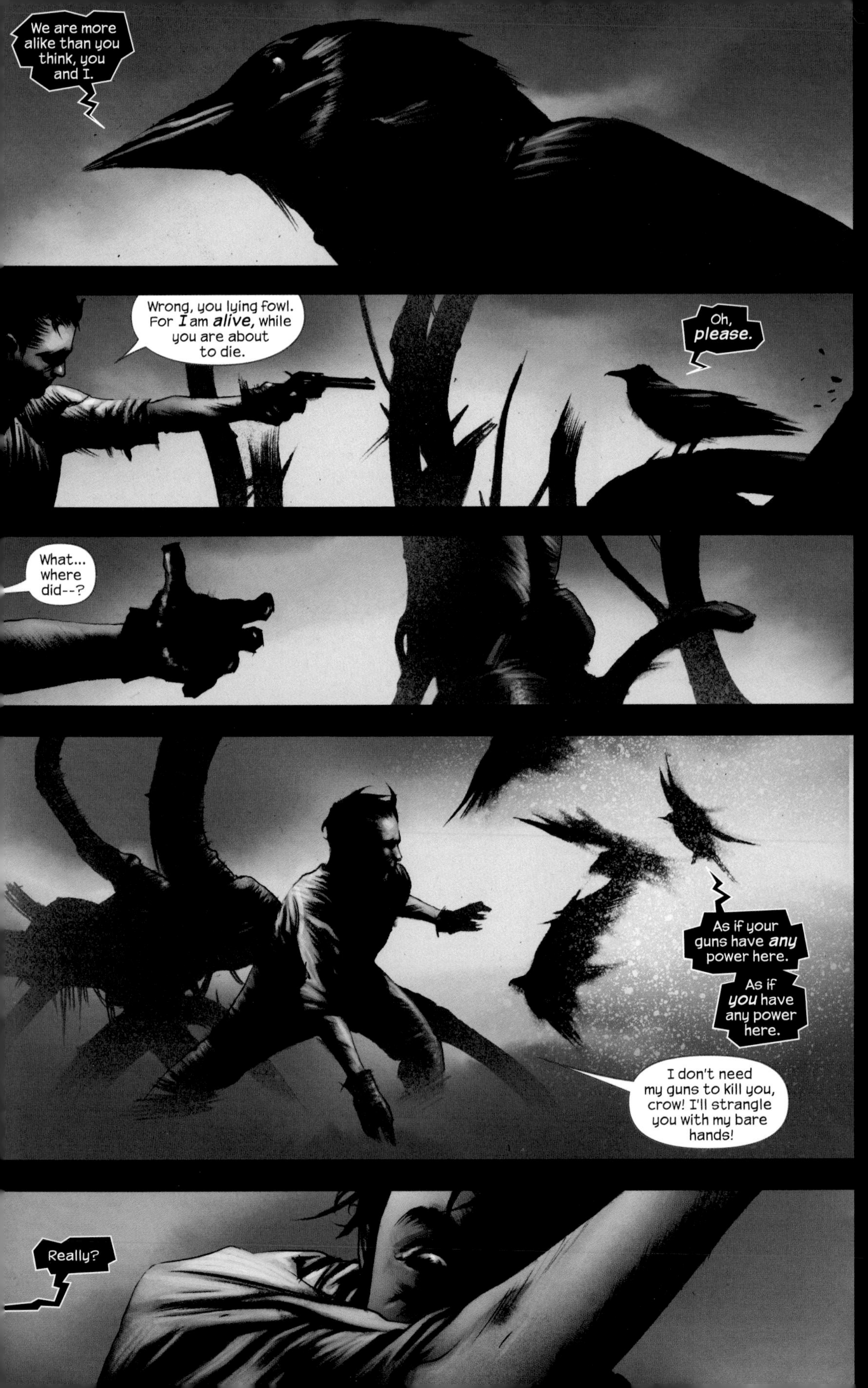

We are more alike than you think, you and I.
Wrong, you lying fowl. For I am alive, while you are about to die.
Oh, please.
What... where did--?
As if your guns have any power here.
As if you have any power here.
I don't need my guns to kill you, crow! I'll strangle you with my bare hands!
Really?

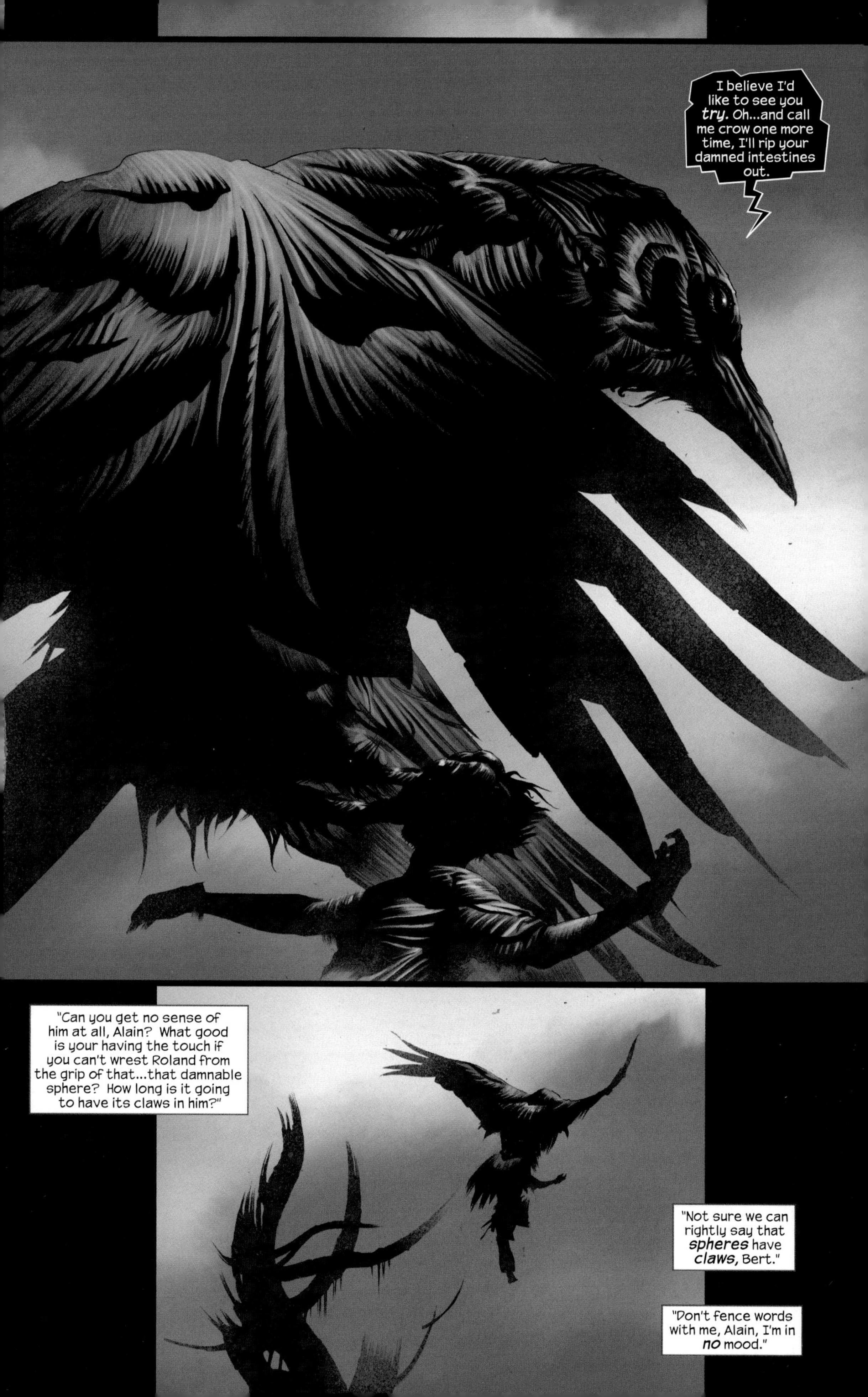
I believe I'd like to see you *try.* Oh...and call me crow one more time, I'll rip your damned intestines out.
"Can you get no sense of him at all, Alain? What good is your having the touch if you can't wrest Roland from the grip of that...that damnable sphere? How long is it going to have its claws in him?"
"Not sure we can rightly say that *spheres* have *claws,* Bert."
"Don't fence words with me, Alain, I'm in *no* mood."

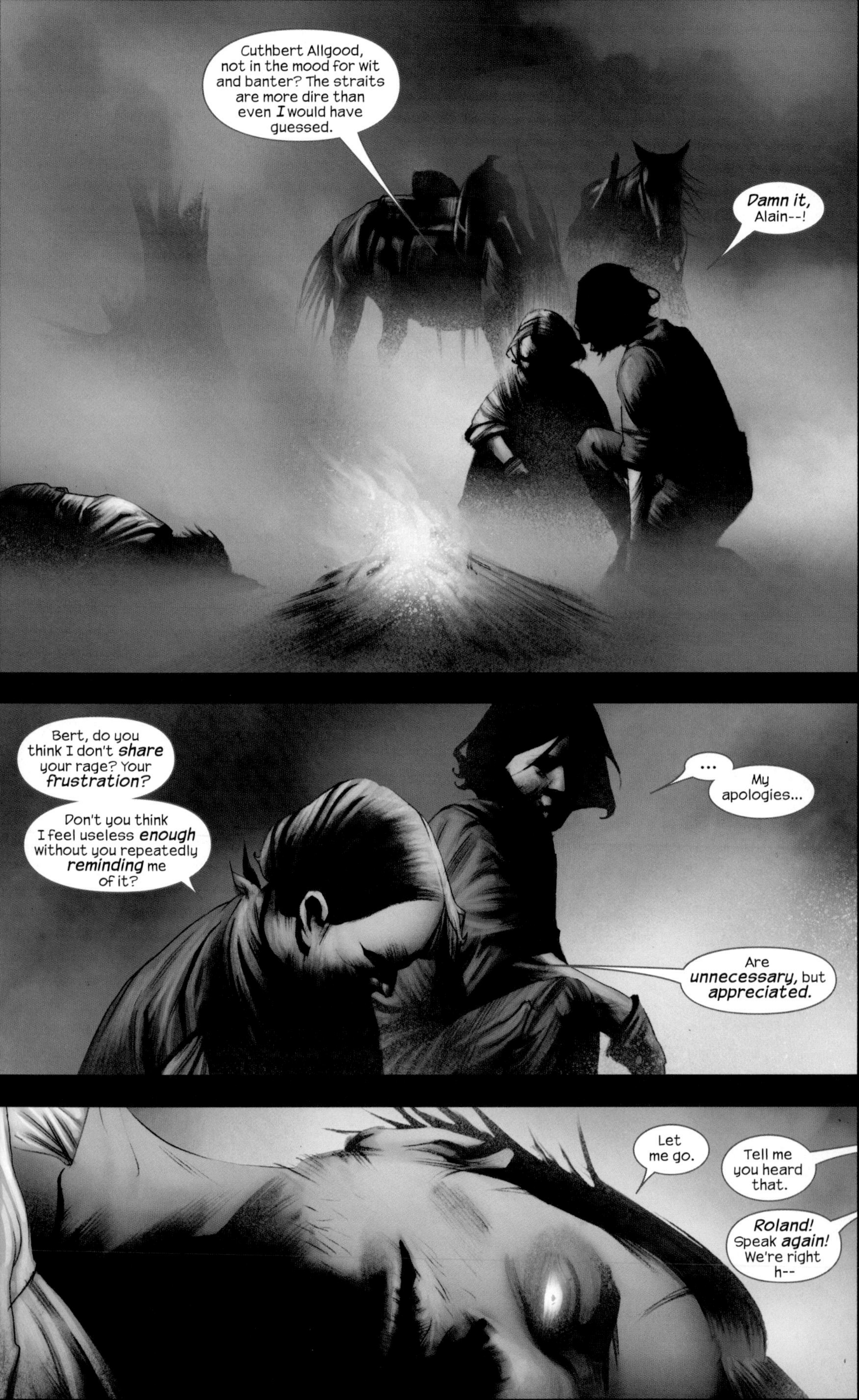
Cuthbert Allgood, not in the mood for wit and banter? The straits are more dire than even *I* would have guessed.
Damn it, Alain--!
Bert, do you think I don't *share* your rage? Your *frustration*?
Don't you think I feel useless *enough* without you repeatedly *reminding* me of it?
... My apologies...
Are *unnecessary,* but *appreciated.*
Let me go.
Tell me you heard that.
Roland! Speak *again!* We're right h--

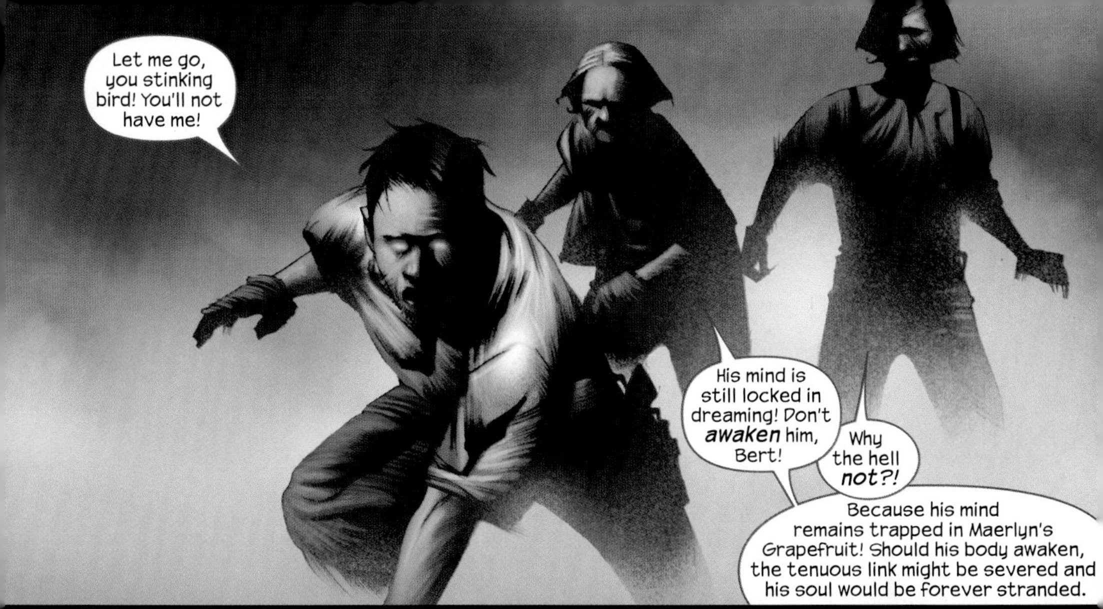
Let me go, you stinking bird! You'll not have me!
His mind is still locked in dreaming! Don't *awaken* him, Bert!
Why the hell *not?!*
Because his mind remains trapped in Maerlyn's Grapefruit! Should his body awaken, the tenuous link might be severed and his soul would be forever stranded.

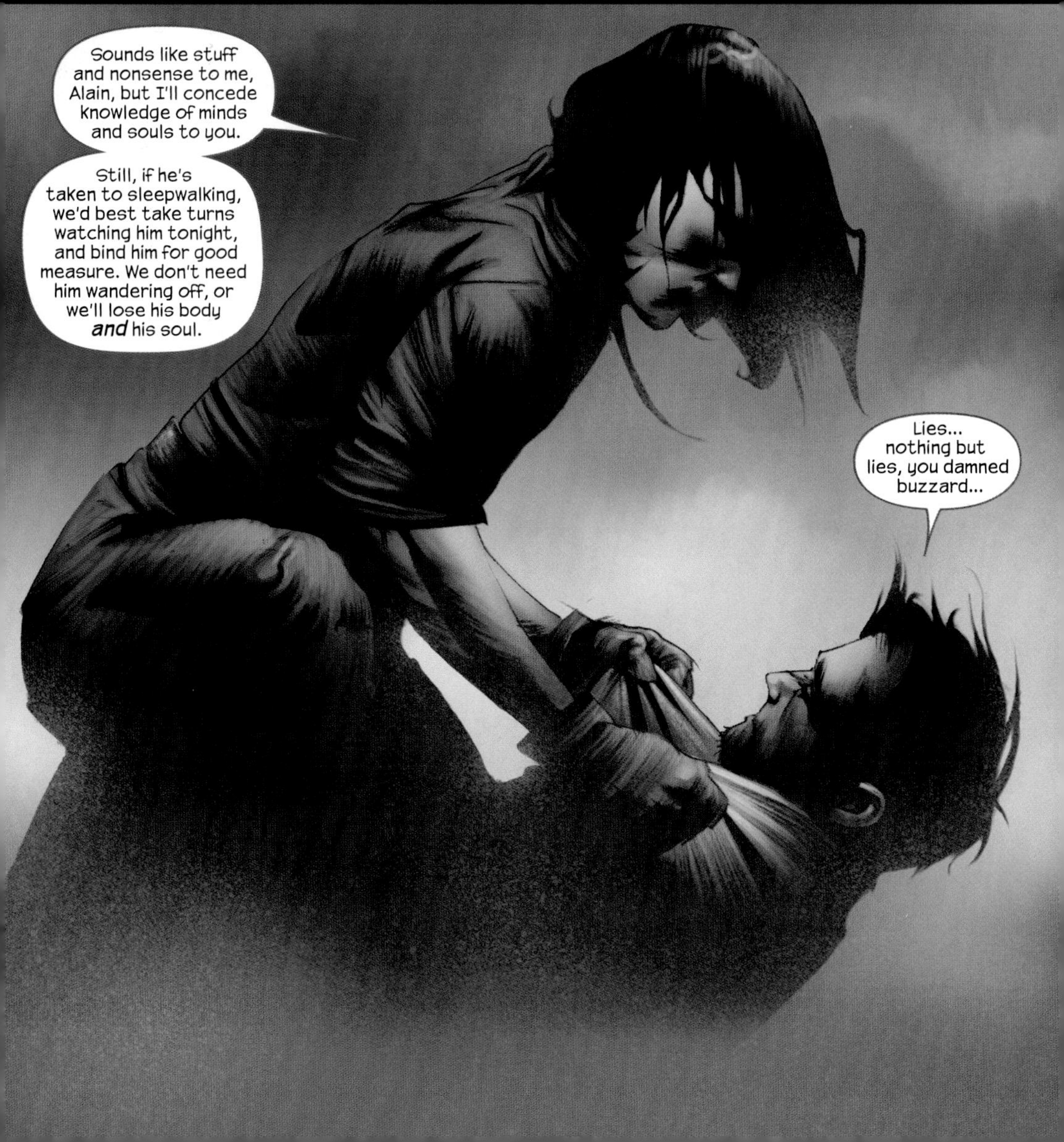
Sounds like stuff and nonsense to me, Alain, but I'll concede knowledge of minds and souls to you.
Still, if he's taken to sleepwalking, we'd best take turns watching him tonight, and bind him for good measure. We don't need him wandering off, or we'll lose his body *and* his soul.
Lies... nothing but lies, you damned buzzard...

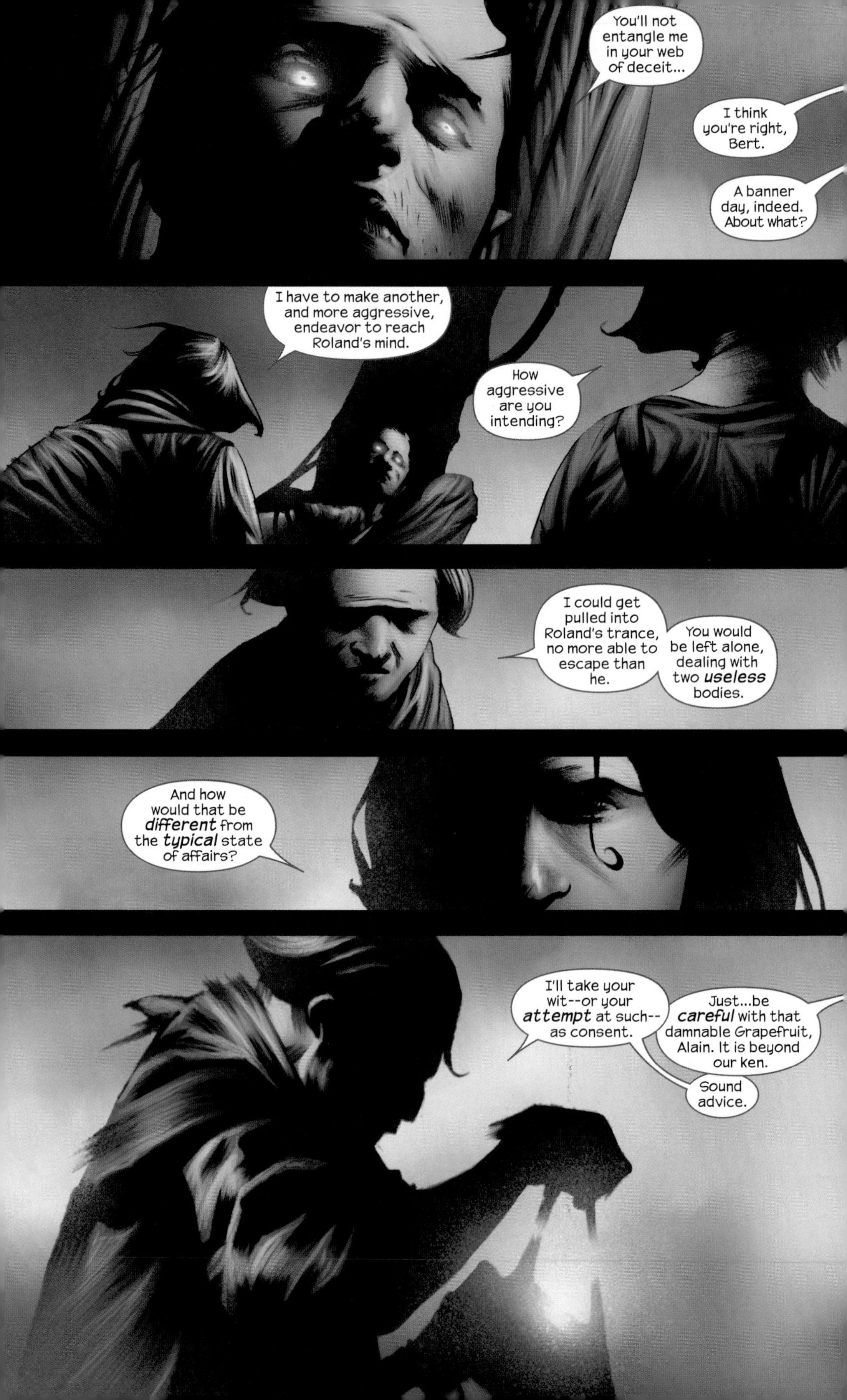
You'll not entangle me in your web of deceit...
I think you're right, Bert.
A banner day, indeed. About what?
I have to make another, and more aggressive, endeavor to reach Roland's mind.
How aggressive are you intending?
I could get pulled into Roland's trance, no more able to escape than he.
You would be left alone, dealing with two *useless* bodies.
And how would that be *different* from the *typical* state of affairs?
I'll take your wit--or your *attempt* at such--as consent.
Just...be *careful* with that damnable Grapefruit, Alain. It is beyond our ken.
Sound advice.

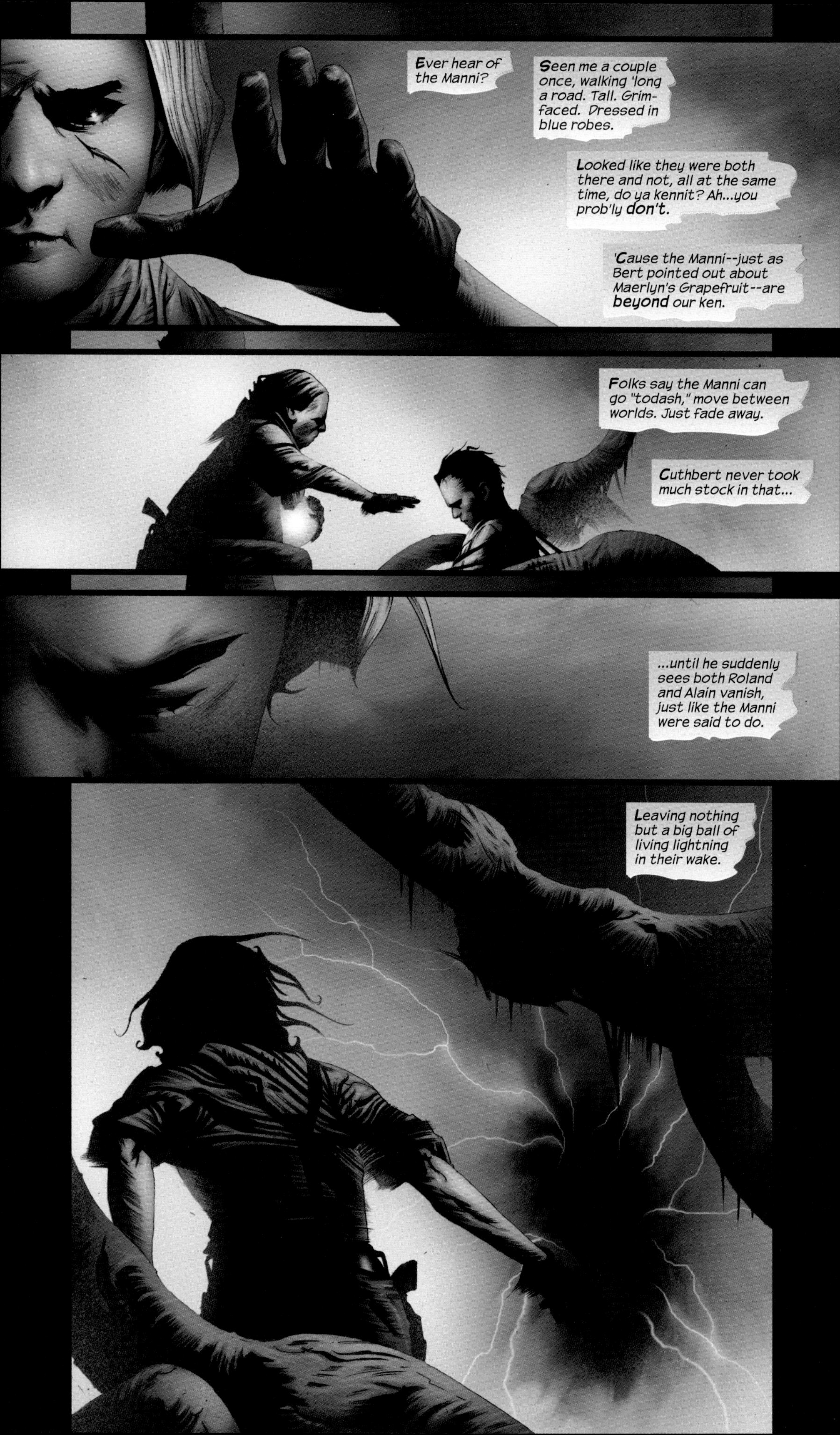
Ever hear of the Manni?
Seen me a couple once, walking 'long a road. Tall. Grim-faced. Dressed in blue robes.
Looked like they were both there and not, all at the same time, do ya kennit? Ah...you prob'ly don't.
'Cause the Manni--just as Bert pointed out about Maerlyn's Grapefruit--are beyond our ken.
Folks say the Manni can go "todash," move between worlds. Just fade away.
Cuthbert never took much stock in that...
...until he suddenly sees both Roland and Alain vanish, just like the Manni were said to do.
Leaving nothing but a big ball of living lightning in their wake.

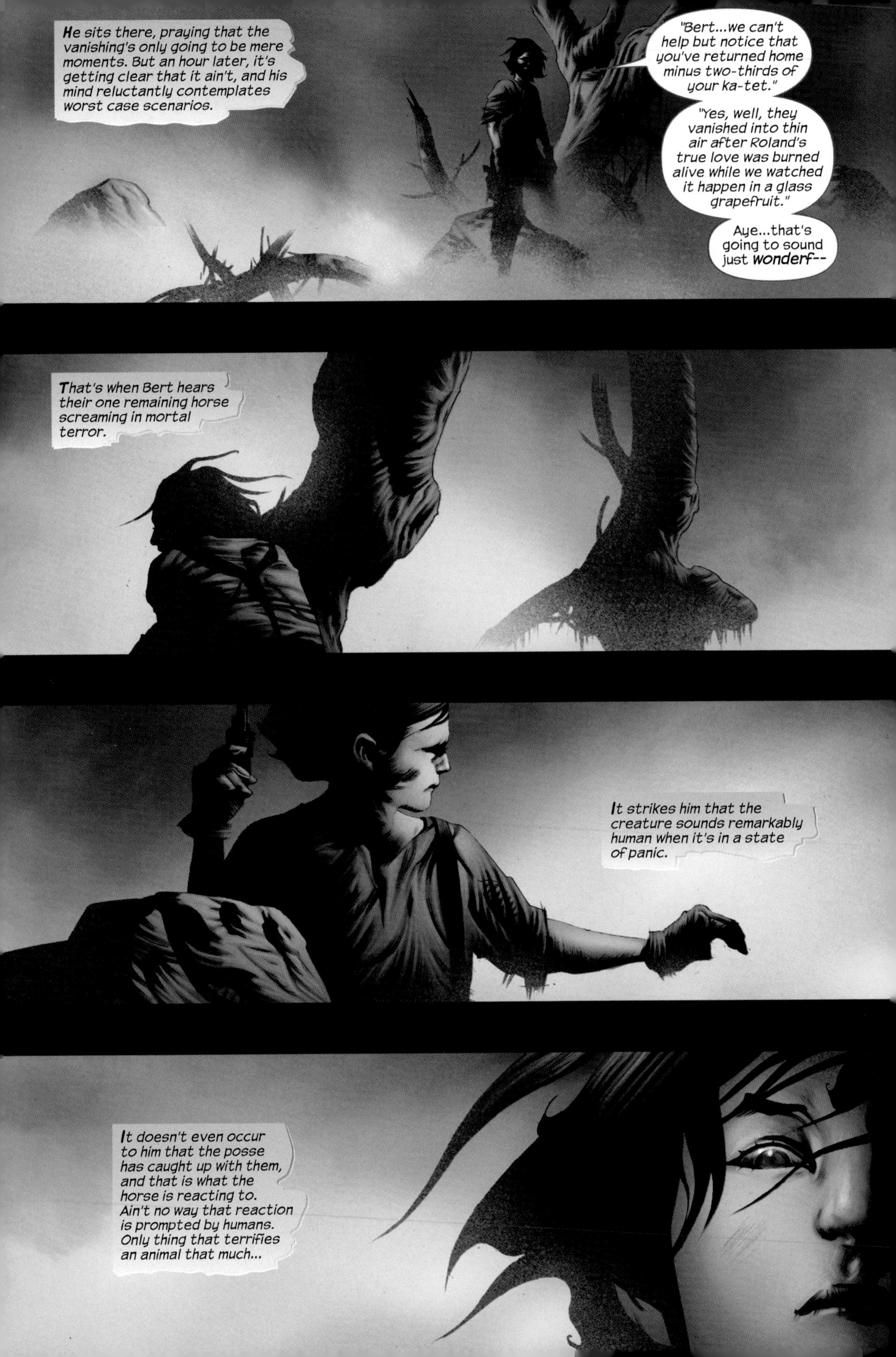
He sits there, praying that the vanishing's only going to be mere moments. But an hour later, it's getting clear that it ain't, and his mind reluctantly contemplates worst case scenarios.
"Bert...we can't help but notice that you've returned home minus two-thirds of your ka-tet."
"Yes, well, they vanished into thin air after Roland's true love was burned alive while we watched it happen in a glass grapefruit."
Aye...that's going to sound just wonderf--
That's when Bert hears their one remaining horse screaming in mortal terror.
It strikes him that the creature sounds remarkably human when it's in a state of panic.
It doesn't even occur to him that the posse has caught up with them, and that is what the horse is reacting to. Ain't no way that reaction is prompted by humans. Only thing that terrifies an animal that much...

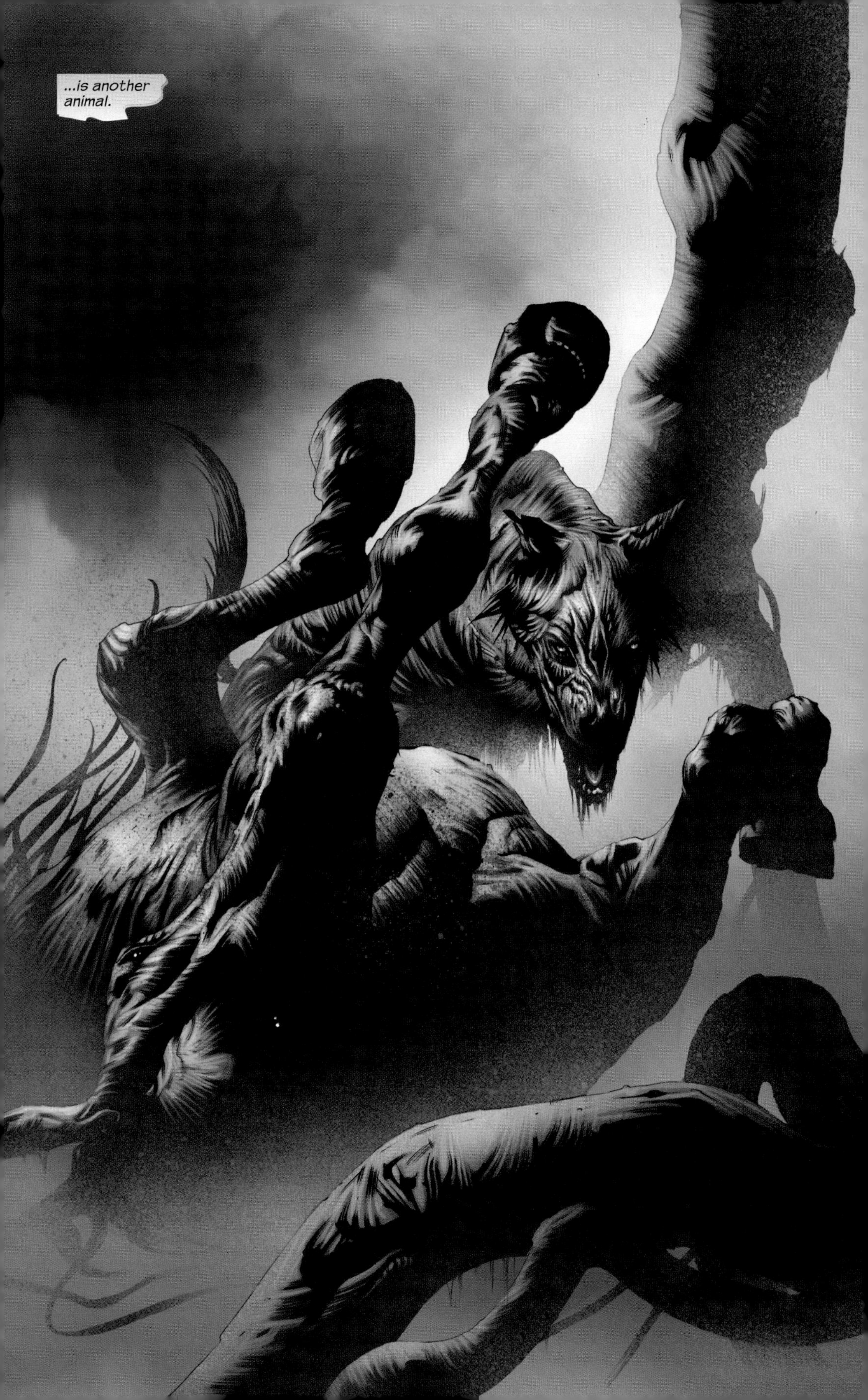
...is another animal.

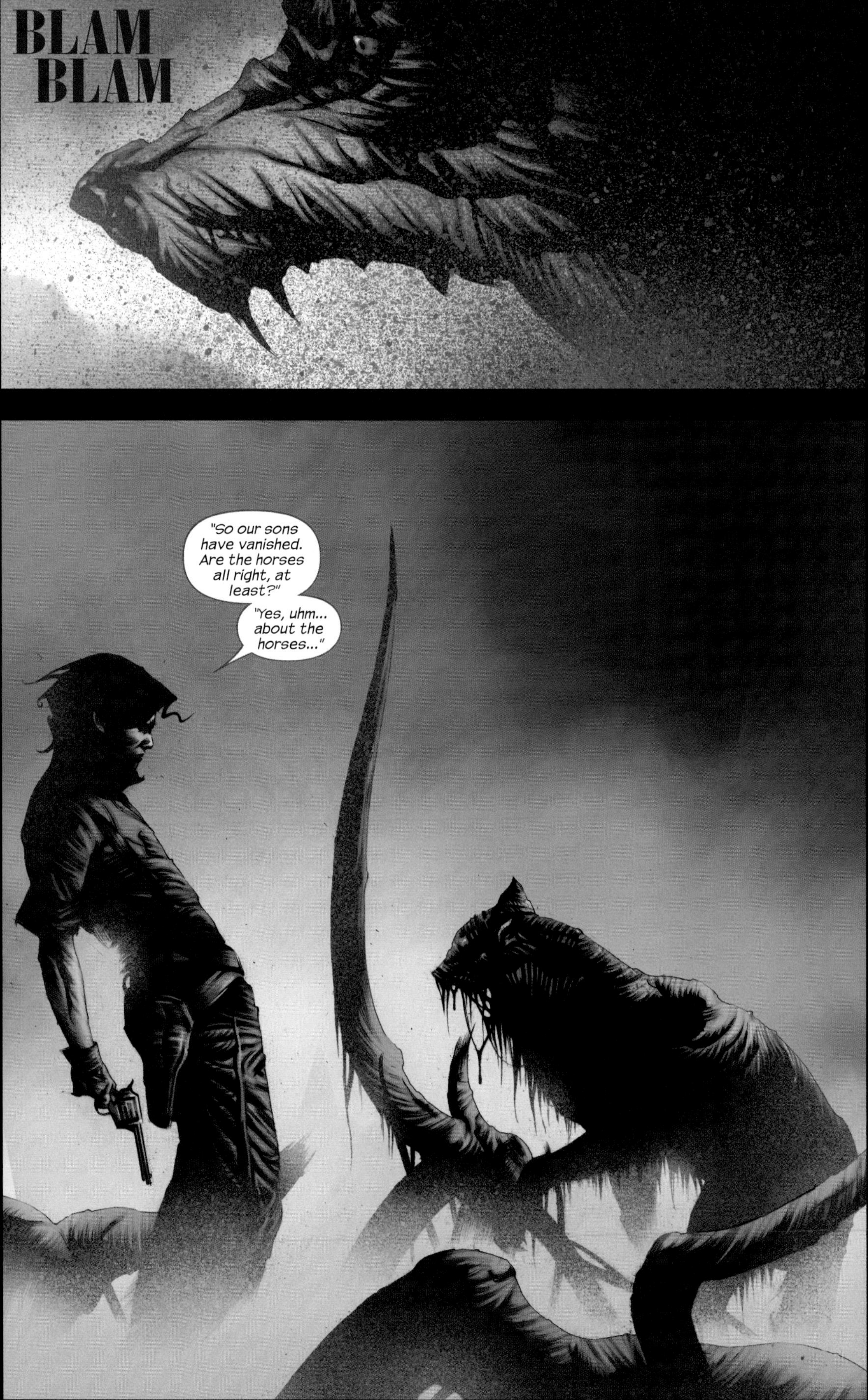
BLAM
BLAM
"So our sons have vanished. Are the horses all right, at least?"
"Yes, uhm... about the horses..."

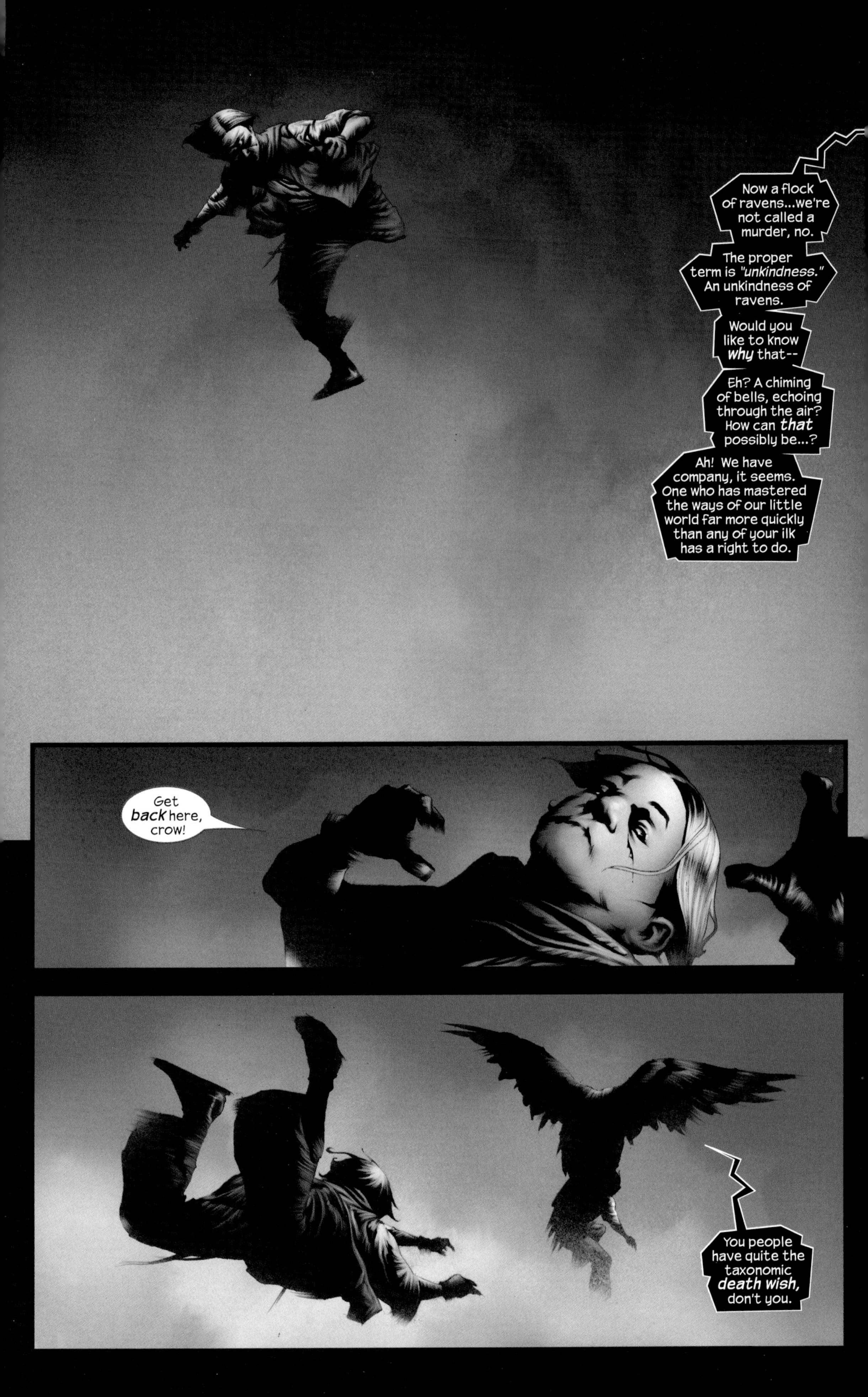
Now a flock of ravens...we're not called a murder, no.
The proper term is "unkindness." An unkindness of ravens.
Would you like to know why that--
Eh? A chiming of bells, echoing through the air? How can that possibly be...?
Ah! We have company, it seems. One who has mastered the ways of our little world far more quickly than any of your ilk has a right to do.
Get back here, crow!
You people have quite the taxonomic death wish, don't you.

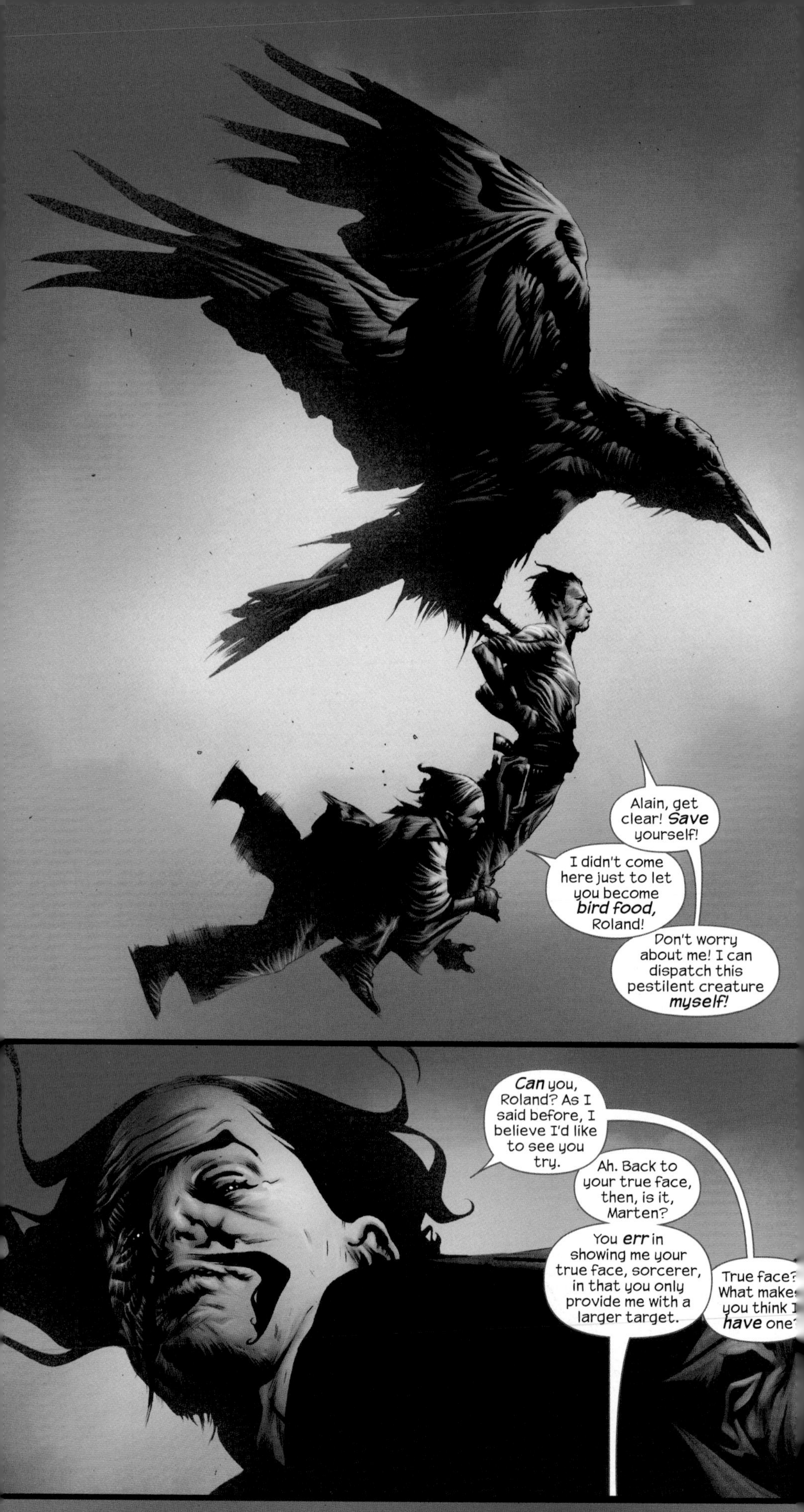

Alain, get clear! Save yourself!
I didn't come here just to let you become bird food, Roland!
Don't worry about me! I can dispatch this pestilent creature myself!
Can you, Roland? As I said before, I believe I'd like to see you try.
Ah. Back to your true face, then, is it, Marten?
You err in showing me your true face, sorcerer, in that you only provide me with a larger target.
True face? What make you think I have one

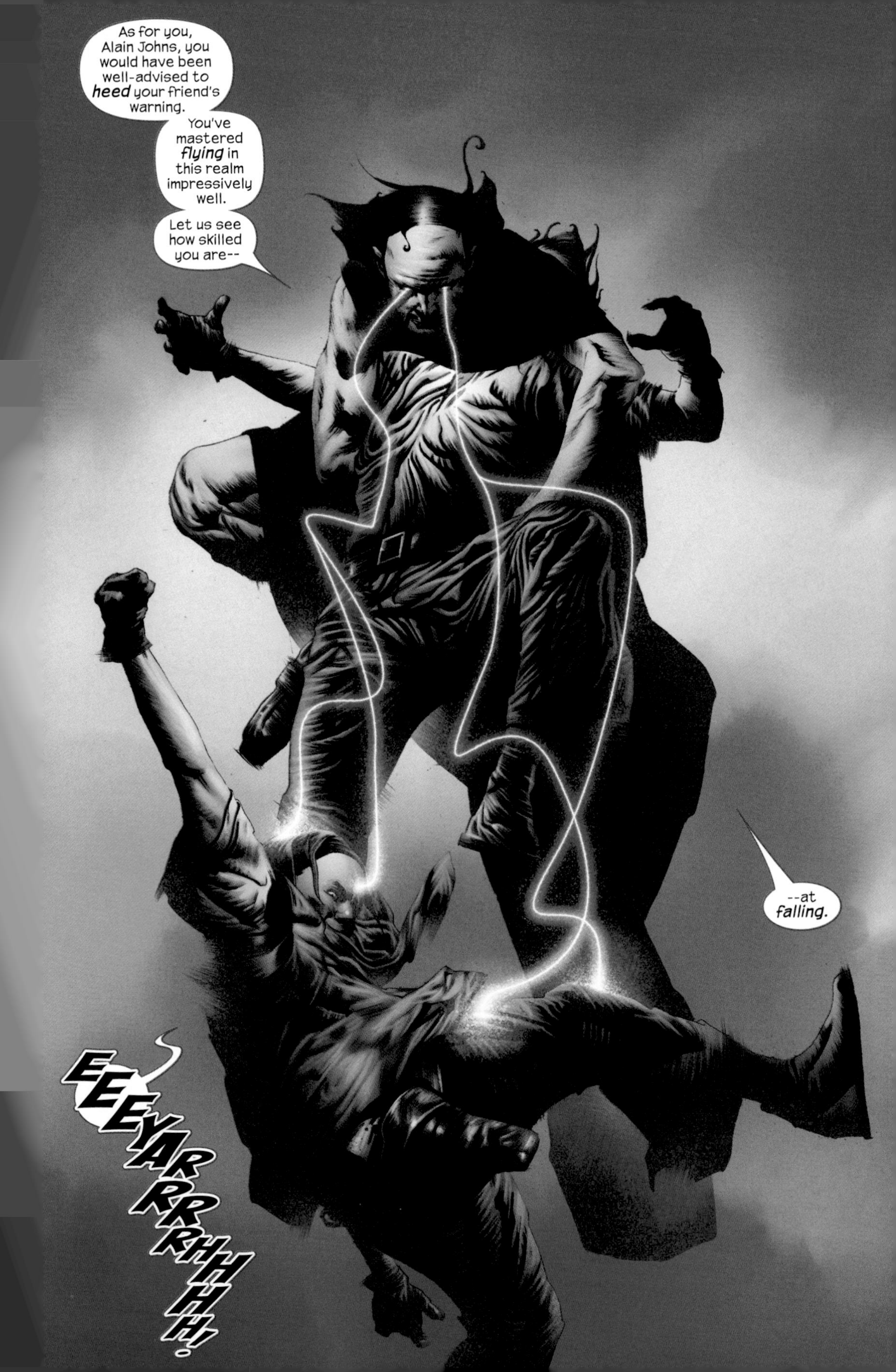
As for you, Alain Johns, you would have been well-advised to **heed** your friend's warning.
You've mastered ***flying*** in this realm impressively well.
Let us see how skilled you are--
--at ***falling.***
EEEYARRRRHHHH!

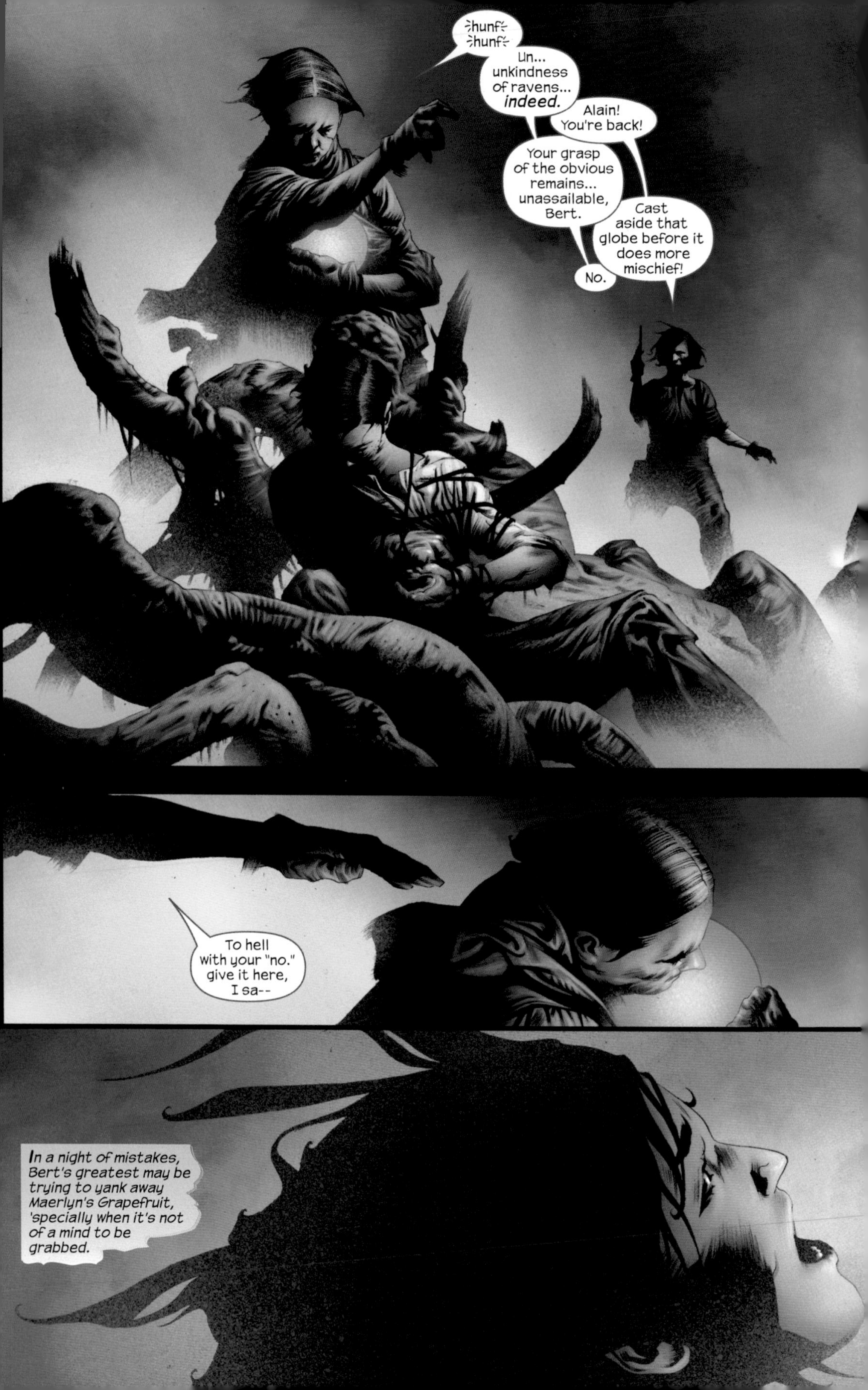

hunf hunf
Un... unkindness of ravens... *indeed.*
Alain! You're back!
Your grasp of the obvious remains... unassailable, Bert.
Cast aside that globe before it does more mischief!
No.
To hell with your "no." give it here, I sa--
In a night of mistakes, Bert's greatest may be trying to yank away Maerlyn's Grapefruit, 'specially when it's not of a mind to be grabbed.

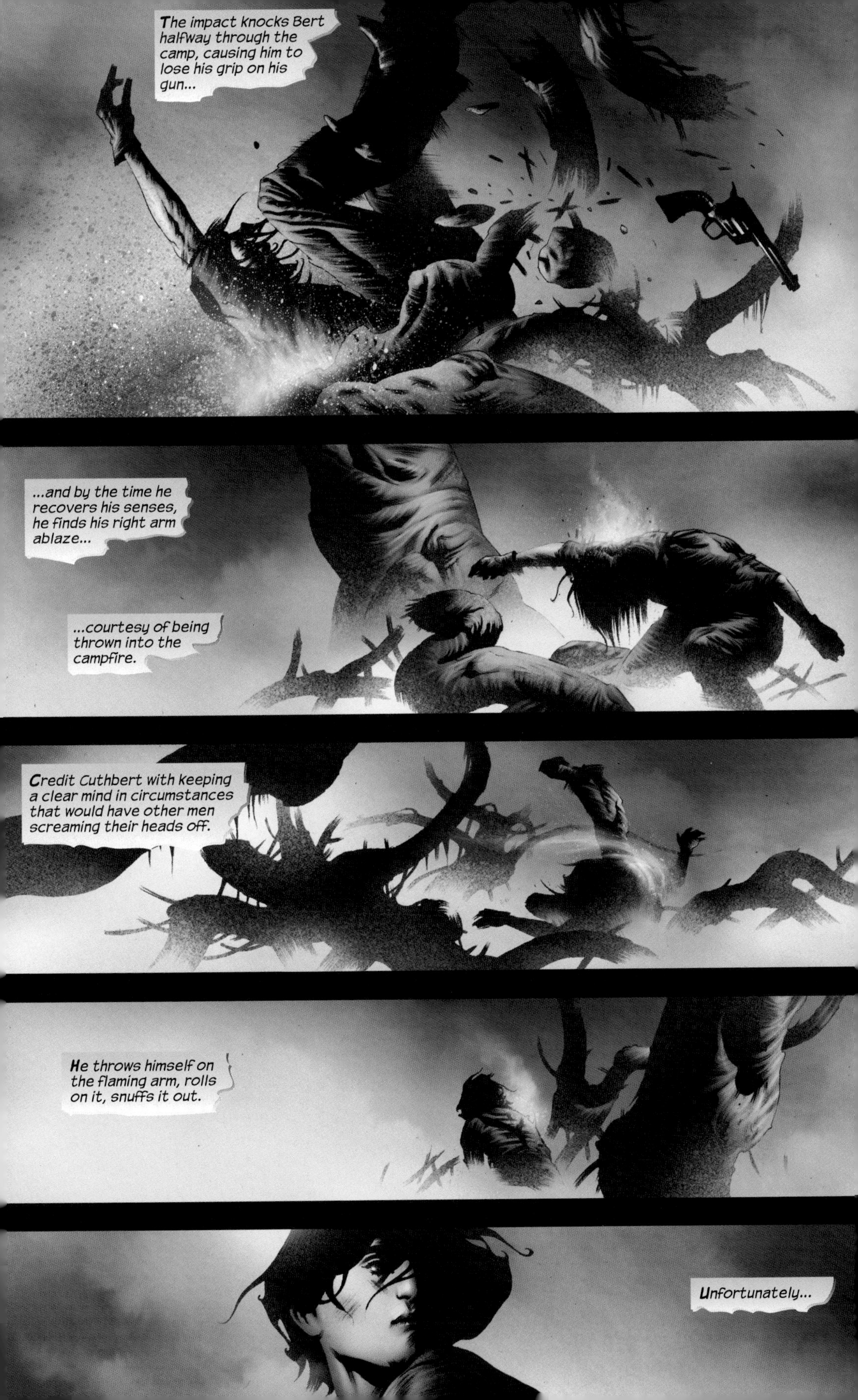
The impact knocks Bert halfway through the camp, causing him to lose his grip on his gun...
...and by the time he recovers his senses, he finds his right arm ablaze...
...courtesy of being thrown into the campfire.
Credit Cuthbert with keeping a clear mind in circumstances that would have other men screaming their heads off.
He throws himself on the flaming arm, rolls on it, snuffs it out.
Unfortunately...

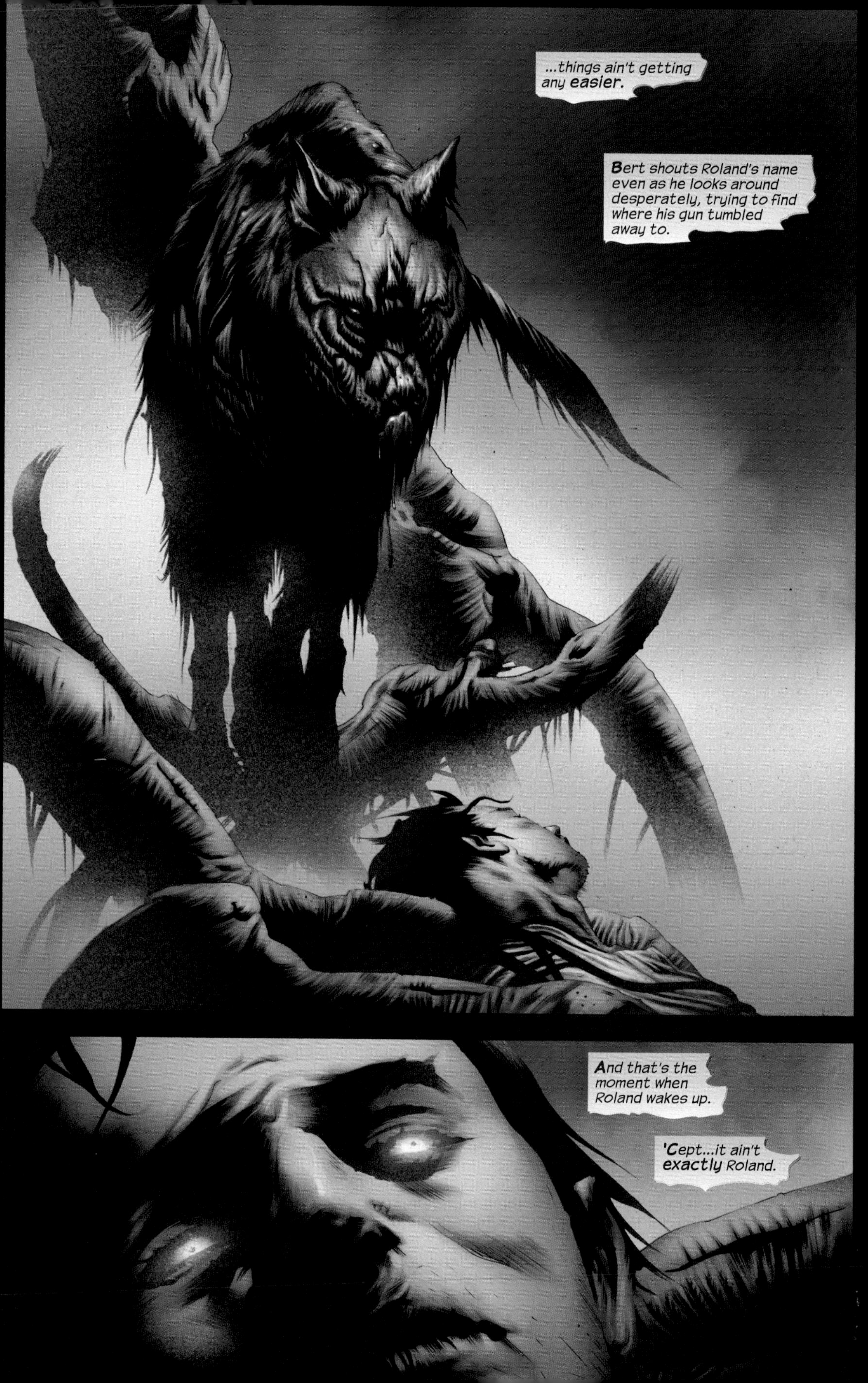
...things ain't getting any easier.
Bert shouts Roland's name even as he looks around desperately, trying to find where his gun tumbled away to.
And that's the moment when Roland wakes up.
'Cept...it ain't exactly Roland.

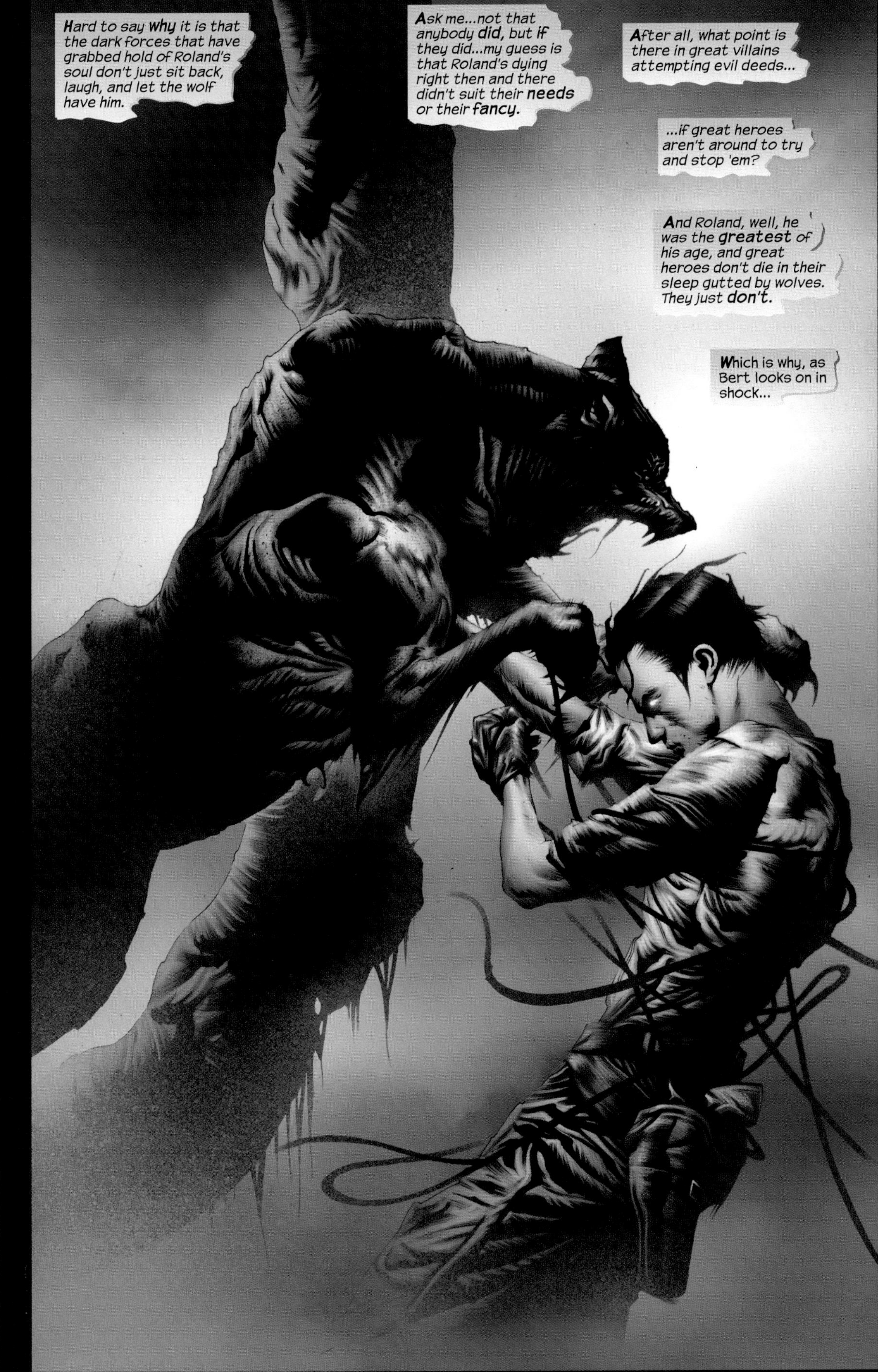
Hard to say why it is that the dark forces that have grabbed hold of Roland's soul don't just sit back, laugh, and let the wolf have him.
Ask me...not that anybody did, but if they did...my guess is that Roland's dying right then and there didn't suit their needs or their fancy.
After all, what point is there in great villains attempting evil deeds...
...if great heroes aren't around to try and stop 'em?
And Roland, well, he was the greatest of his age, and great heroes don't die in their sleep gutted by wolves. They just don't.
Which is why, as Bert looks on in shock...

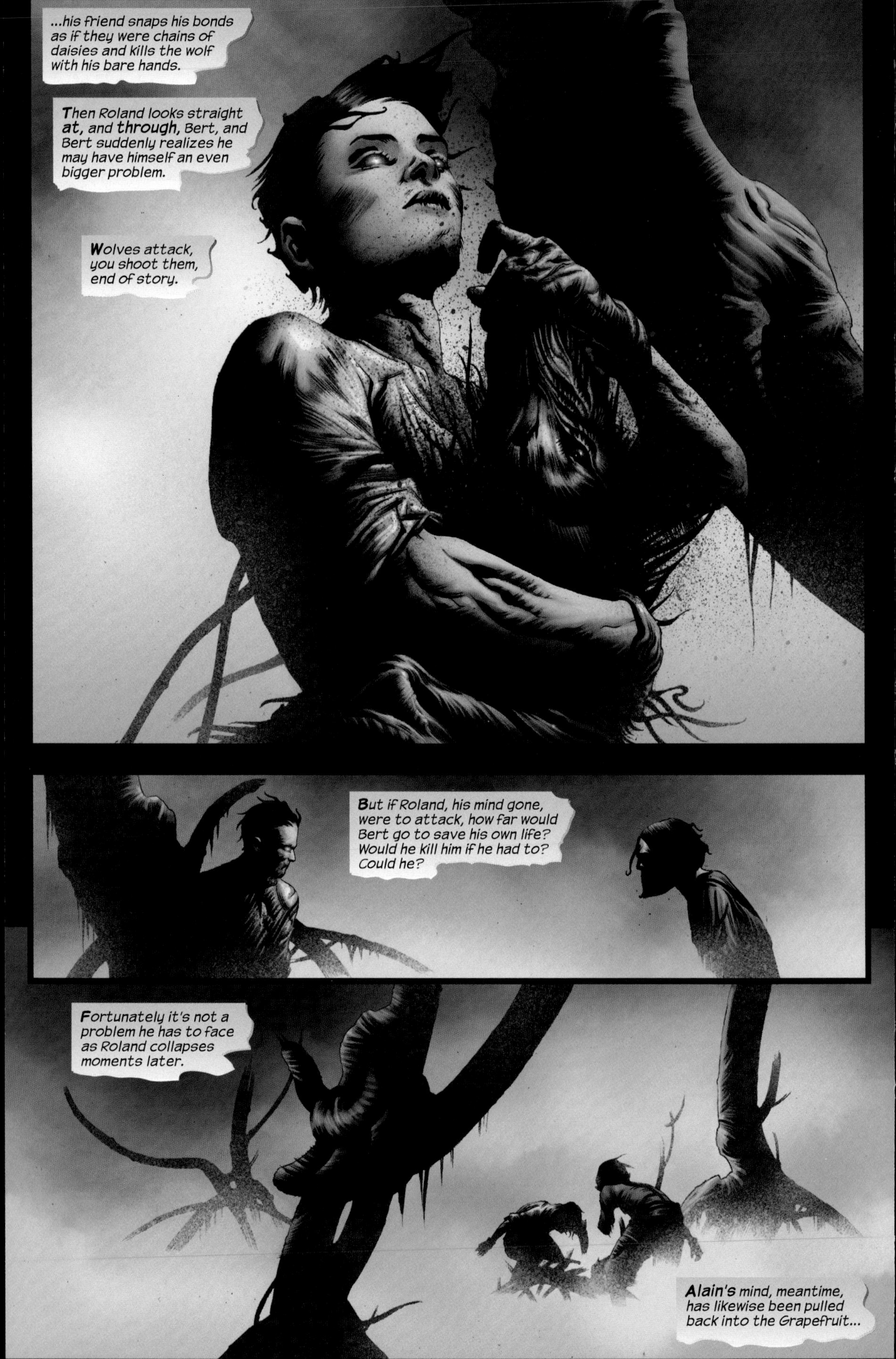

...his friend snaps his bonds as if they were chains of daisies and kills the wolf with his bare hands.
Then Roland looks straight at, and through, Bert, and Bert suddenly realizes he may have himself an even bigger problem.
Wolves attack, you shoot them, end of story.
But if Roland, his mind gone, were to attack, how far would Bert go to save his own life? Would he kill him if he had to? Could he?
Fortunately it's not a problem he has to face as Roland collapses moments later.
Alain's mind, meantime, has likewise been pulled back into the Grapefruit...

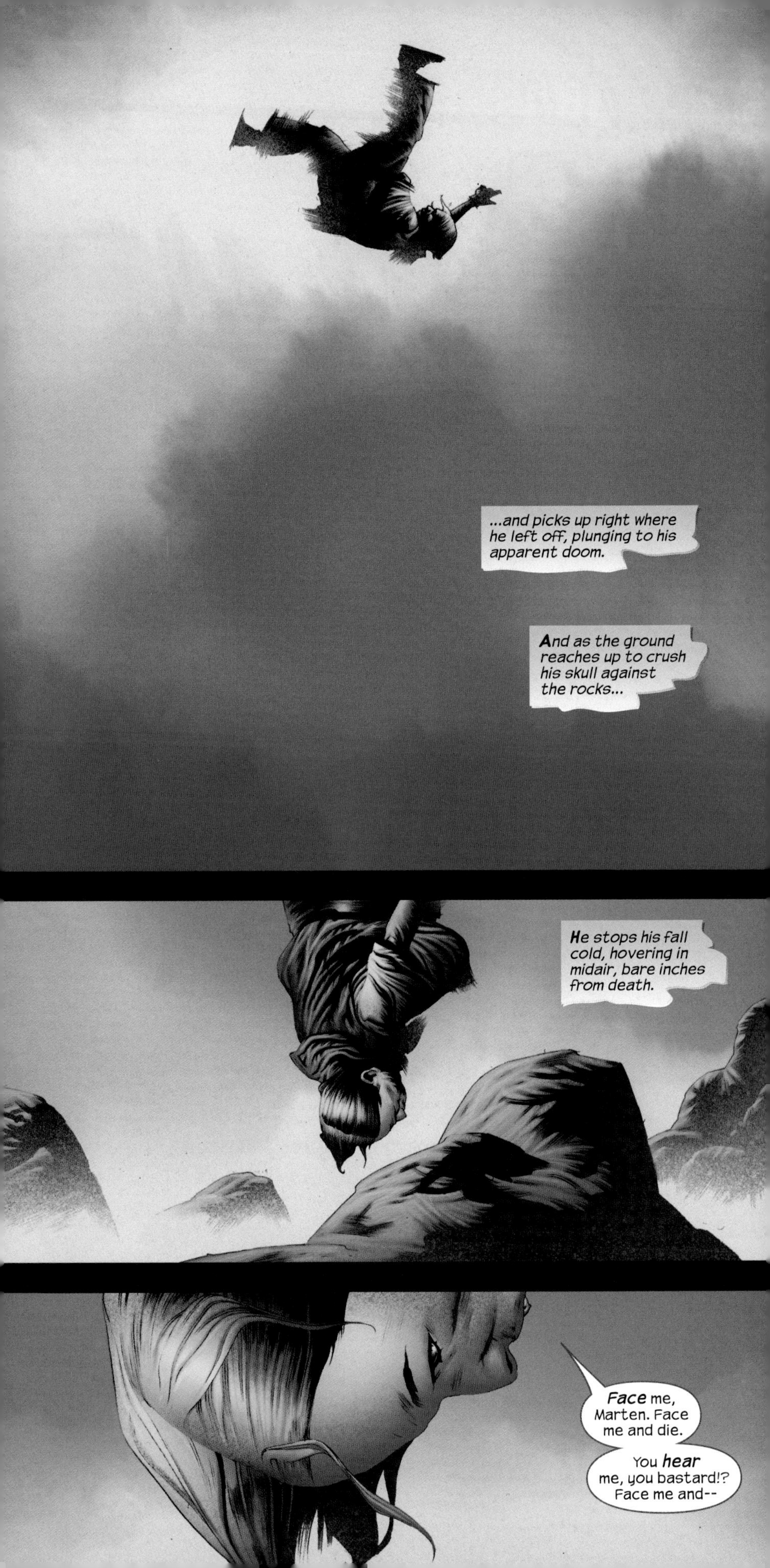
...and picks up right where he left off, plunging to his apparent doom.
And as the ground reaches up to crush his skull against the rocks...
He stops his fall cold, hovering in midair, bare inches from death.
Face me, Marten. Face me and die.
You hear me, you bastard!? Face me and--

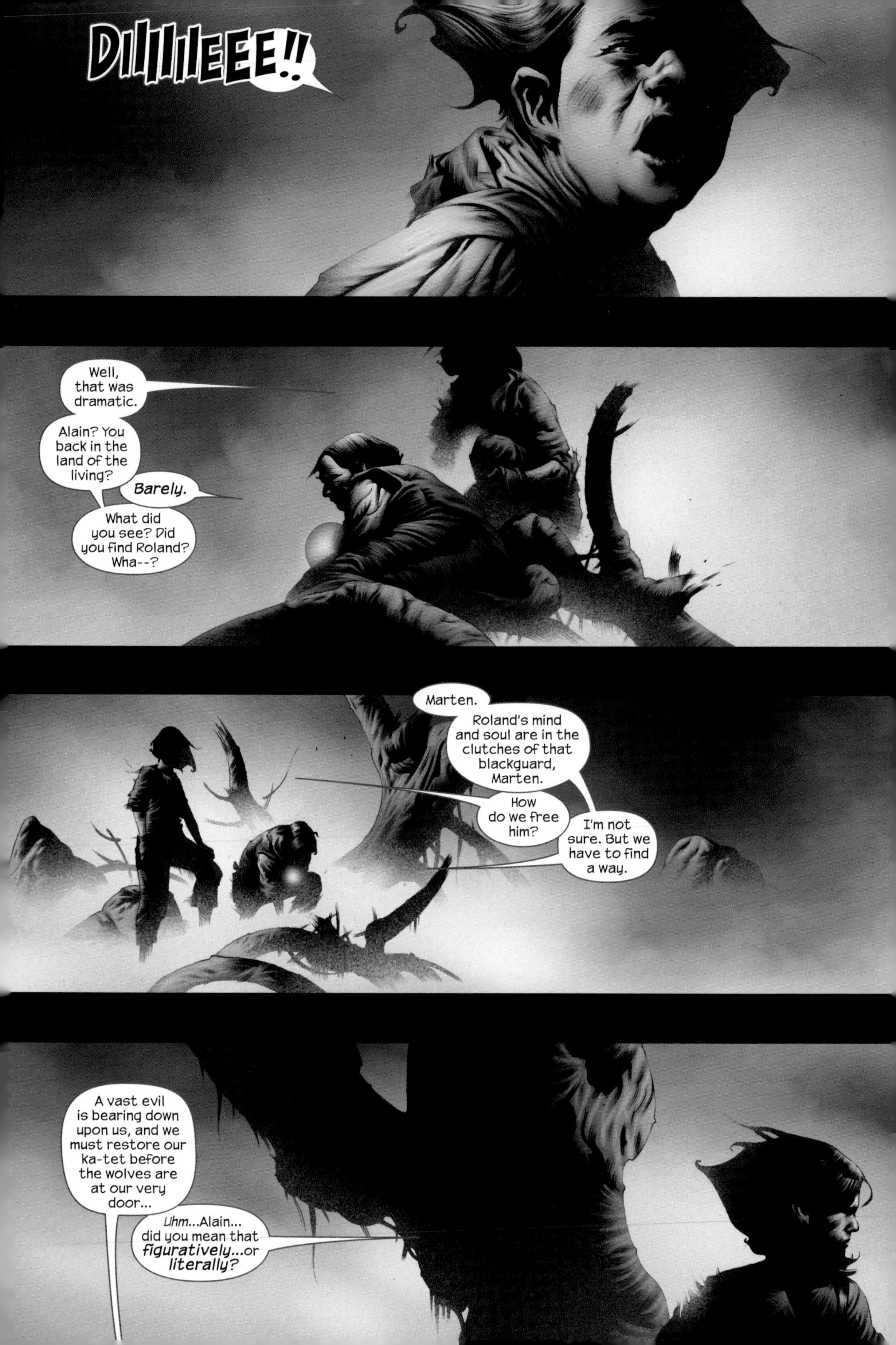
DIIIIIEEE!!
Well, that was dramatic.
Alain? You back in the land of the living?
Barely.
What did you see? Did you find Roland? Wha--?
Marten.
Roland's mind and soul are in the clutches of that blackguard, Marten.
How do we free him?
I'm not sure. But we have to find a way.
A vast evil is bearing down upon us, and we must restore our ka-tet before the wolves are at our very door...
Uhm...Alain... did you mean that figuratively...or literally?

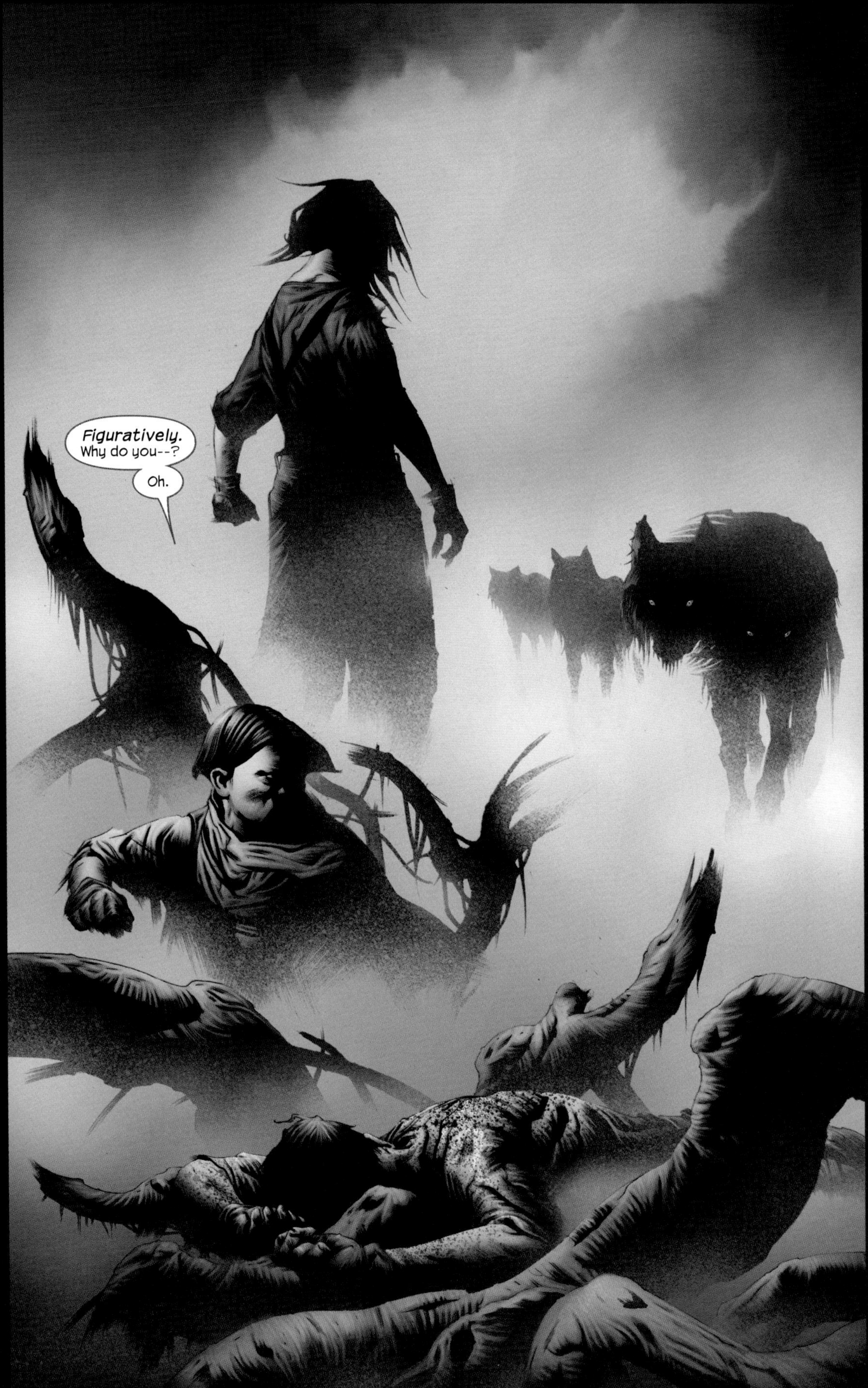
Figuratively.
Why do you--?
Oh.

STEPHEN KING

THE DARK TOWER

THE LONG ROAD HOME

CHAPTER FOUR

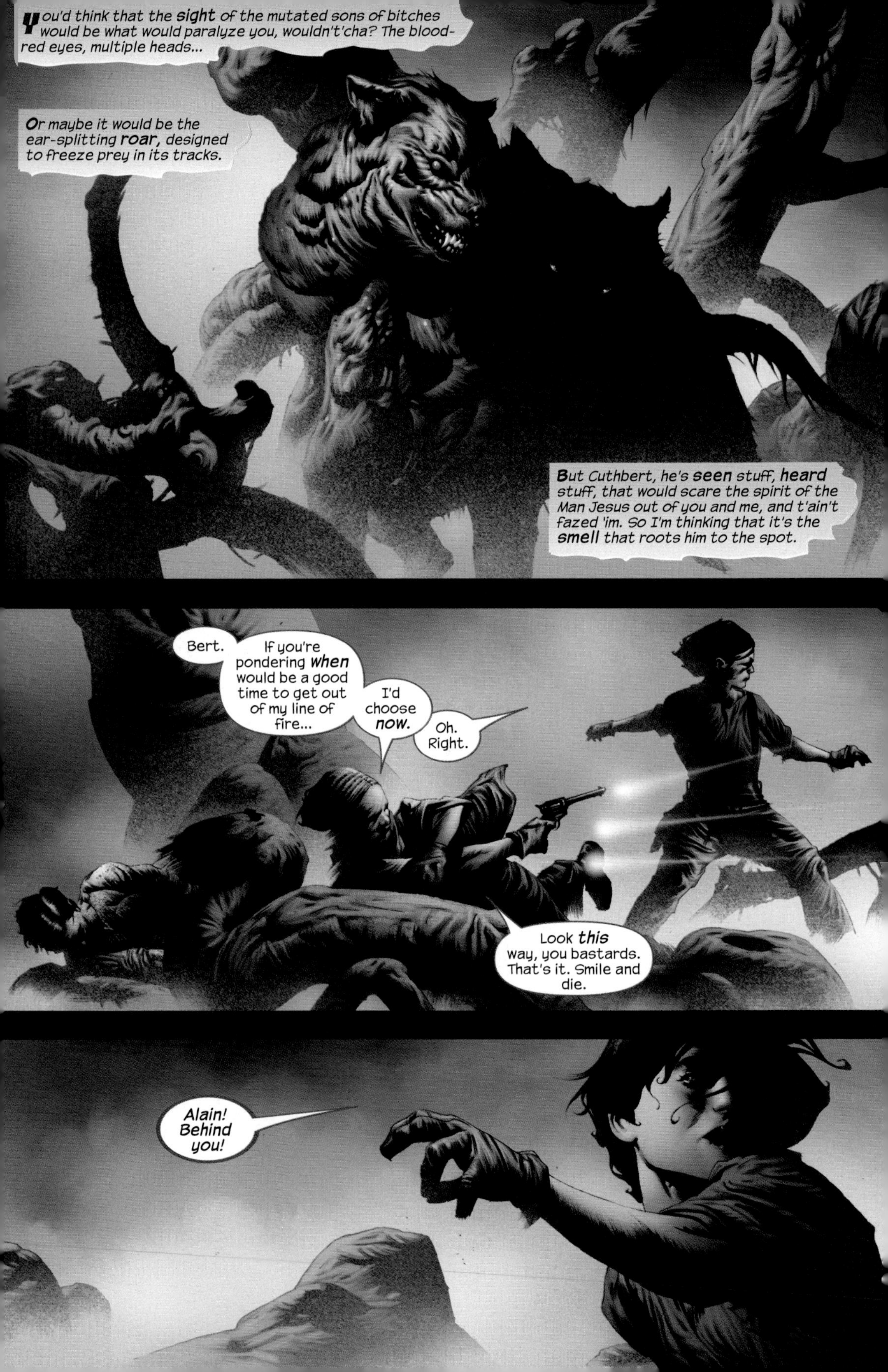
You'd think that the sight of the mutated sons of bitches would be what would paralyze you, wouldn't'cha? The blood-red eyes, multiple heads...
Or maybe it would be the ear-splitting roar, designed to freeze prey in its tracks.
But Cuthbert, he's seen stuff, heard stuff, that would scare the spirit of the Man Jesus out of you and me, and t'ain't fazed 'im. So I'm thinking that it's the smell that roots him to the spot.
Bert.
If you're pondering when would be a good time to get out of my line of fire...
I'd choose now.
Oh. Right.
Look this way, you bastards. That's it. Smile and die.
Alain! Behind you!

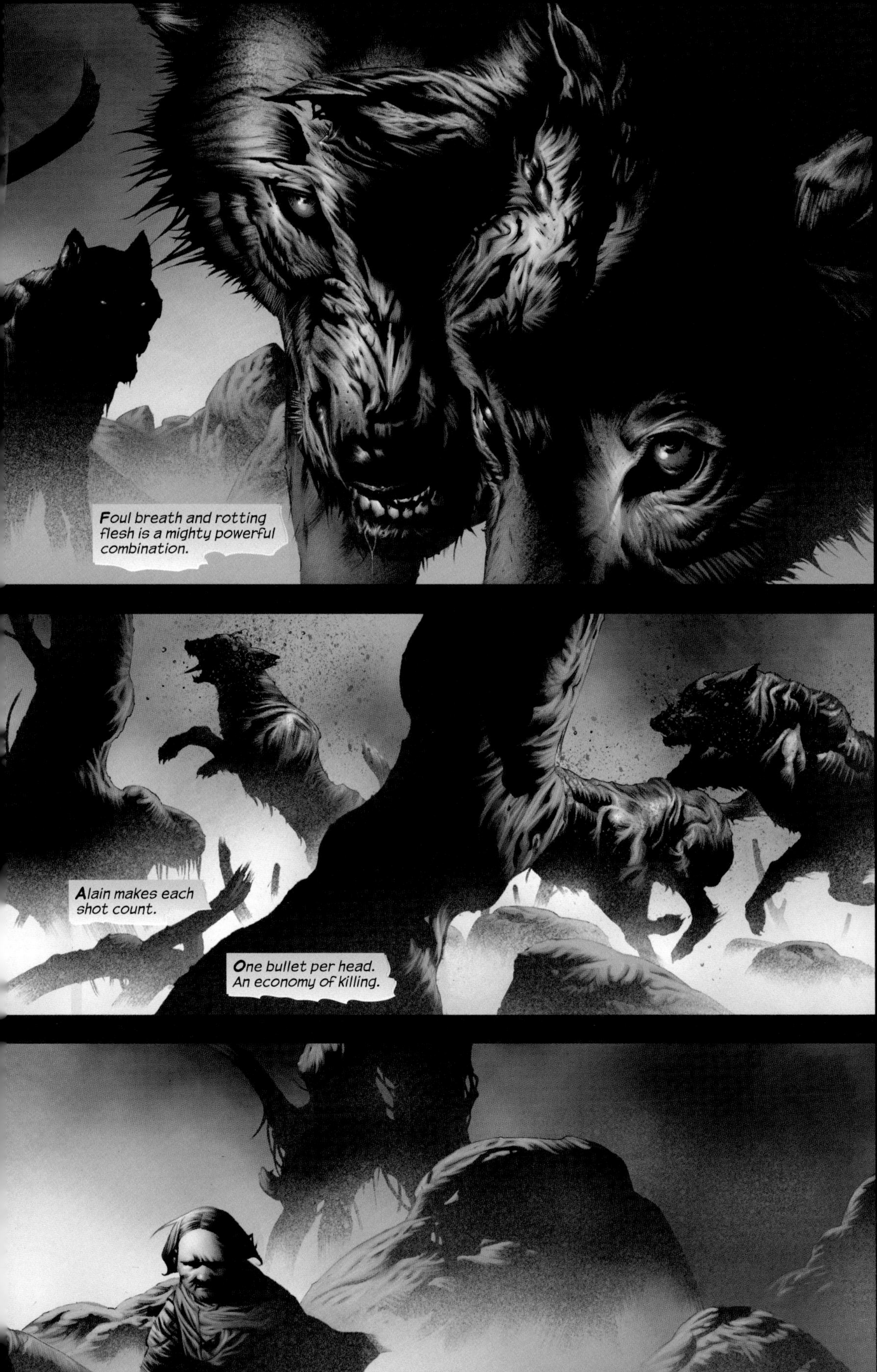
Foul breath and rotting flesh is a mighty powerful combination.
Alain makes each shot count.
One bullet per head. An economy of killing.

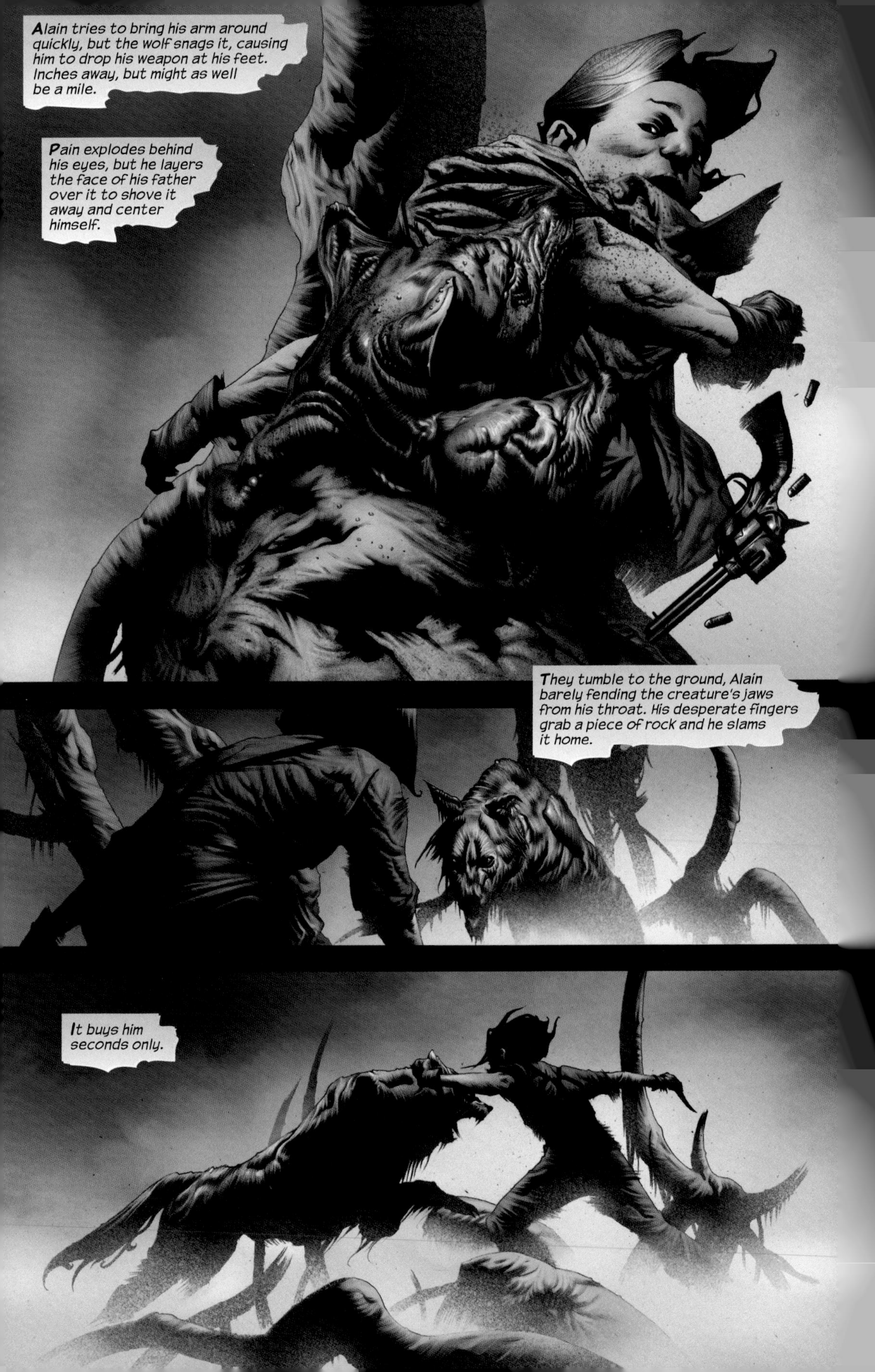
Alain tries to bring his arm around quickly, but the wolf snags it, causing him to drop his weapon at his feet. Inches away, but might as well be a mile.
Pain explodes behind his eyes, but he layers the face of his father over it to shove it away and center himself.
They tumble to the ground, Alain barely fending the creature's jaws from his throat. His desperate fingers grab a piece of rock and he slams it home.
It buys him seconds only.

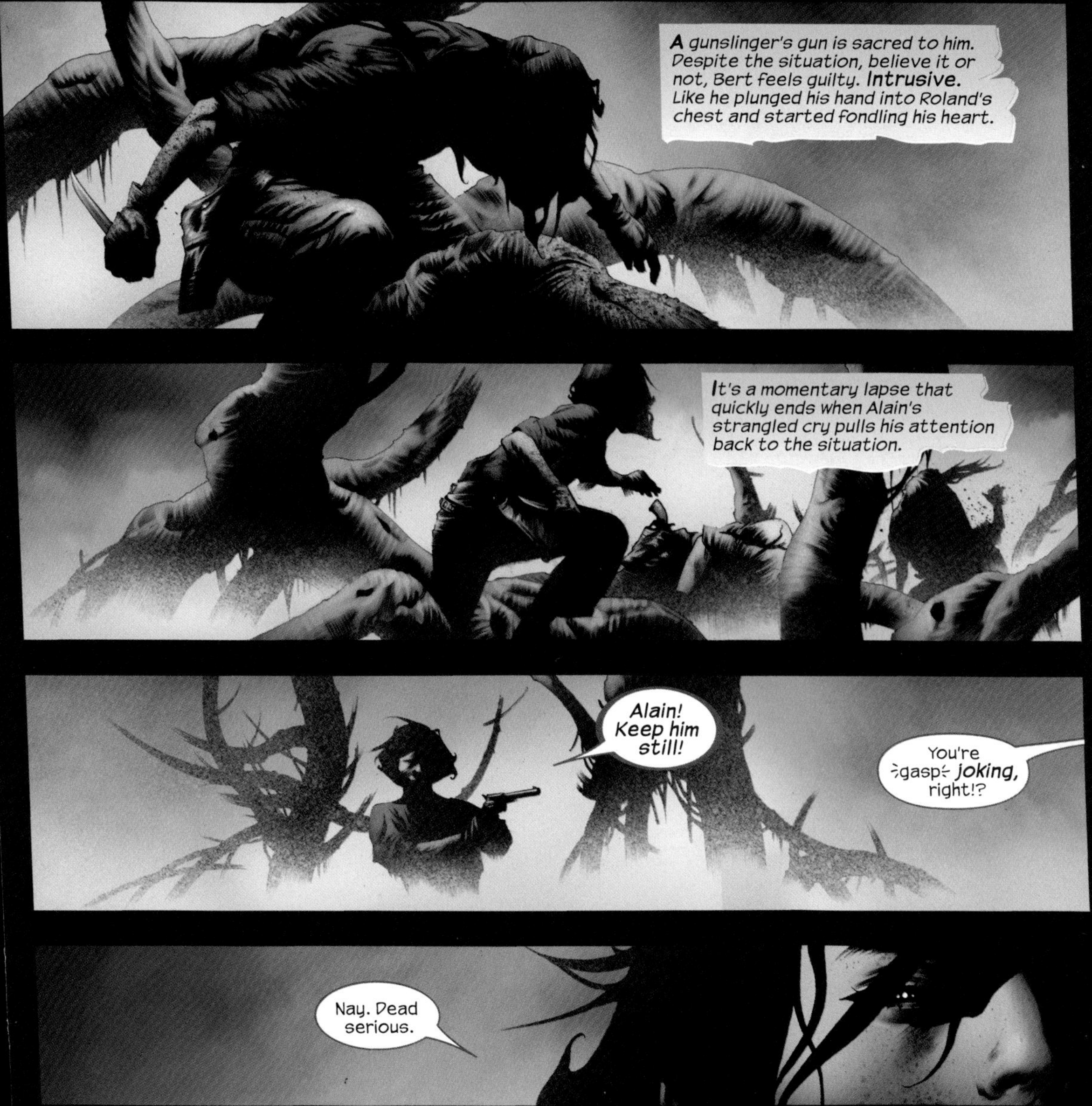
A gunslinger's gun is sacred to him. Despite the situation, believe it or not, Bert feels guilty. Intrusive. Like he plunged his hand into Roland's chest and started fondling his heart.
It's a momentary lapse that quickly ends when Alain's strangled cry pulls his attention back to the situation.
Alain! Keep him still!
You're -gasp- joking, right!?
Nay. Dead serious.

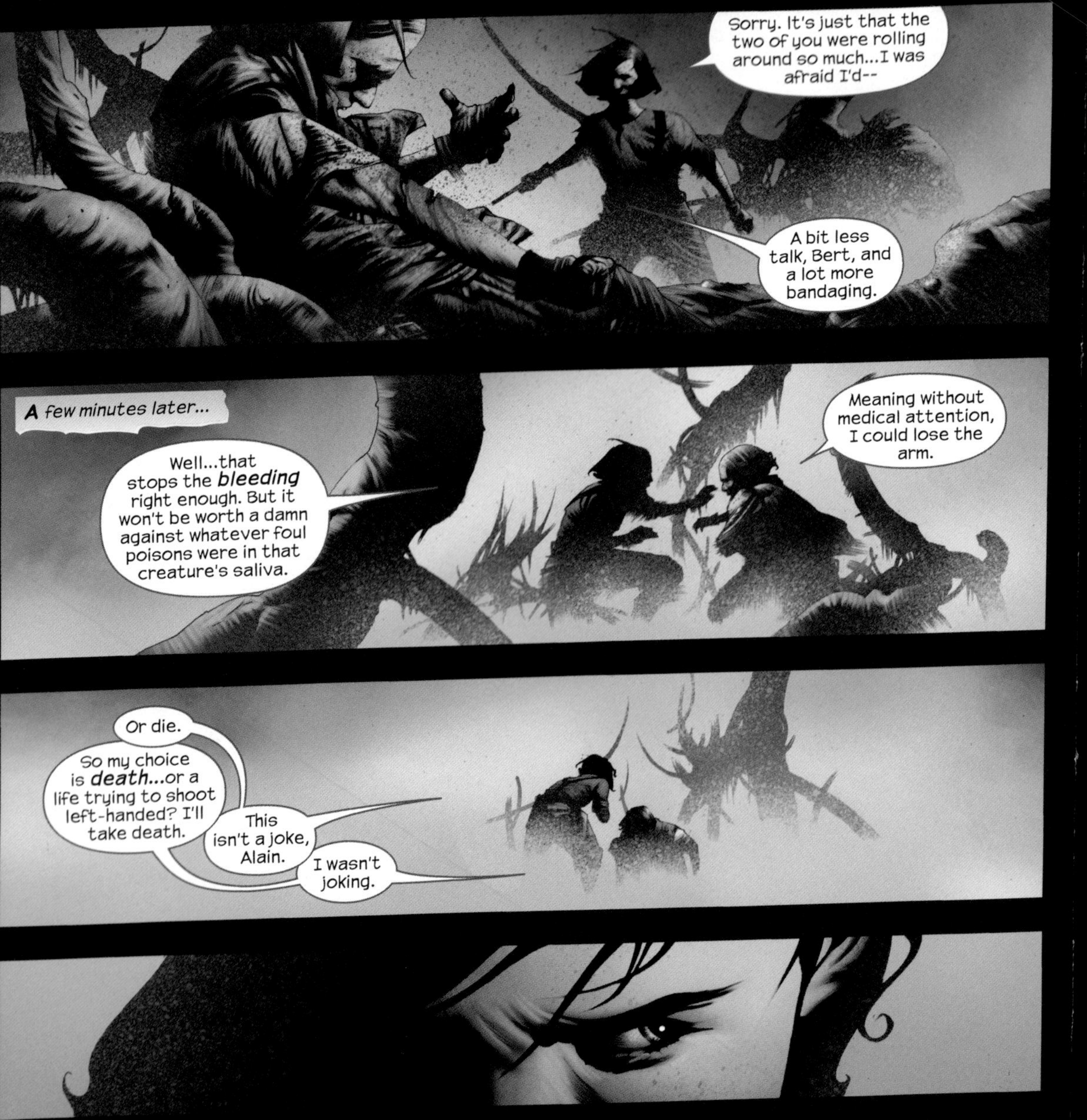

Sorry. It's just that the two of you were rolling around so much...I was afraid I'd--
A bit less talk, Bert, and a lot more bandaging.
A few minutes later...
Well...that stops the *bleeding* right enough. But it won't be worth a damn against whatever foul poisons were in that creature's saliva.
Meaning without medical attention, I could lose the arm.
Or die.
So my choice is *death*...or a life trying to shoot left-handed? I'll take death.
This isn't a joke, Alain.
I wasn't joking.

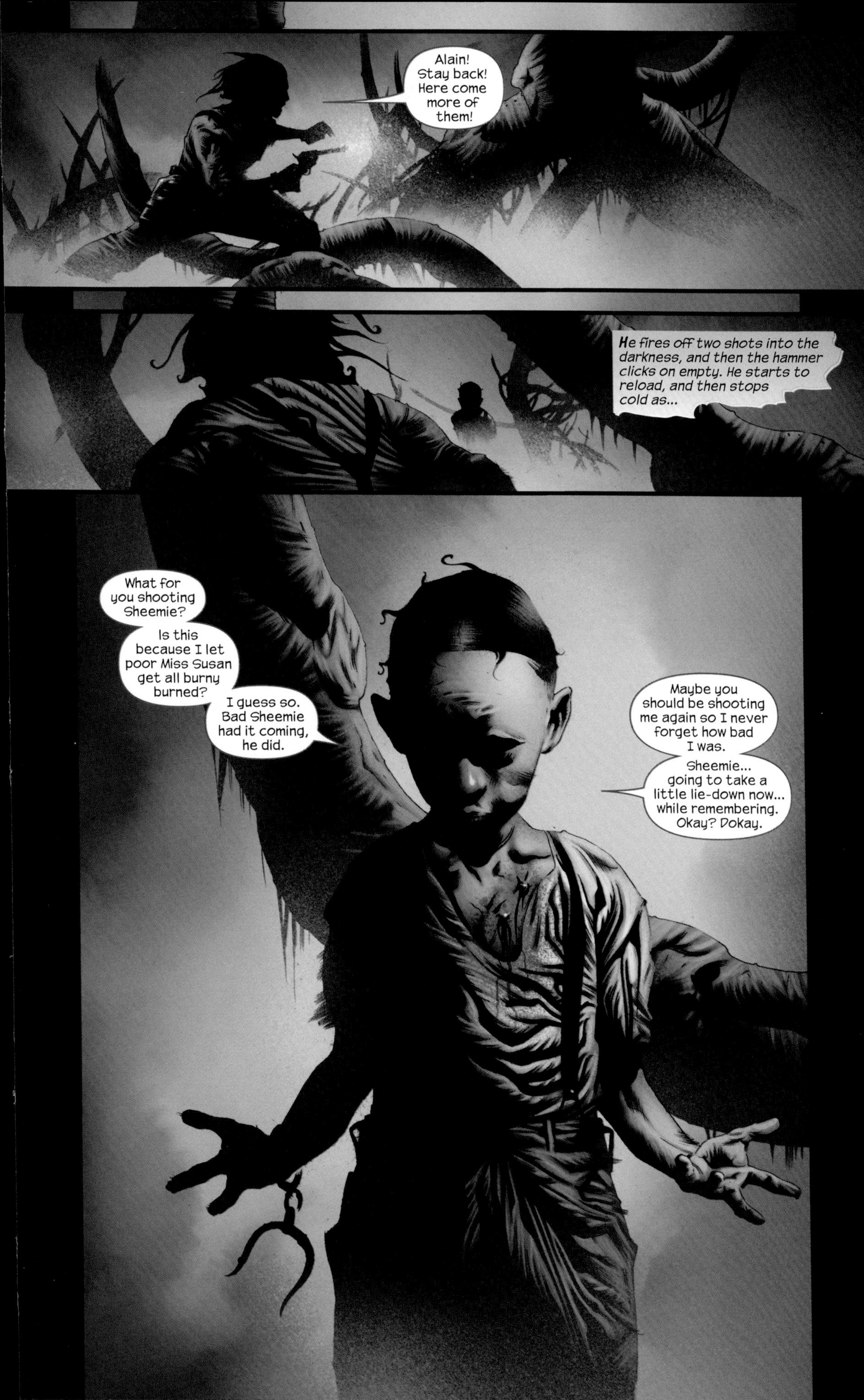
Alain! Stay back! Here come more of them!
He fires off two shots into the darkness, and then the hammer clicks on empty. He starts to reload, and then stops cold as...
What for you shooting Sheemie?
Is this because I let poor Miss Susan get all burny burned?
I guess so. Bad Sheemie had it coming, he did.
Maybe you should be shooting me again so I never forget how bad I was.
Sheemie... going to take a little lie-down now... while remembering. Okay? Dokay.

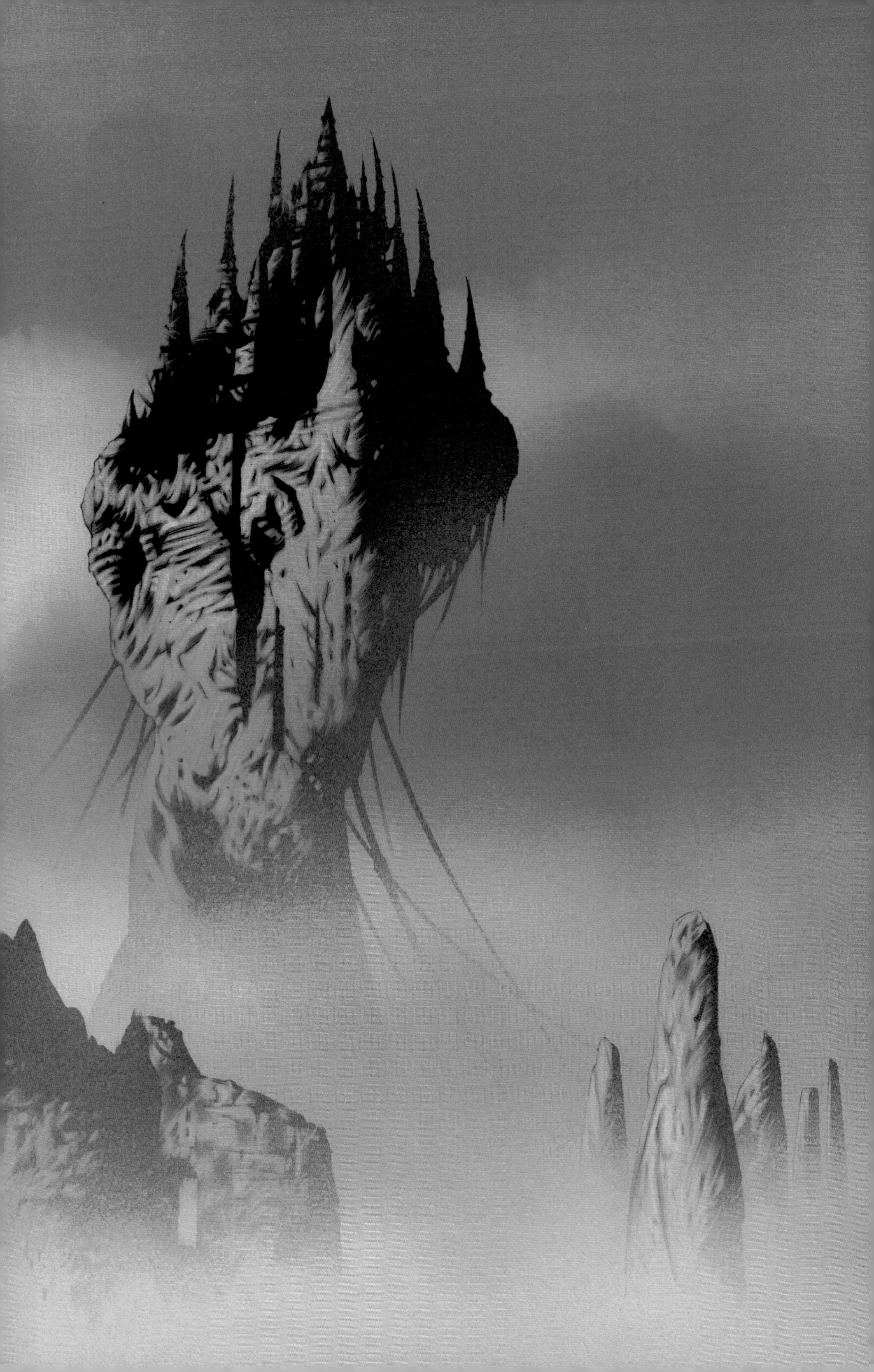

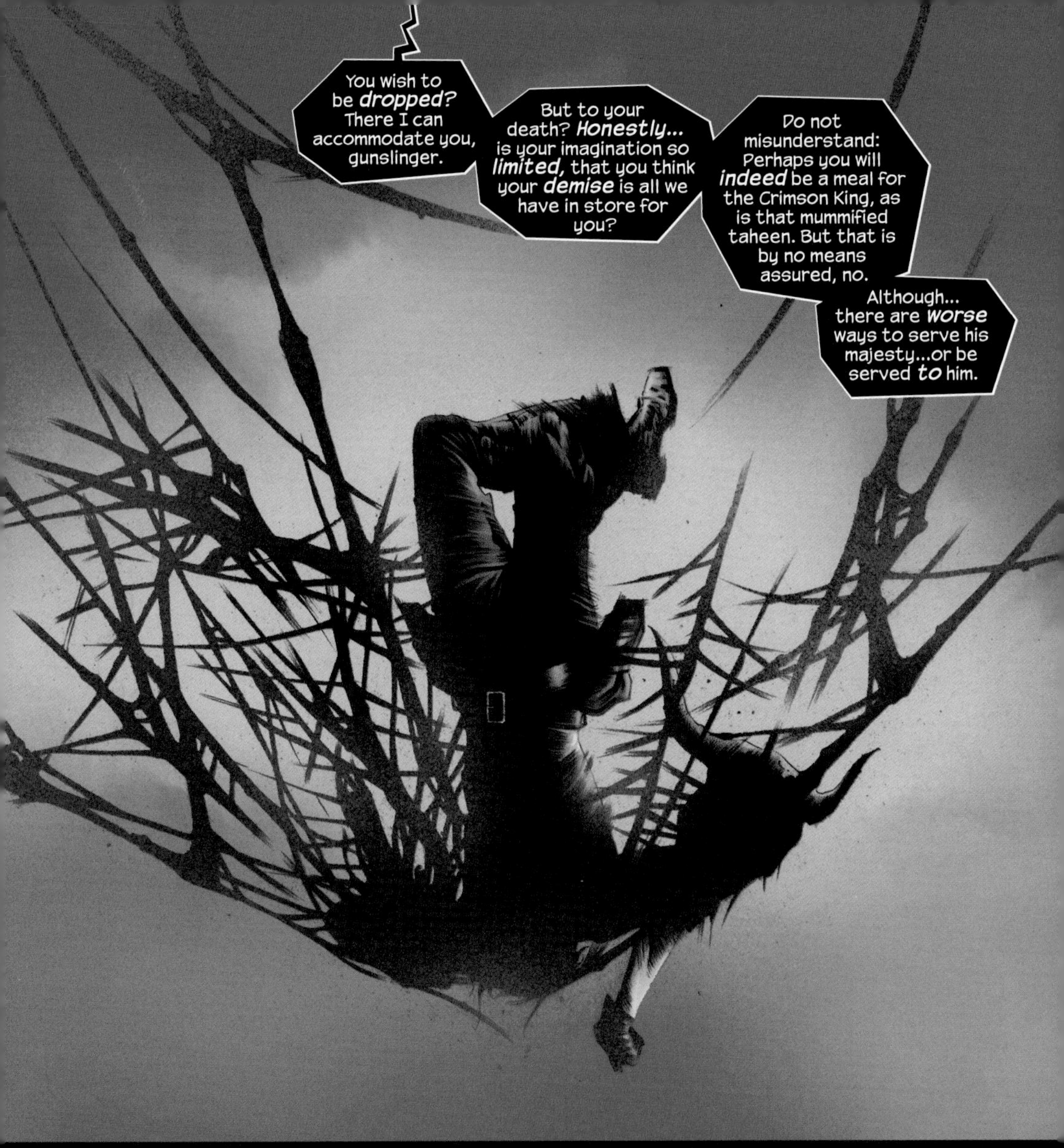

You wish to be *dropped?* There I can accommodate you, gunslinger.
But to your death? *Honestly...* is your imagination so *limited,* that you think your *demise* is all we have in store for you?
Do not misunderstand: Perhaps you will *indeed* be a meal for the Crimson King, as is that mummified taheen. But that is by no means assured, no.
Although... there are *worse* ways to serve his majesty...or be served *to* him.

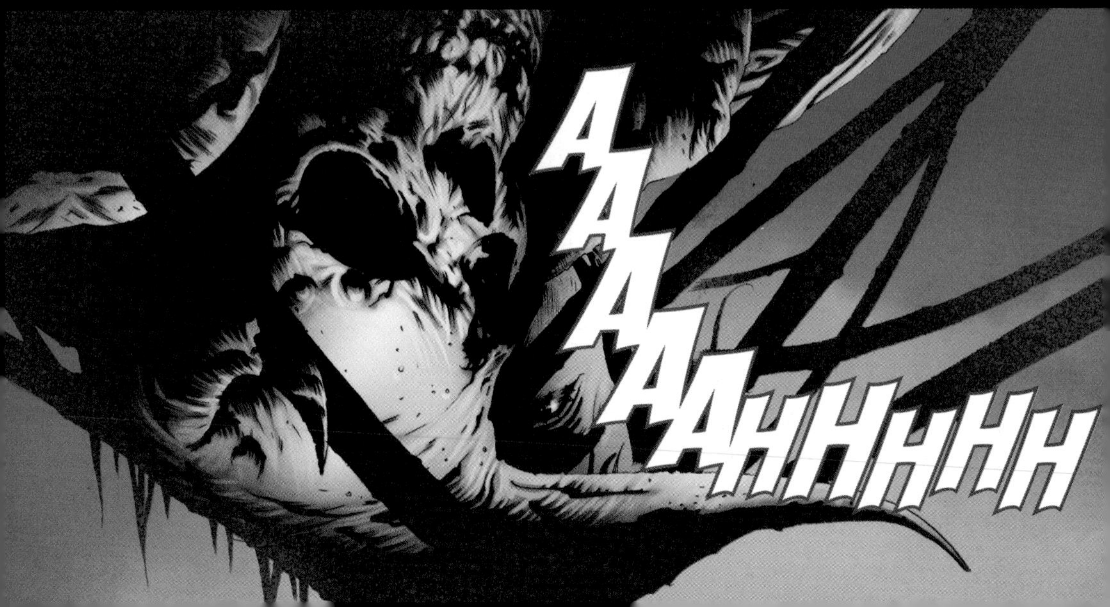

AAAAAAHHHHHH

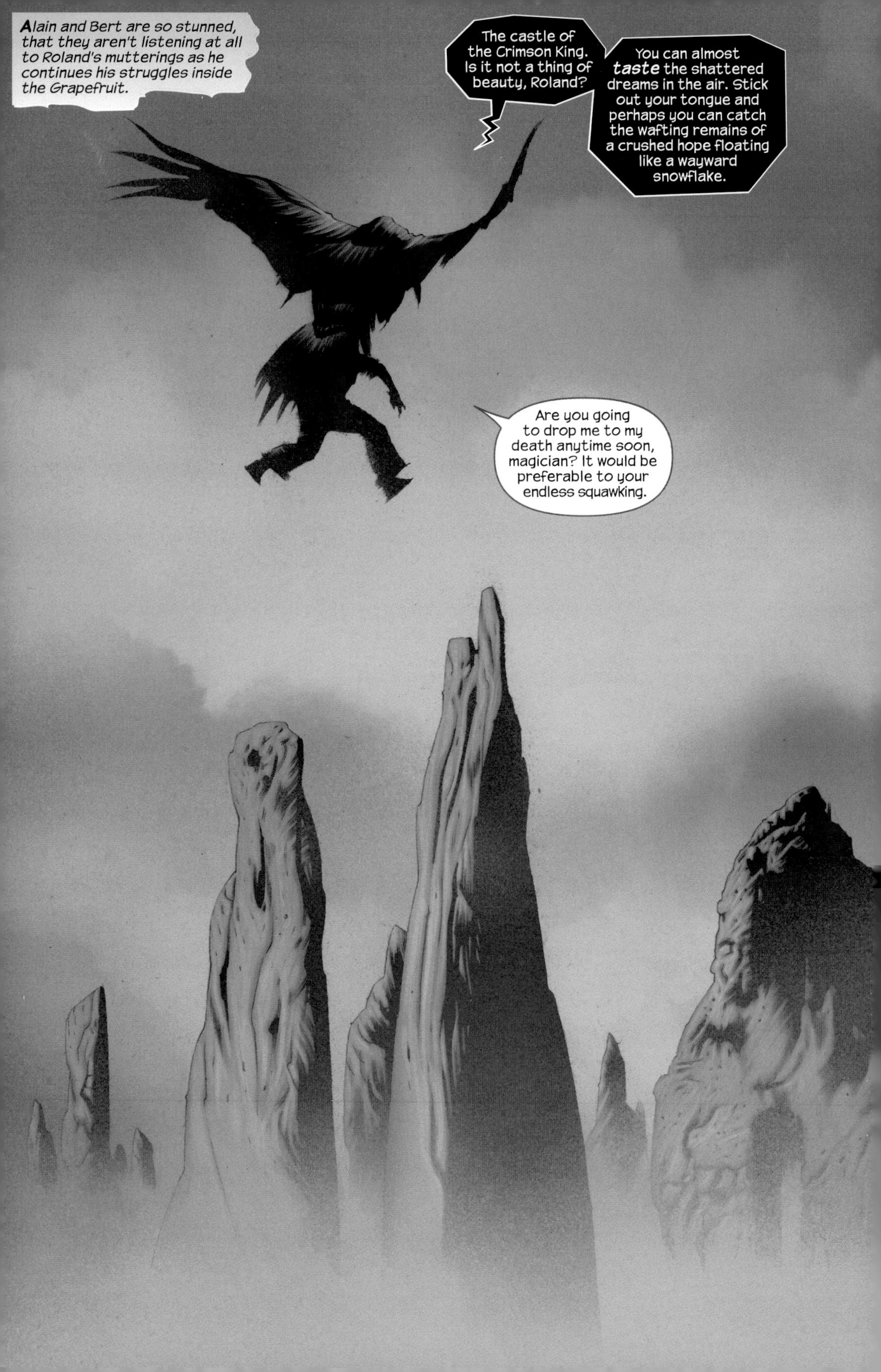
Alain and Bert are so stunned, that they aren't listening at all to Roland's mutterings as he continues his struggles inside the Grapefruit.
The castle of the Crimson King. Is it not a thing of beauty, Roland?
You can almost taste the shattered dreams in the air. Stick out your tongue and perhaps you can catch the wafting remains of a crushed hope floating like a wayward snowflake.
Are you going to drop me to my death anytime soon, magician? It would be preferable to your endless squawking.

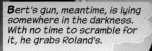

Bert's gun, meantime, is lying somewhere in the darkness. With no time to scramble for it, he grabs Roland's.

A gunslinger's gun is sacred to him. Despite the situation, believe it or not, Bert feels guilty. **Intrusive.** Like he plunged his hand into Roland's chest and started fondling his heart.

It's a momentary lapse that quickly ends when Alain's strangled cry pulls his attention back to the situation.

Alain! Keep him still!

You're ÷gasp÷ *joking*, right!?

Nay. Dead serious.

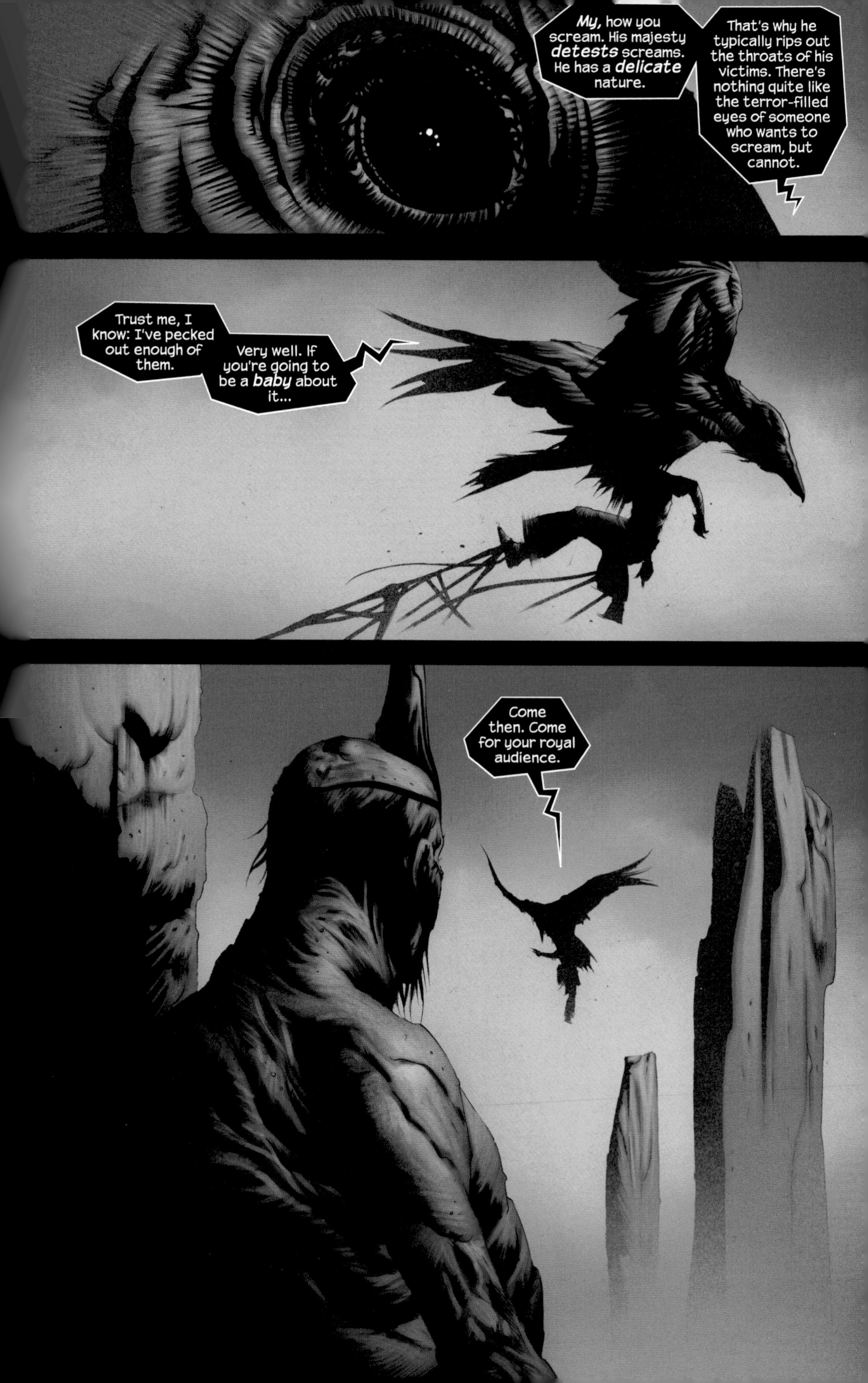
My, how you scream. His majesty detests screams. He has a delicate nature.
That's why he typically rips out the throats of his victims. There's nothing quite like the terror-filled eyes of someone who wants to scream, but cannot.
Trust me, I know: I've pecked out enough of them.
Very well. If you're going to be a baby about it...
Come then. Come for your royal audience.

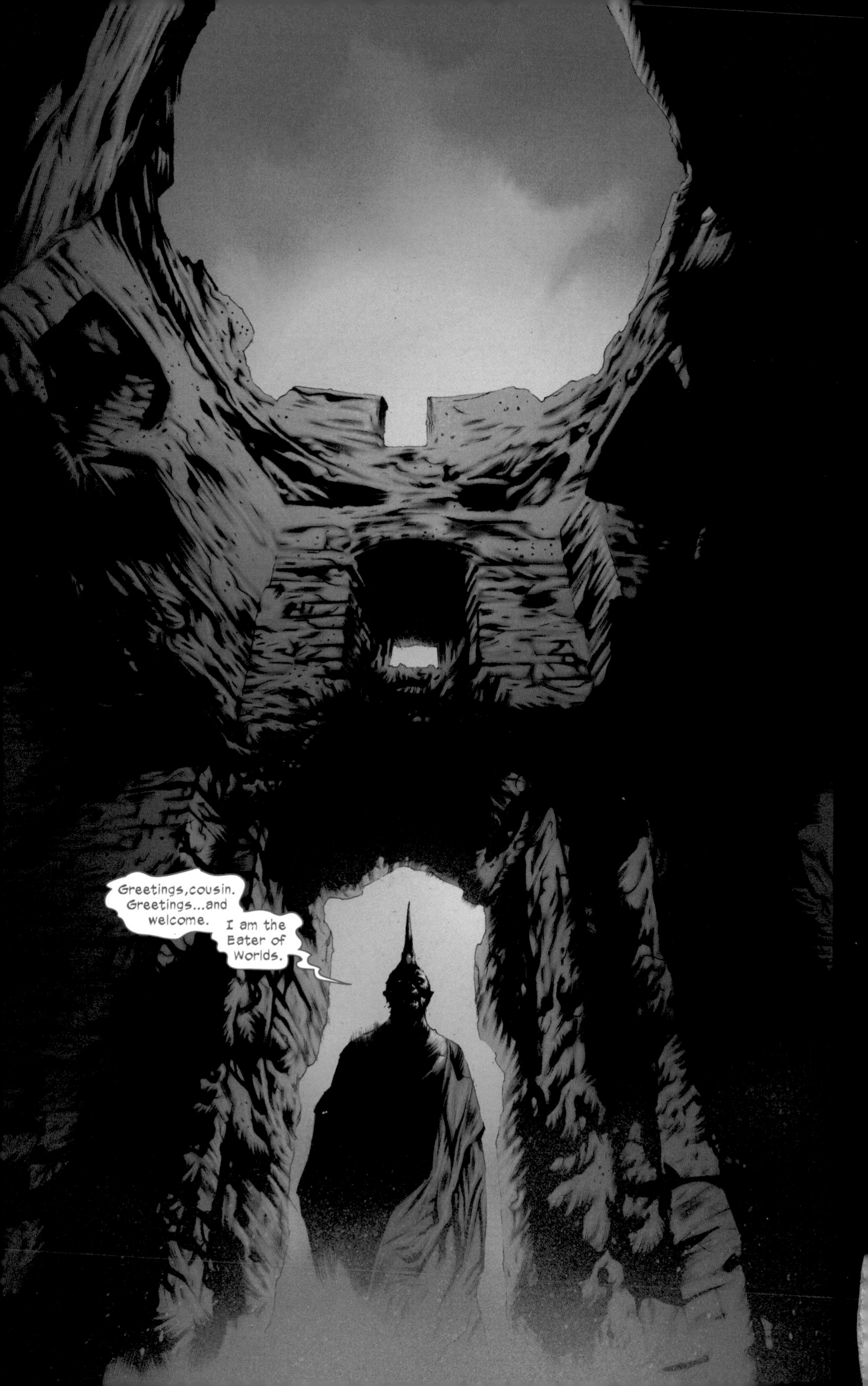
Greetings, cousin. Greetings...and welcome.
I am the Eater of Worlds.

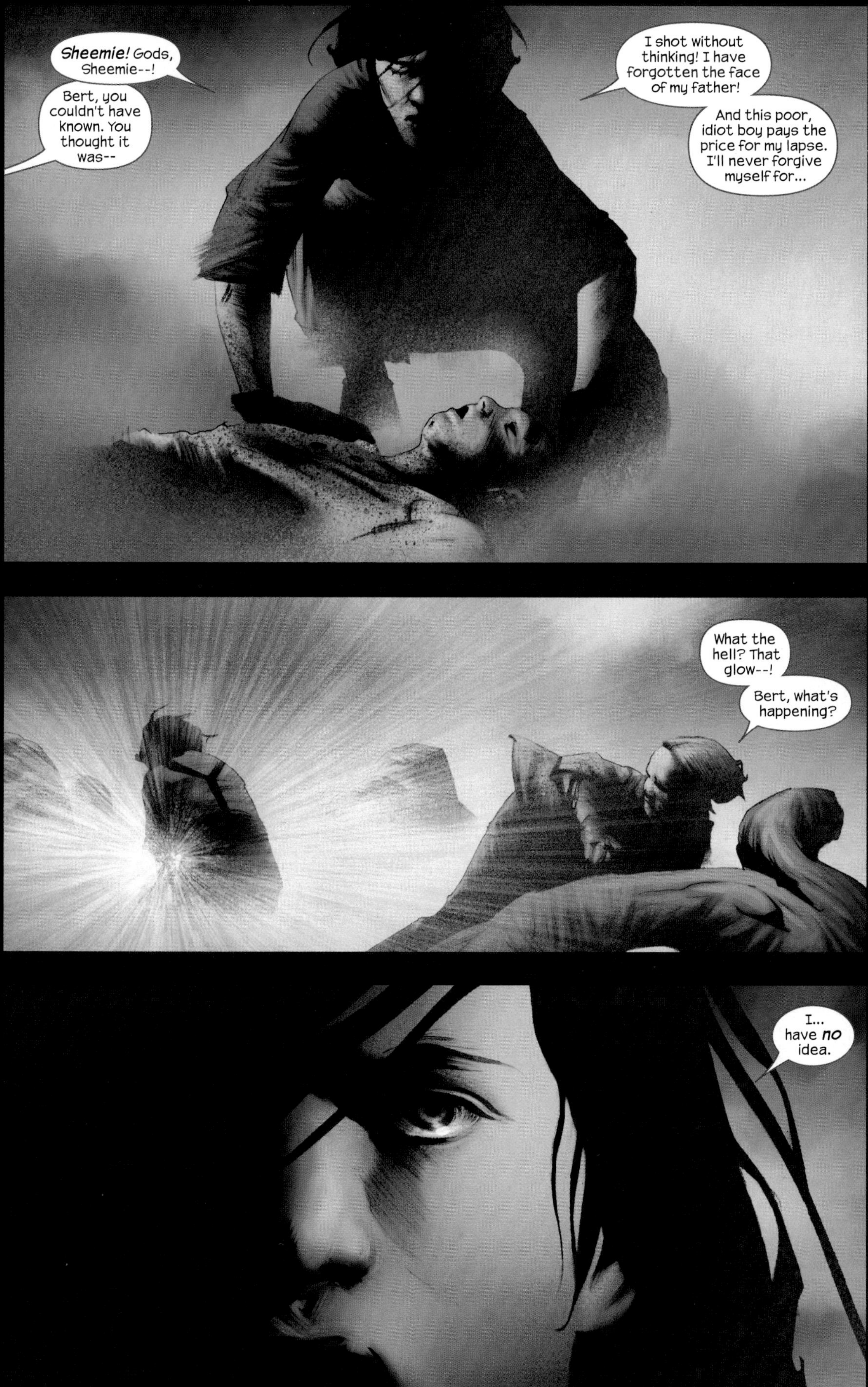

Sheemie! Gods, Sheemie--!
Bert, you couldn't have known. You thought it was--
I shot without thinking! I have forgotten the face of my father!
And this poor, idiot boy pays the price for my lapse. I'll never forgive myself for...
What the hell? That glow--!
Bert, what's happening?
I... have *no* idea.

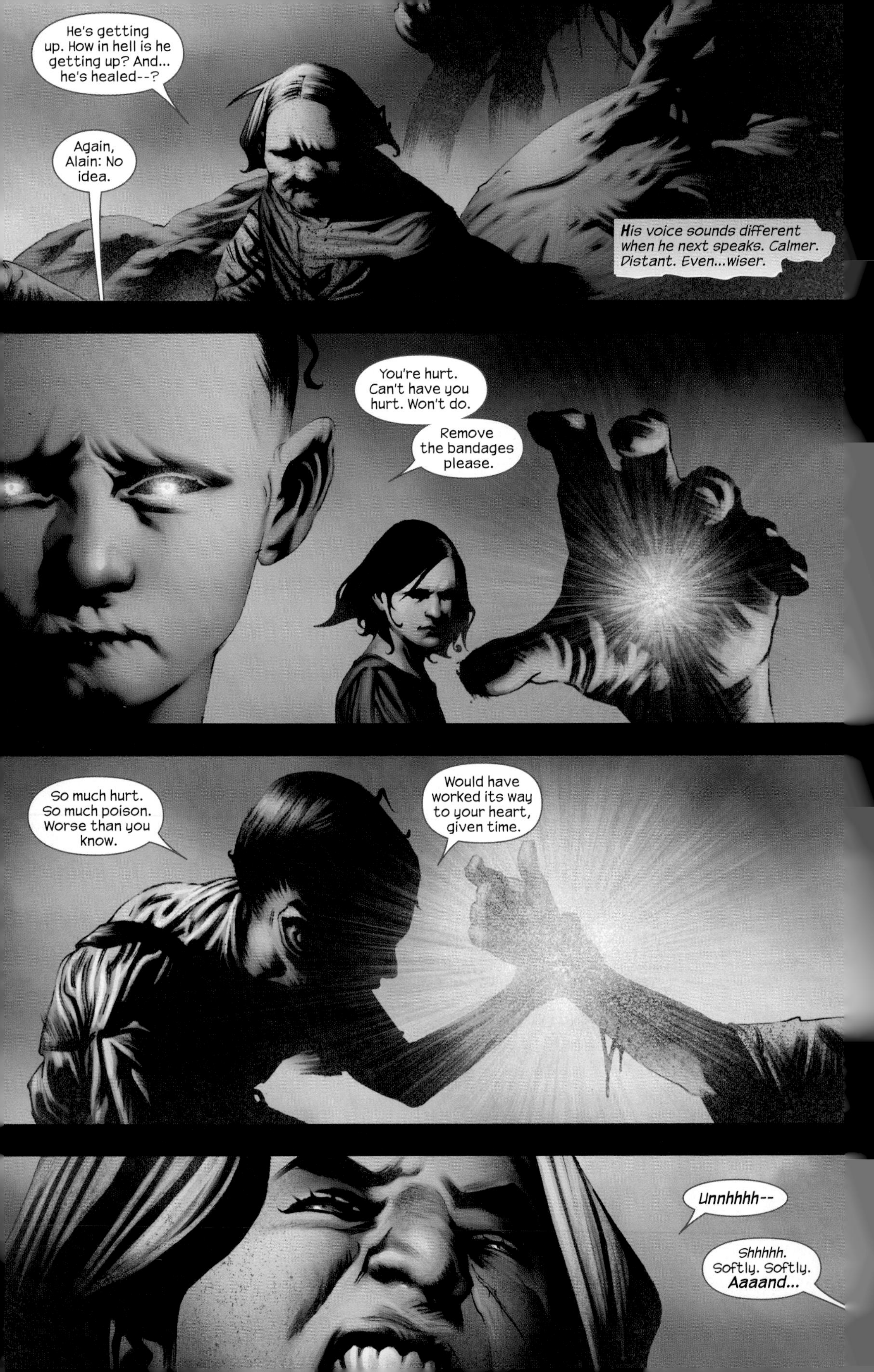
He's getting up. How in hell is he getting up? And... he's healed--?
Again, Alain: No idea.
His voice sounds different when he next speaks. Calmer. Distant. Even...wiser.
You're hurt. Can't have you hurt. Won't do.
Remove the bandages please.
So much hurt. So much poison. Worse than you know.
Would have worked its way to your heart, given time.
Unnhhhh--
Shhhhh. Softly. Softly. Aaaand...

All better.

You...you *did* it! But I don't understand how...how--

Never mind. Questioning a miracle just tempts the gods to take it back.

Sheemie... do you think you have one more miracle left in you?

Maybe.

Roland's soul is trapped in this damnable sphere. Do you think you can free him?

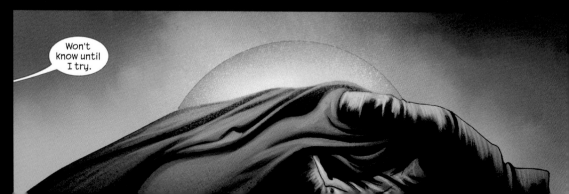

Won't know until I try.

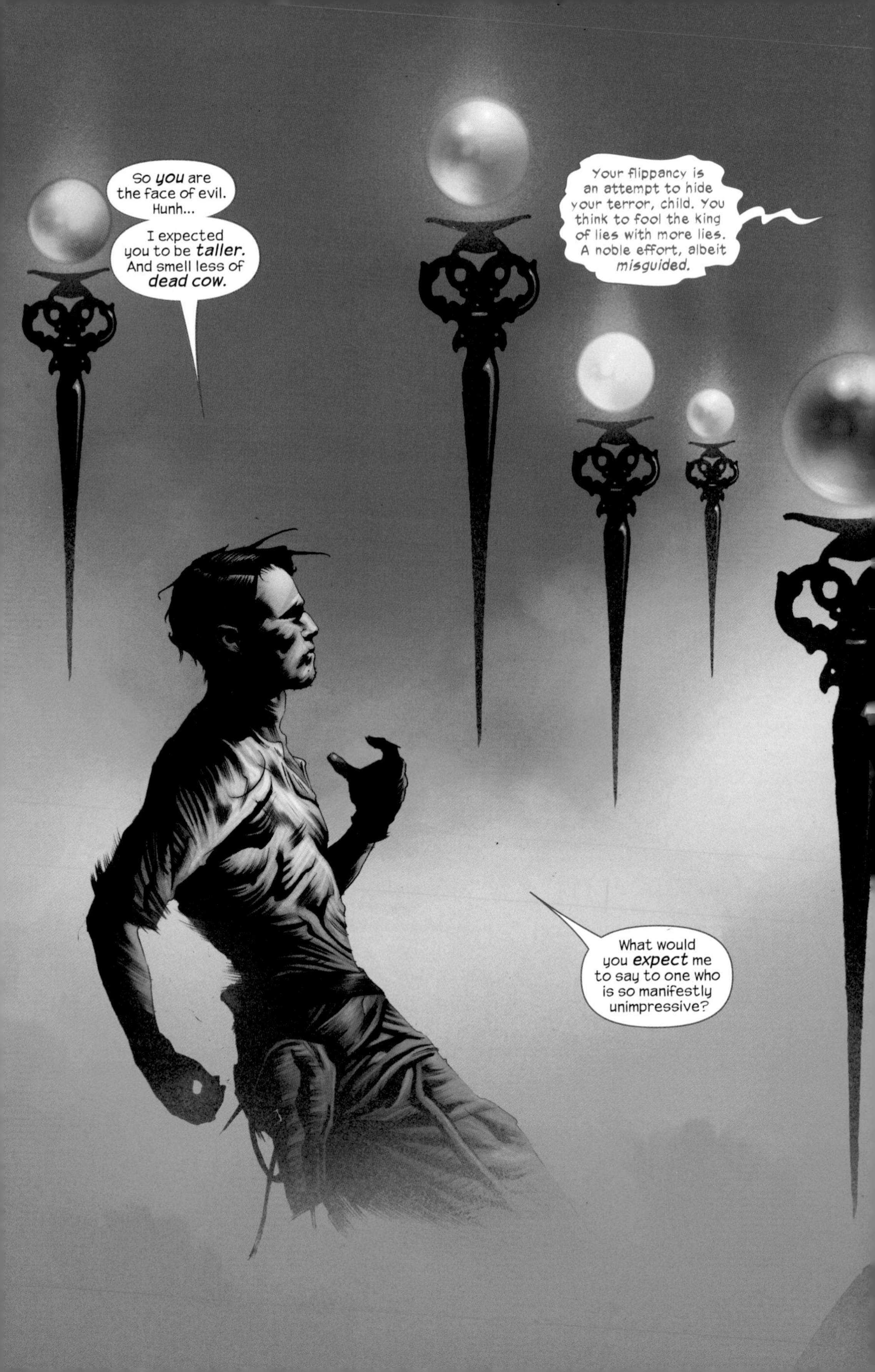
So you are the face of evil. Hunh...
I expected you to be taller. And smell less of dead cow.
Your flippancy is an attempt to hide your terror, child. You think to fool the king of lies with more lies. A noble effort, albeit misguided.
What would you expect me to say to one who is so manifestly unimpressive?

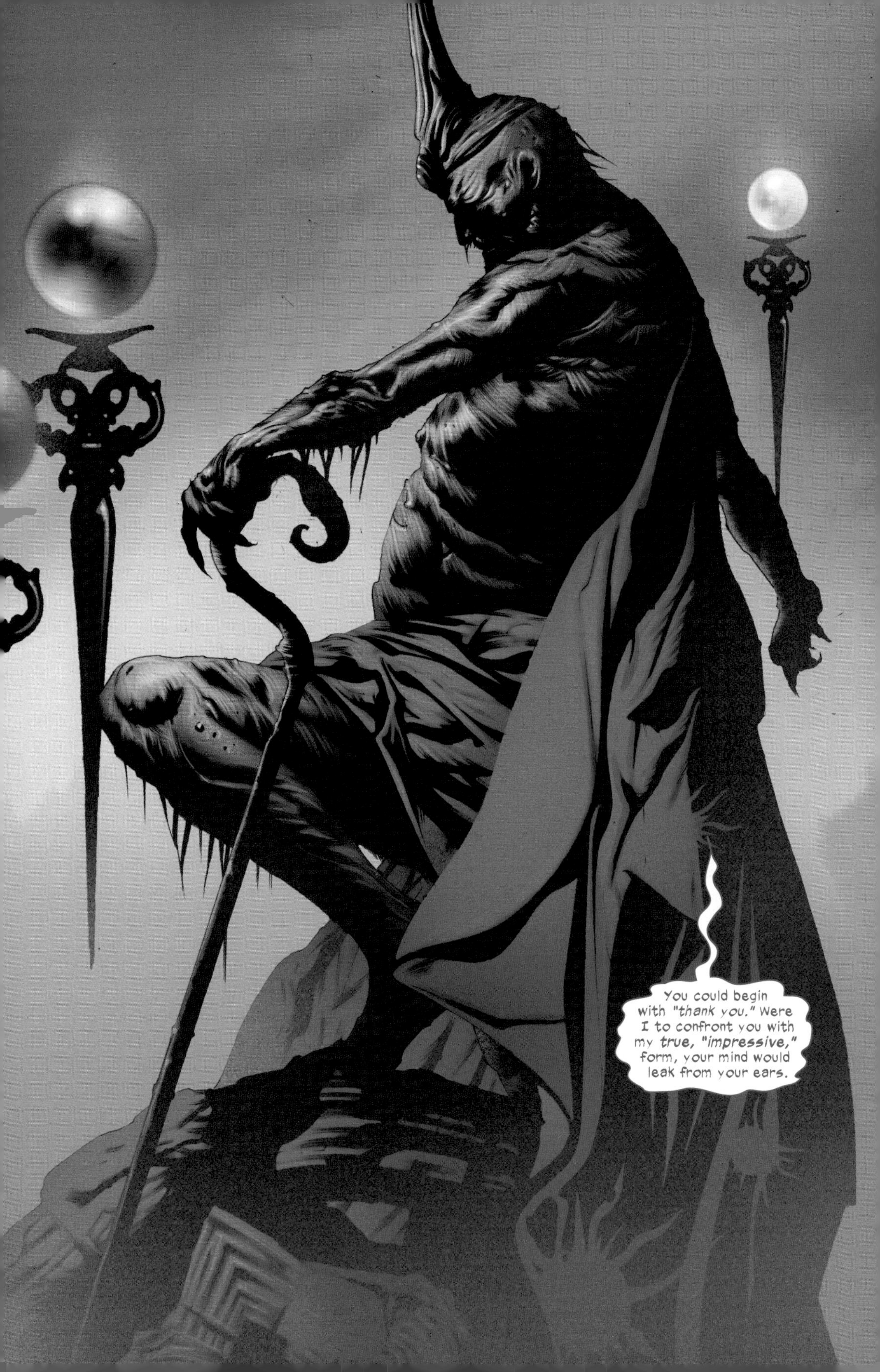
You could begin with "*thank you.*" Were I to confront you with my *true*, "*impressive,*" form, your mind would leak from your ears.

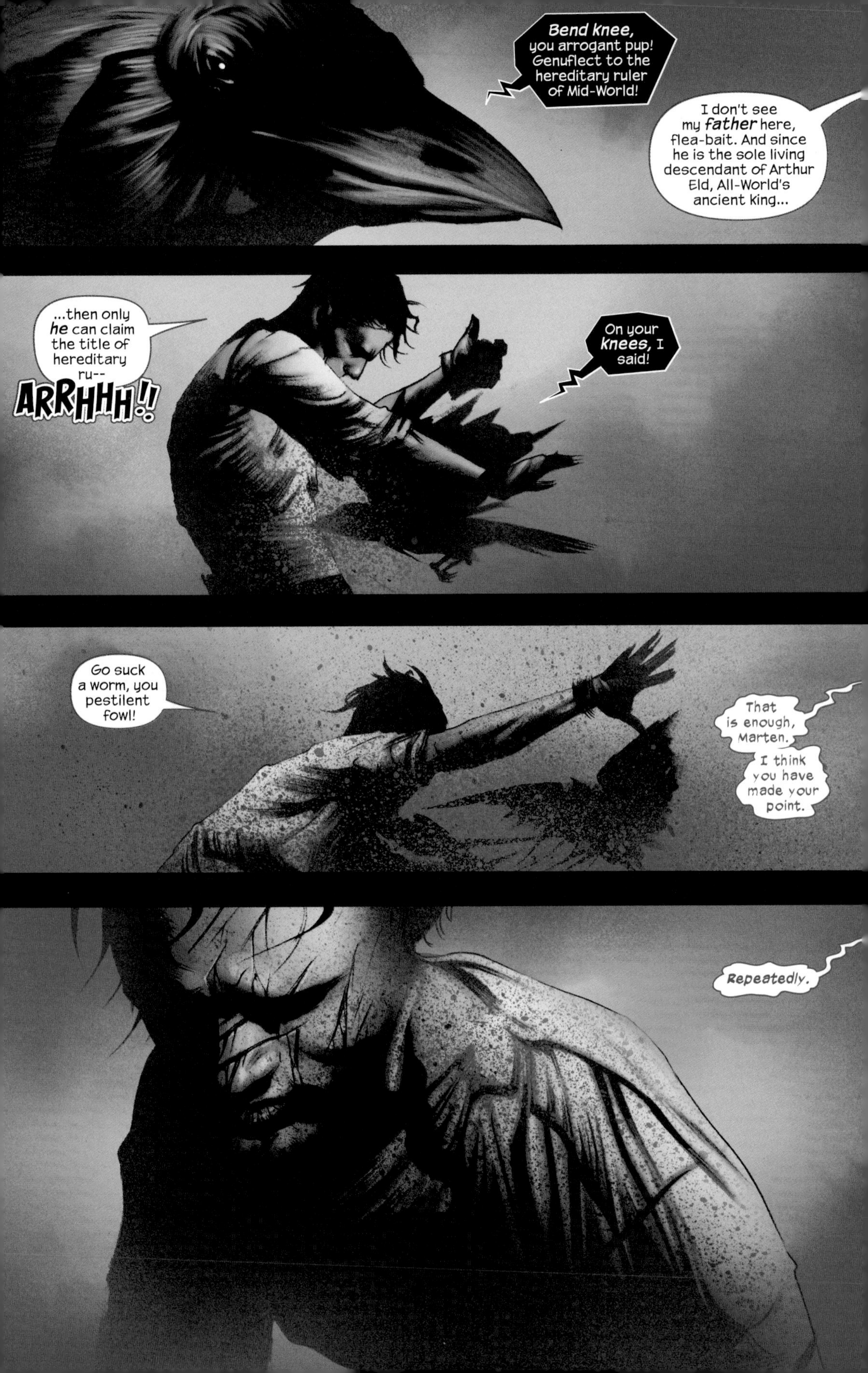

Bend knee, you arrogant pup! Genuflect to the hereditary ruler of Mid-World!
I don't see my father here, flea-bait. And since he is the sole living descendant of Arthur Eld, All-World's ancient king...
...then only he can claim the title of hereditary ru--
ARRHHH!!
On your knees, I said!
Go suck a worm, you pestilent fowl!
That is enough, Marten.
I think you have made your point.
Repeatedly.

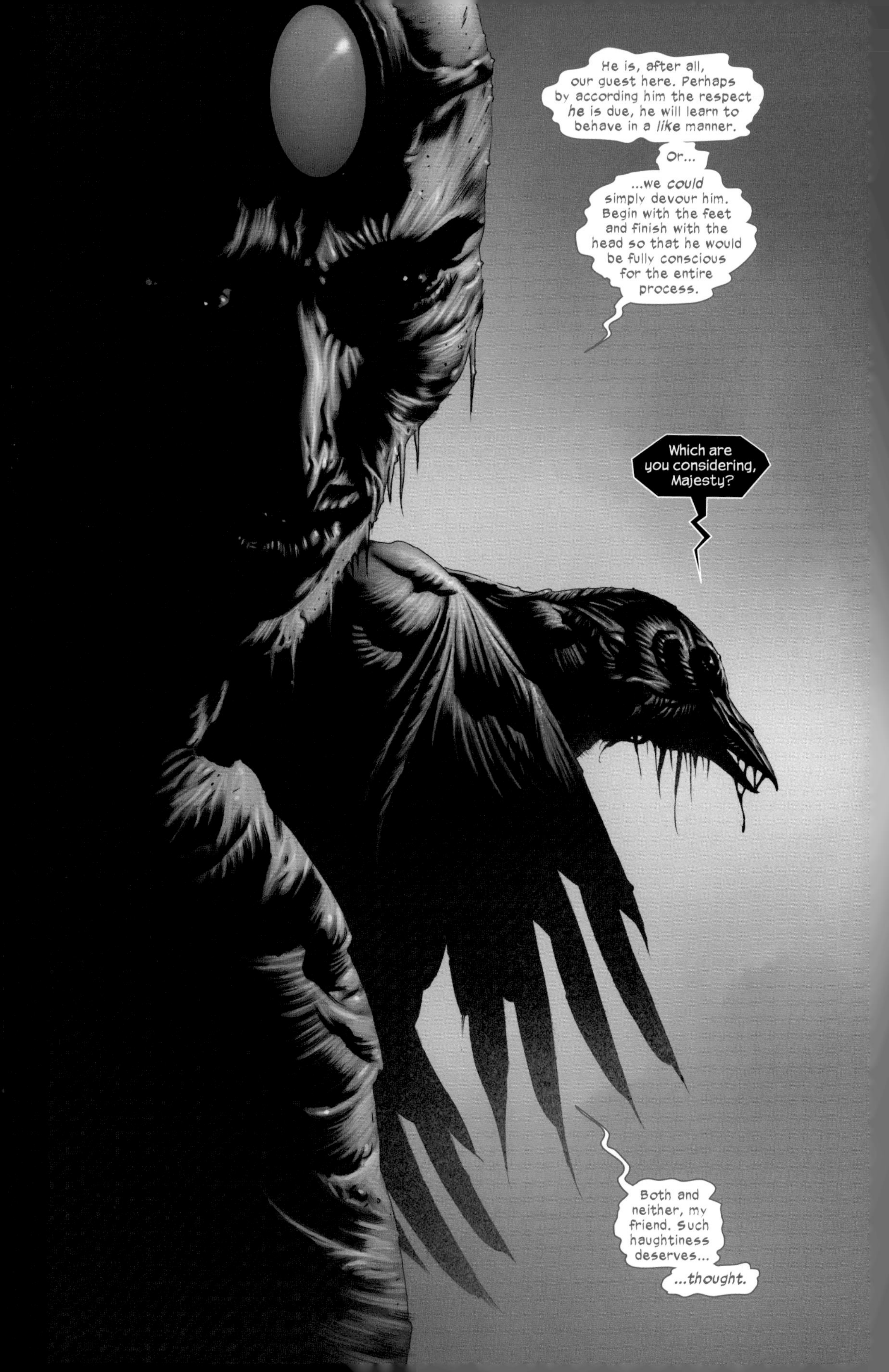
He is, after all, our guest here. Perhaps by according him the respect *he* is due, he will learn to behave in a *like* manner.
Or...
...we *could* simply devour him. Begin with the feet and finish with the head so that he would be fully conscious for the entire process.
Which are you considering, Majesty?
Both and neither, my friend. Such haughtiness deserves...
...*thought.*

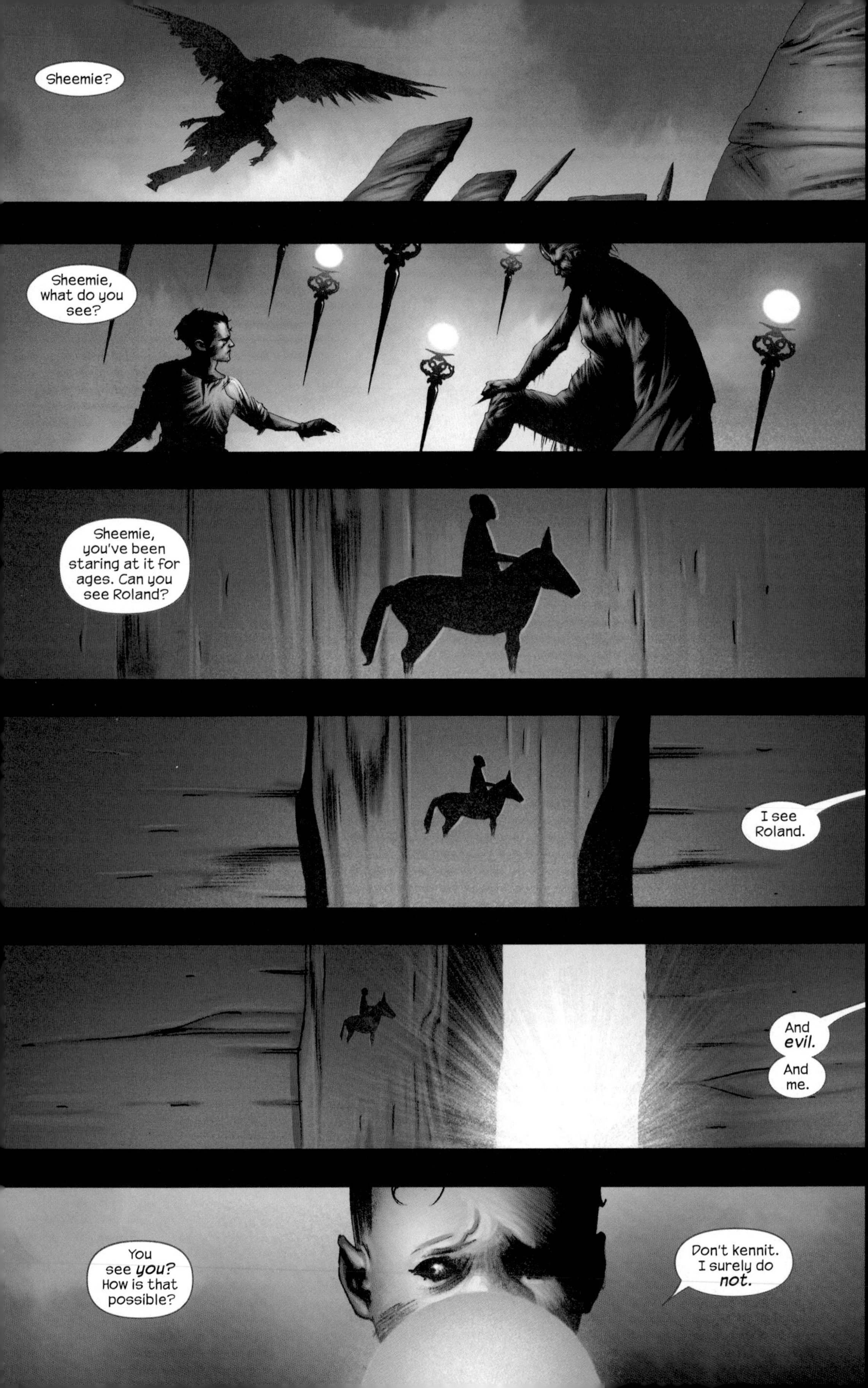
Sheemie?
Sheemie, what do you see?
Sheemie, you've been staring at it for ages. Can you see Roland?
I see Roland.
And *evil.*
And me.
You see *you?* How is that possible?
Don't kennit. I surely do *not.*

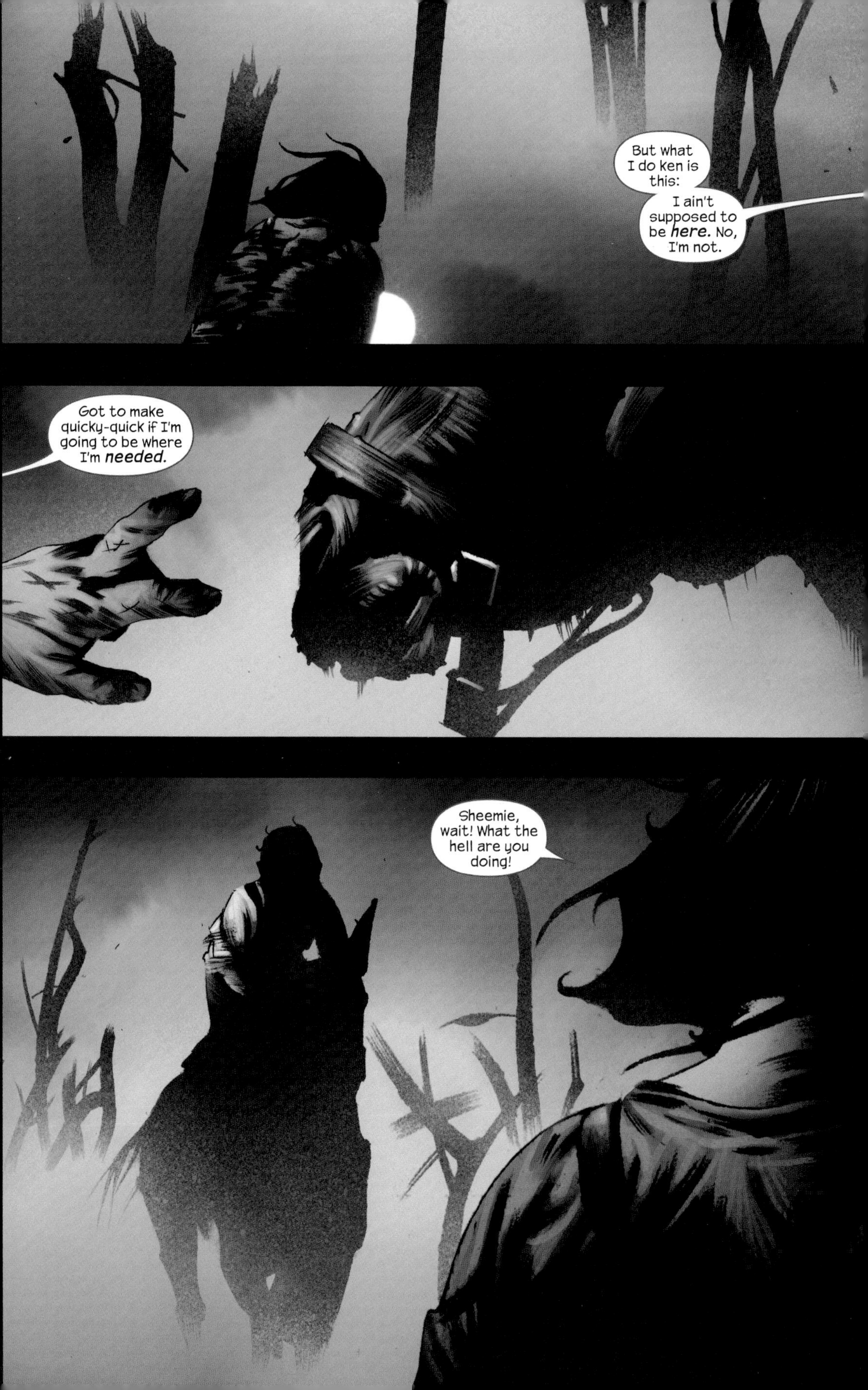
But what I do ken is this:
I ain't supposed to be *here.* No, I'm not.
Got to make quicky-quick if I'm going to be where I'm *needed.*
Sheemie, wait! What the hell are you doing!

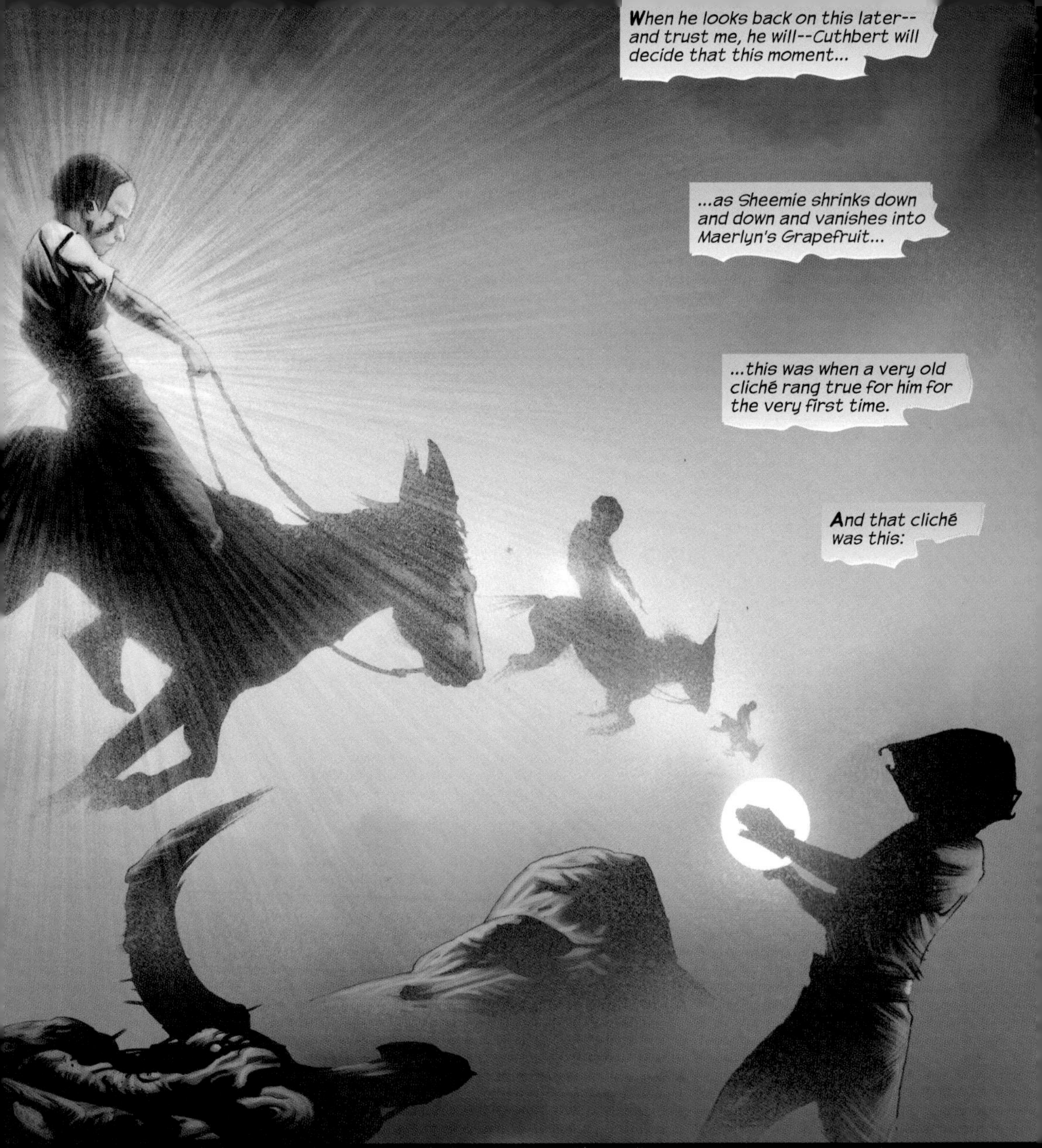
When he looks back on this later--and trust me, he will--Cuthbert will decide that this moment...
...as Sheemie shrinks down and down and vanishes into Maerlyn's Grapefruit...
...this was when a very old cliché rang true for him for the very first time.
And that cliché was this:

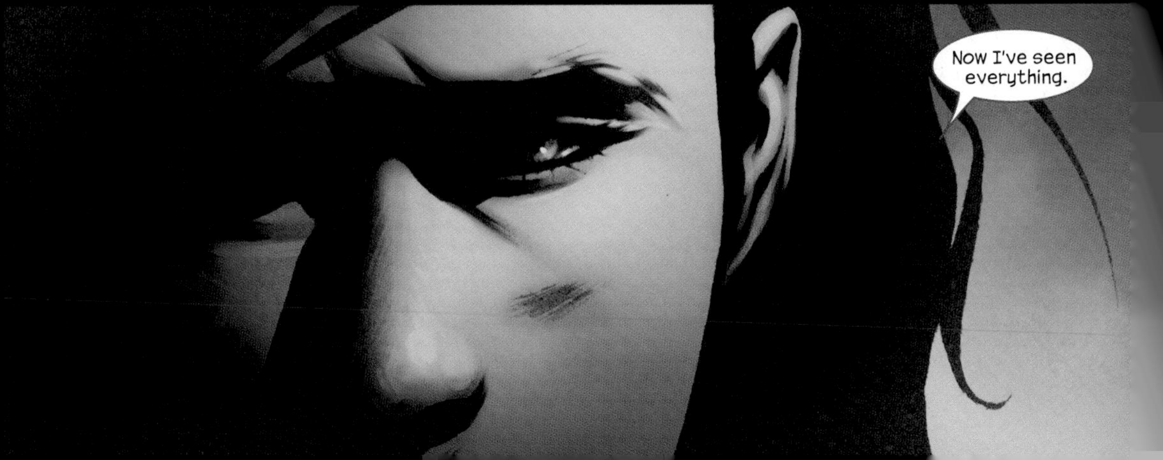
Now I've seen everything.

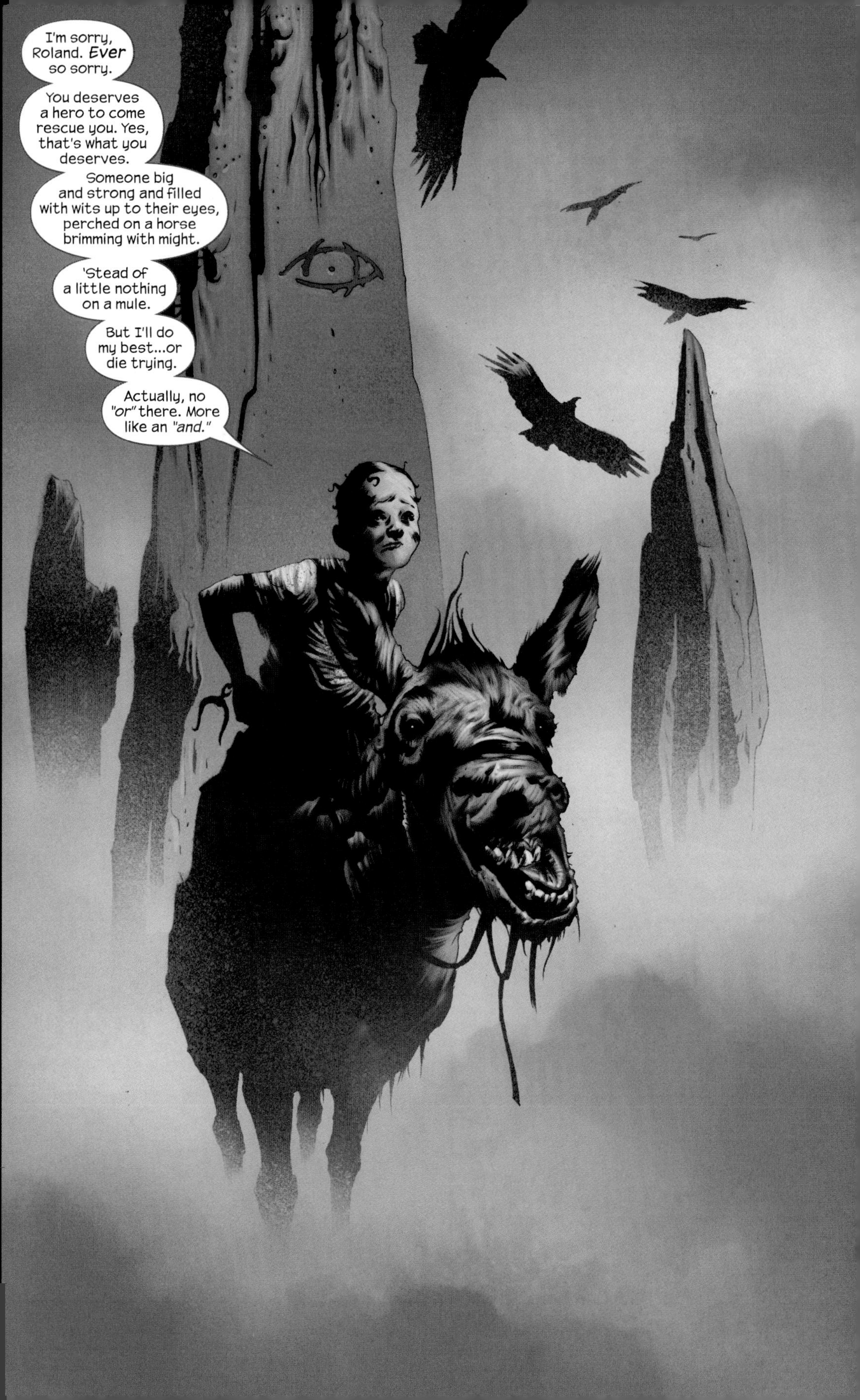
I'm sorry, Roland. *Ever* so sorry.
You deserves a hero to come rescue you. Yes, that's what you deserves.
Someone big and strong and filled with wits up to their eyes, perched on a horse brimming with might.
'Stead of a little nothing on a mule.
But I'll do my best...or die trying.
Actually, no *"or"* there. More like an *"and."*

STEPHEN KING
THE DARK TOWER

THE LONG ROAD HOME

CHAPTER FIVE

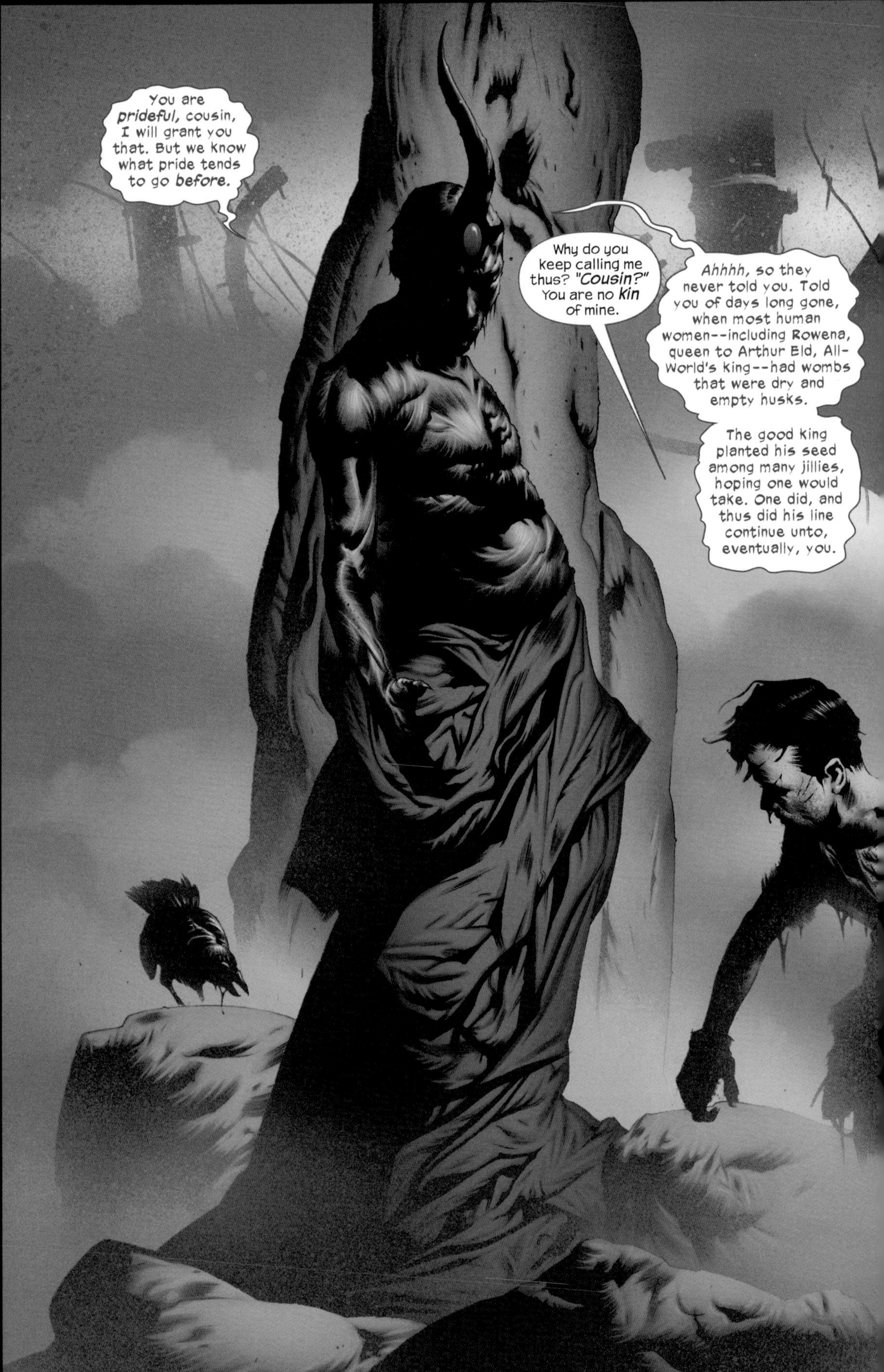
You are prideful, cousin, I will grant you that. But we know what pride tends to go before.
Why do you keep calling me thus? "Cousin?" You are no kin of mine.
Ahhhh, so they never told you. Told you of days long gone, when most human women--including Rowena, queen to Arthur Eld, All-World's king--had wombs that were dry and empty husks.
The good king planted his seed among many jillies, hoping one would take. One did, and thus did his line continue unto, eventually, you.

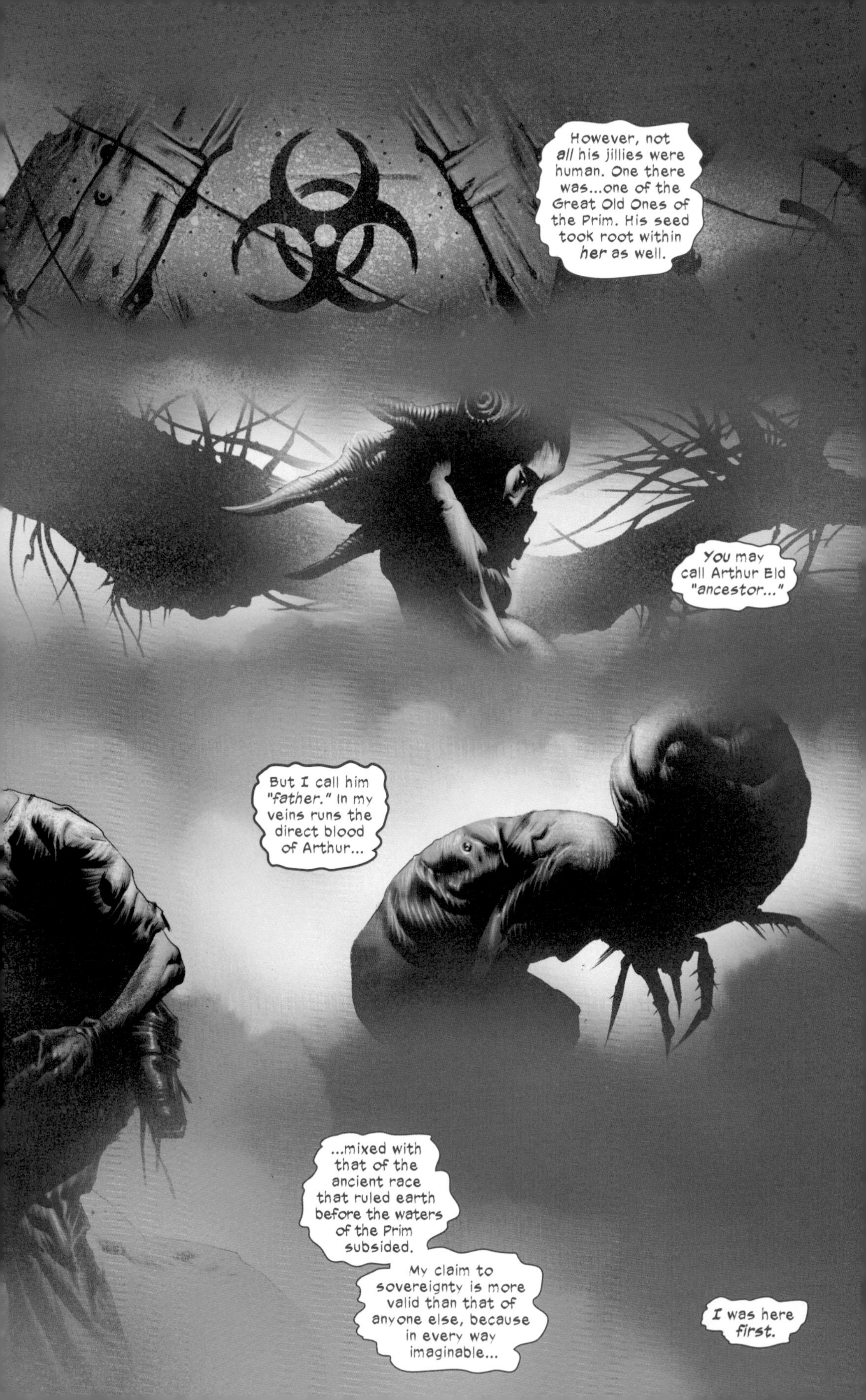
However, not *all* his jillies were human. One there was...one of the Great Old Ones of the Prim. His seed took root within *her* as well.
You may call Arthur Eld *"ancestor..."*
But I call him *"father."* In my veins runs the direct blood of Arthur...
...mixed with that of the ancient race that ruled earth before the waters of the Prim subsided.
My claim to sovereignty is more valid than that of anyone else, because in every way imaginable...
I was here first.

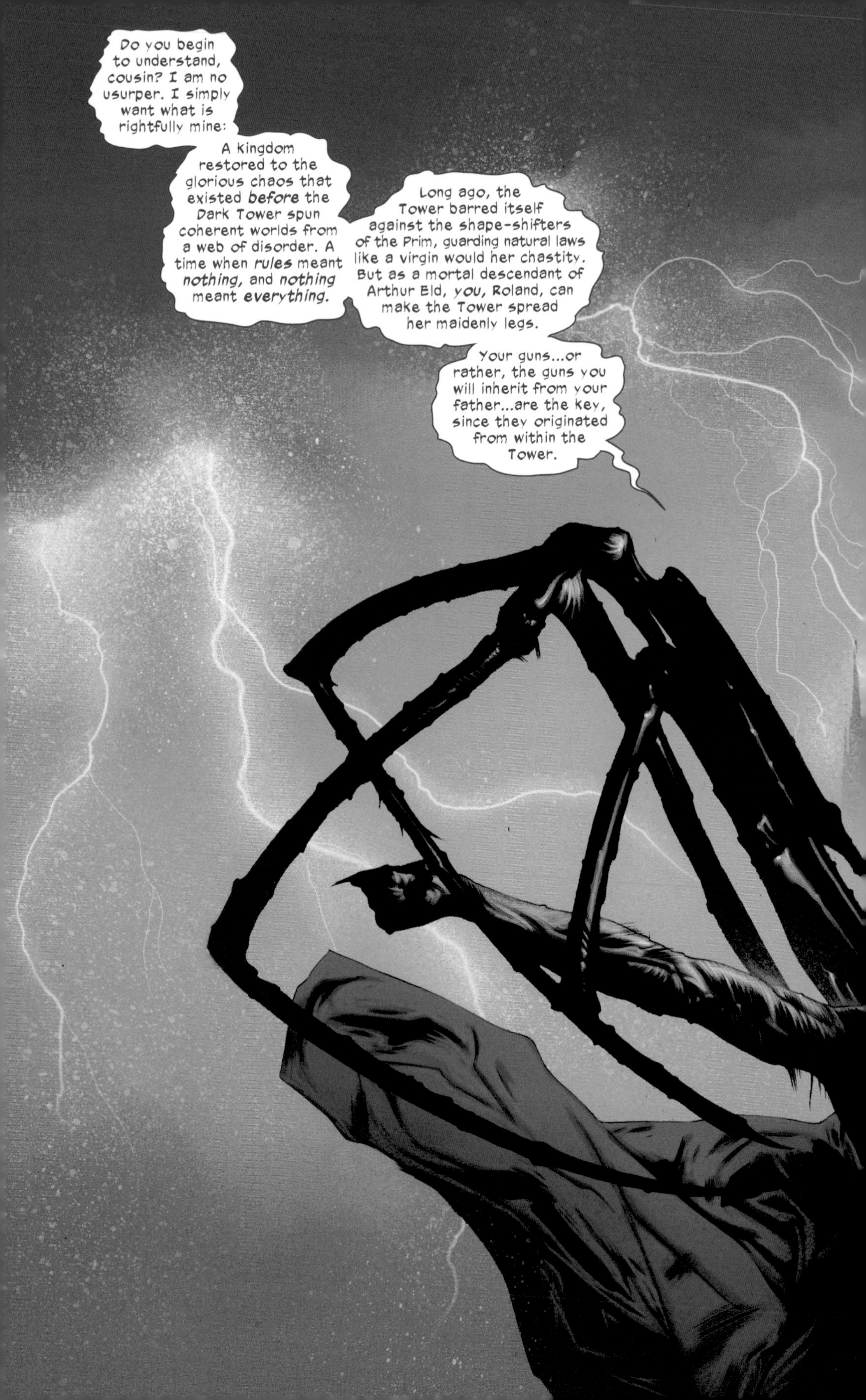
Do you begin to understand, cousin? I am no usurper. I simply want what is rightfully mine:
A kingdom restored to the glorious chaos that existed *before* the Dark Tower spun coherent worlds from a web of disorder. A time when *rules* meant *nothing,* and *nothing* meant *everything.*
Long ago, the Tower barred itself against the shape-shifters of the Prim, guarding natural laws like a virgin would her chastity. But as a mortal descendant of Arthur Eld, *you,* Roland, can make the Tower spread her maidenly legs.
Your guns...or rather, the guns you will inherit from your father...are the key, since they originated from within the Tower.

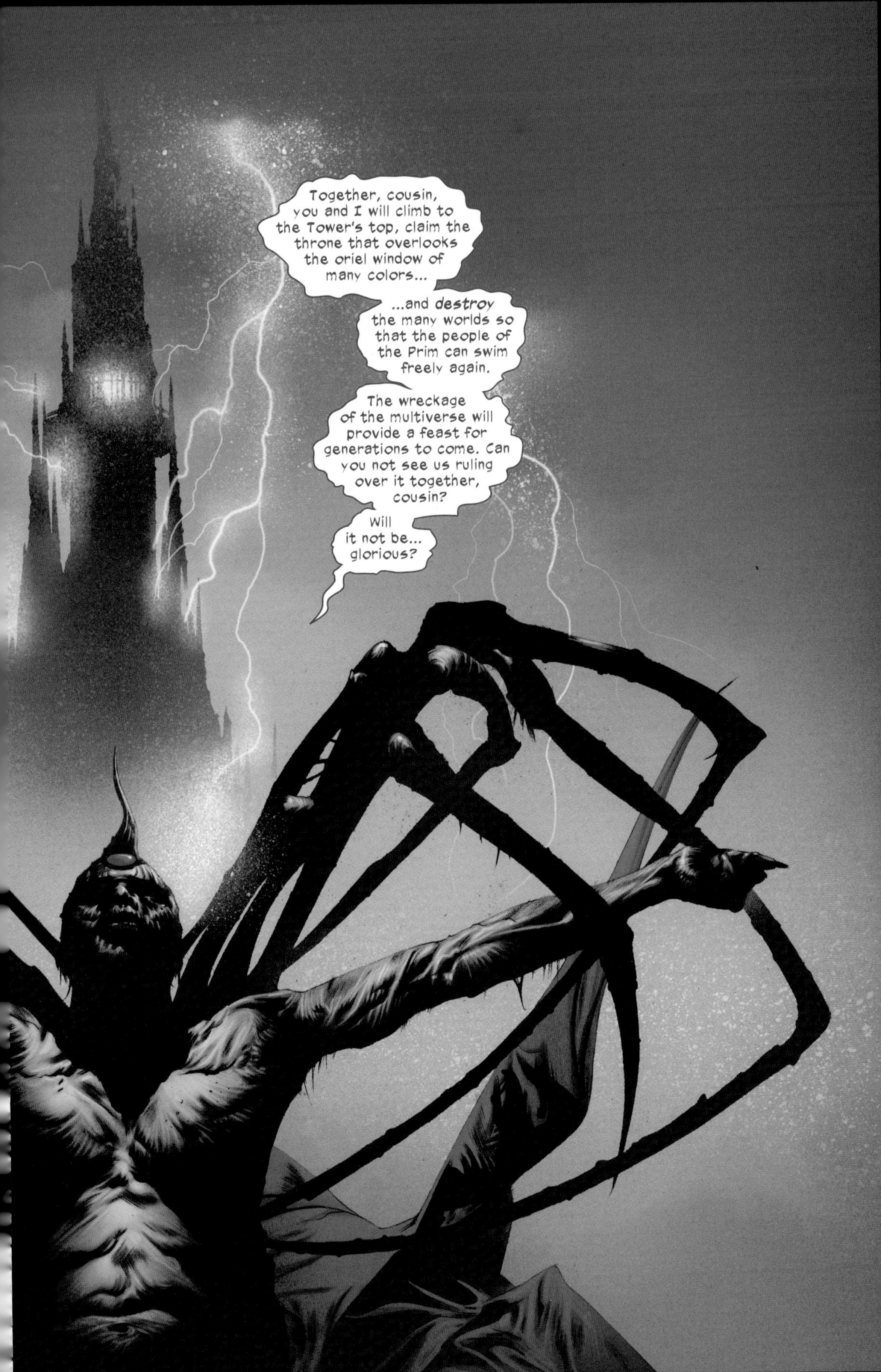
Together, cousin, you and I will climb to the Tower's top, claim the throne that overlooks the oriel window of many colors...
...and *destroy* the many worlds so that the people of the Prim can swim freely again.
The wreckage of the multiverse will provide a feast for generations to come. Can you not see us ruling over it together, cousin?
Will it not be... glorious?

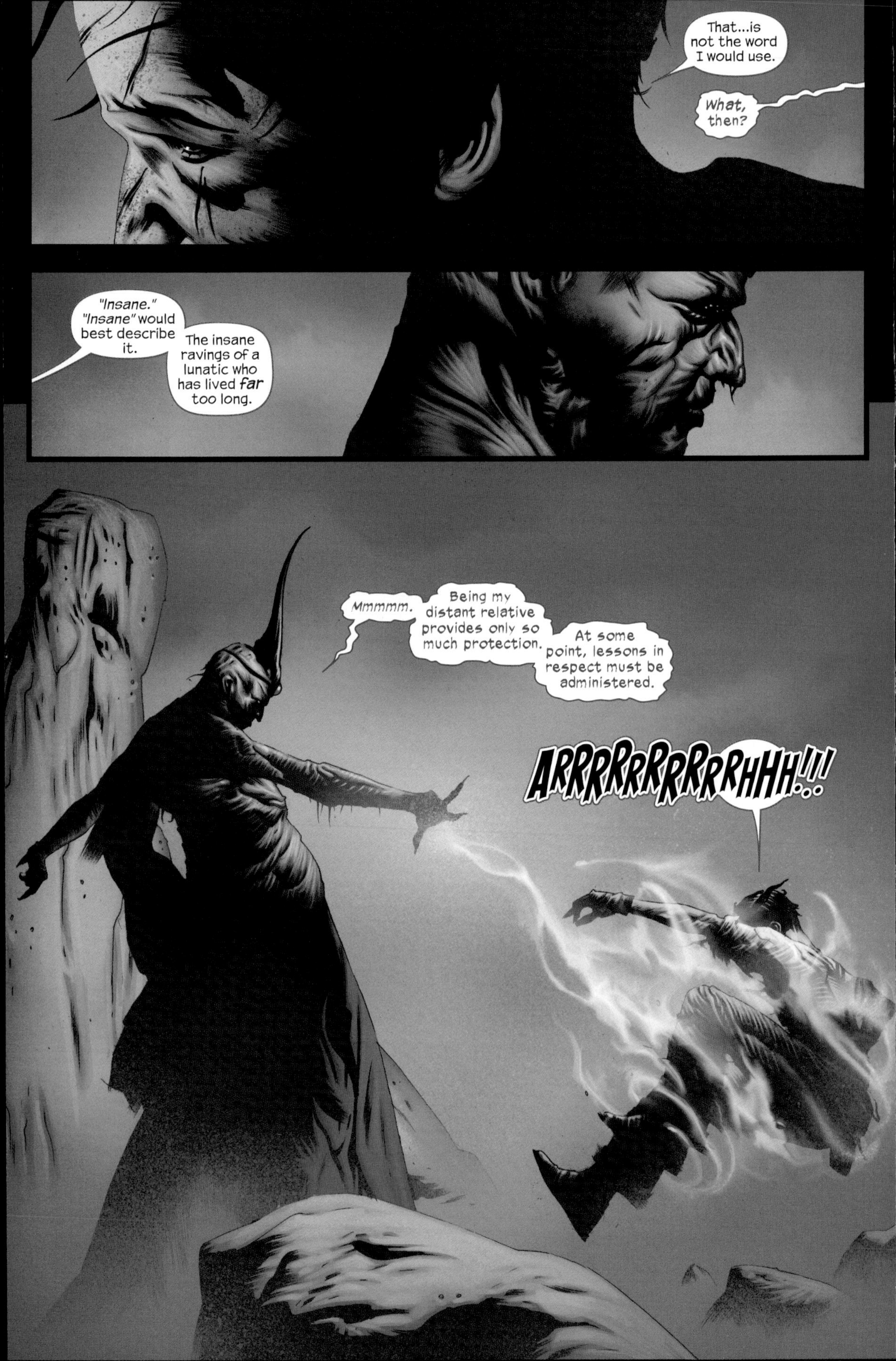

That...is not the word I would use.
What, then?
"*Insane.*" "*Insane*" would best describe it.
The insane ravings of a lunatic who has lived ***far*** too long.
Mmmmm.
Being my distant relative provides only so much protection.
At some point, lessons in respect must be administered.
ARRRRRRRRRRHHH!!!

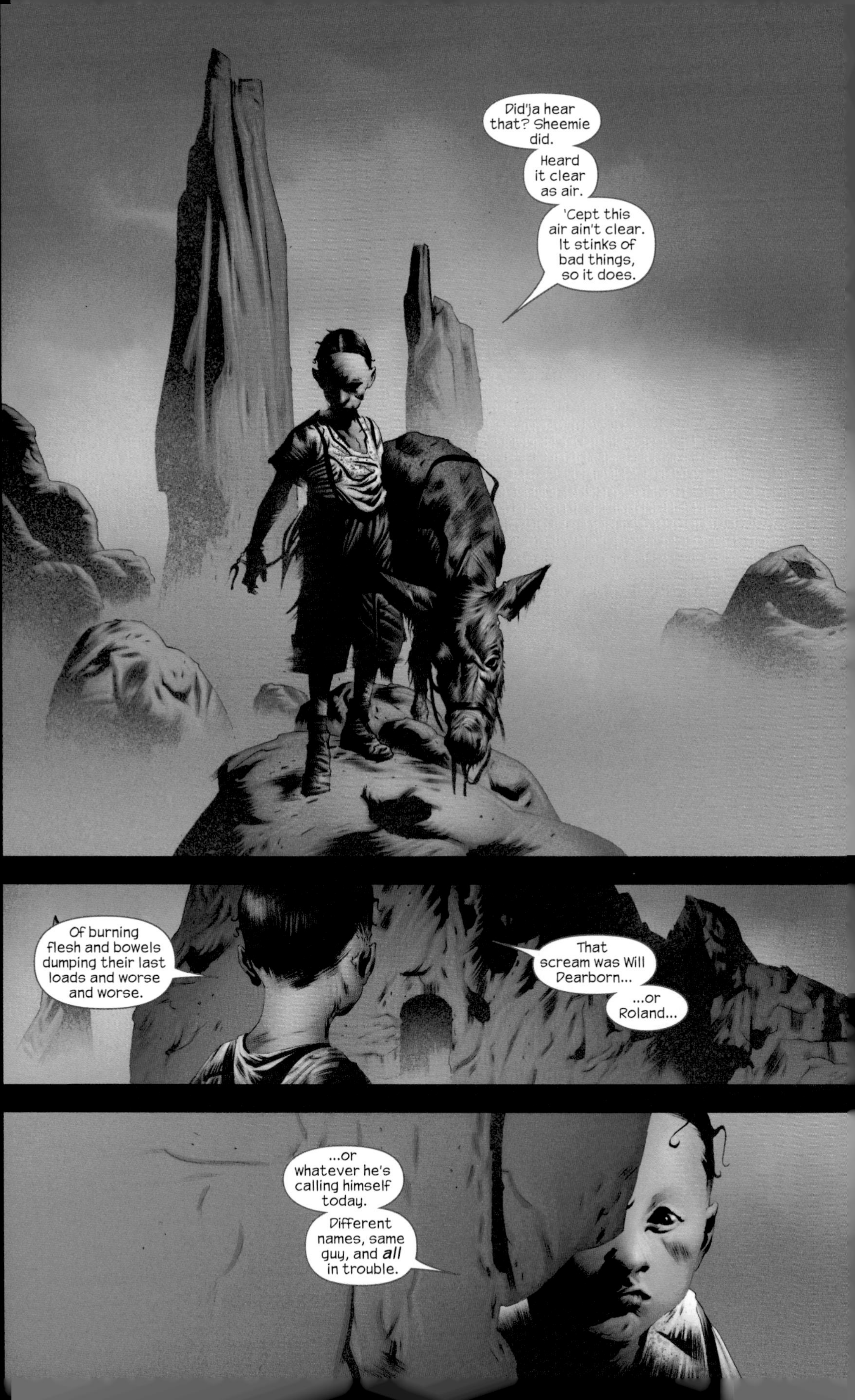
Did'ja hear that? Sheemie did.
Heard it clear as air.
'Cept this air ain't clear. It stinks of bad things, so it does.
Of burning flesh and bowels dumping their last loads and worse and worse.
That scream was Will Dearborn...
...or Roland...
...or whatever he's calling himself today.
Different names, same guy, and *all* in trouble.

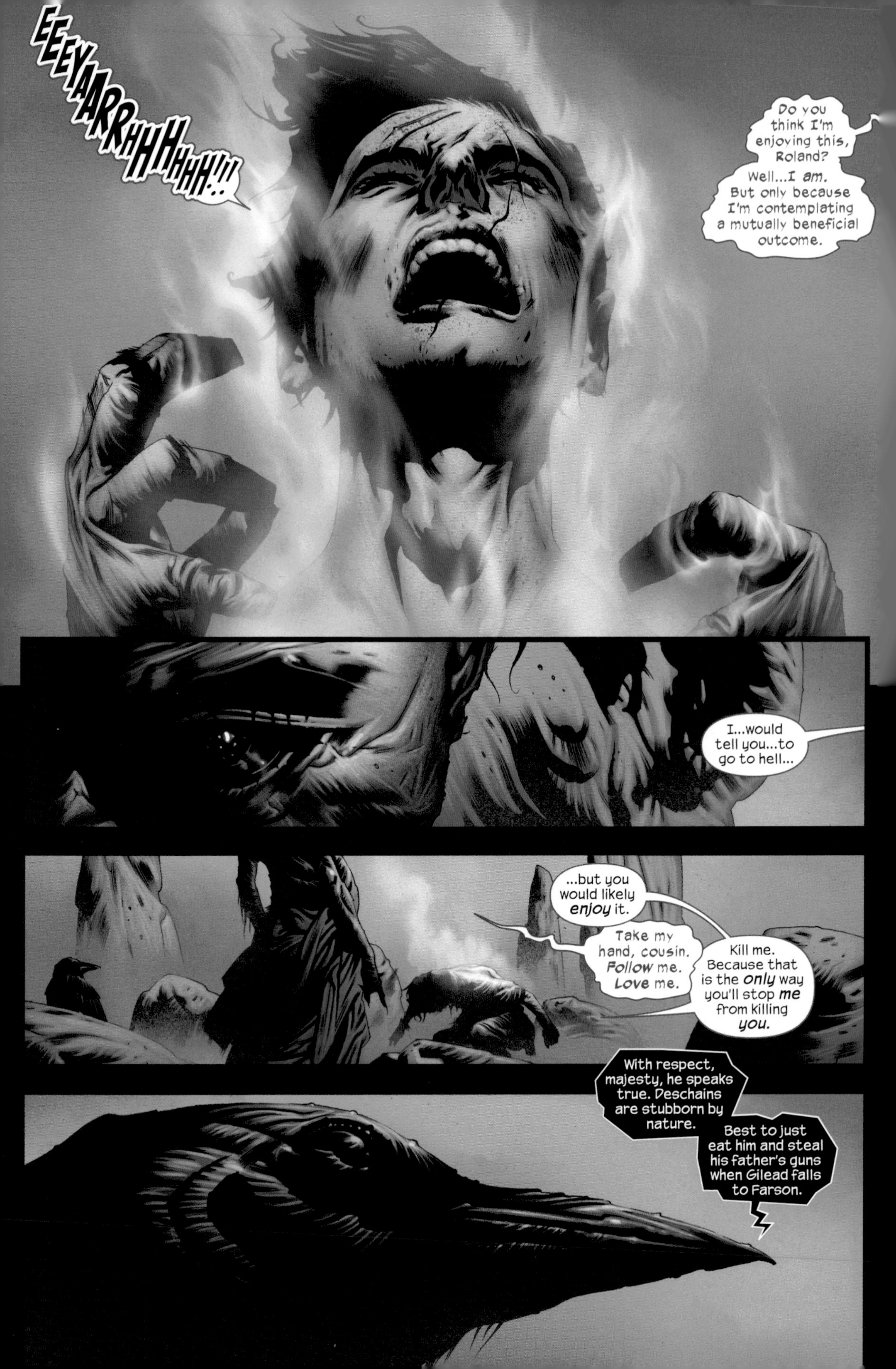
EEEYAARRHHHHHH!!!
Do you think I'm enjoying this, Roland?
Well...I am. But only because I'm contemplating a mutually beneficial outcome.
I...would tell you...to go to hell...
...but you would likely enjoy it.
Take my hand, cousin. Follow me. Love me.
Kill me. Because that is the only way you'll stop me from killing you.
With respect, majesty, he speaks true. Deschains are stubborn by nature.
Best to just eat him and steal his father's guns when Gilead falls to Farson.

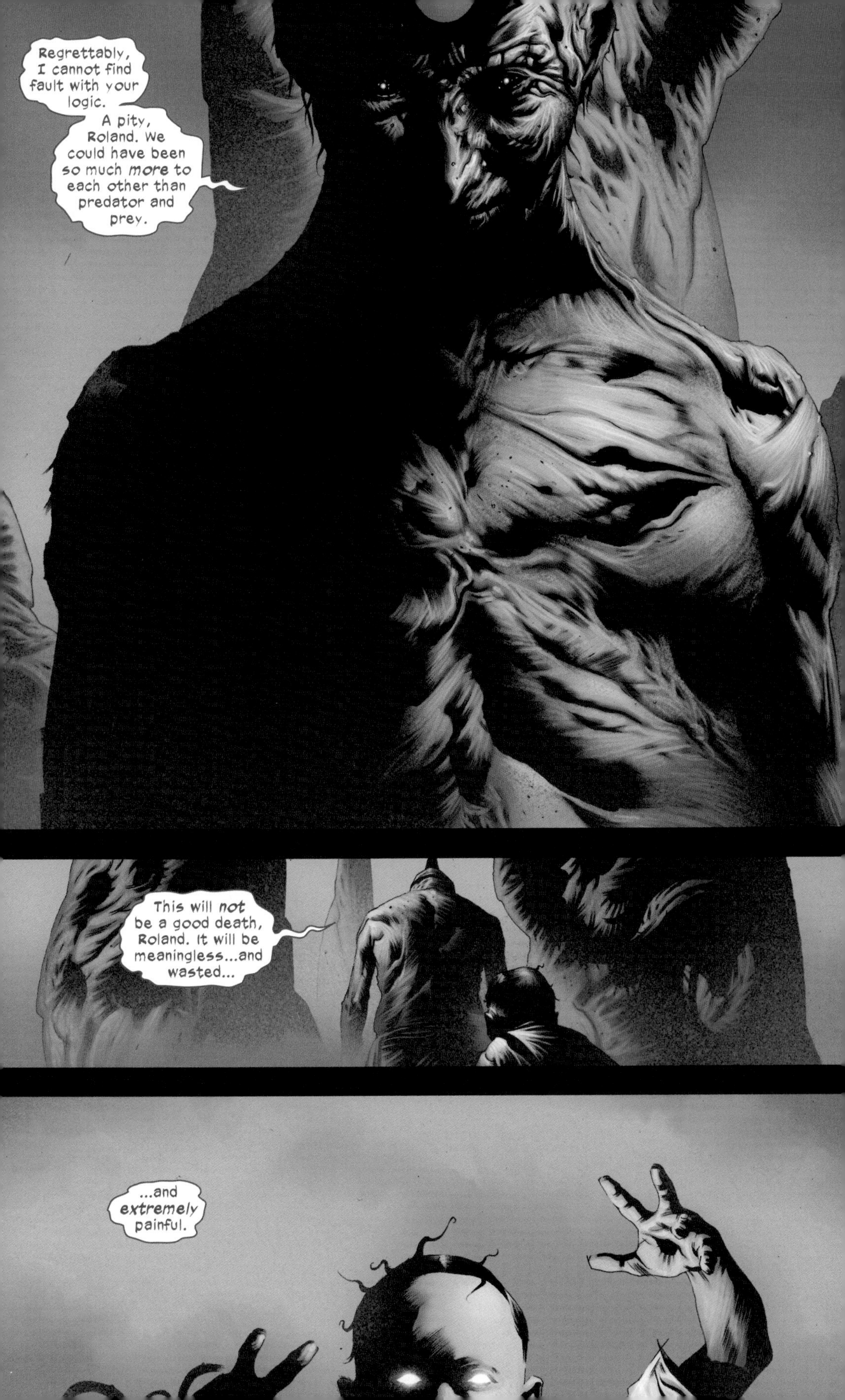

Regrettably, I cannot find fault with your logic.
A pity, Roland. We could have been so much *more* to each other than predator and prey.
This will *not* be a good death, Roland. It will be meaningless...and wasted...
...and *extremely* painful.

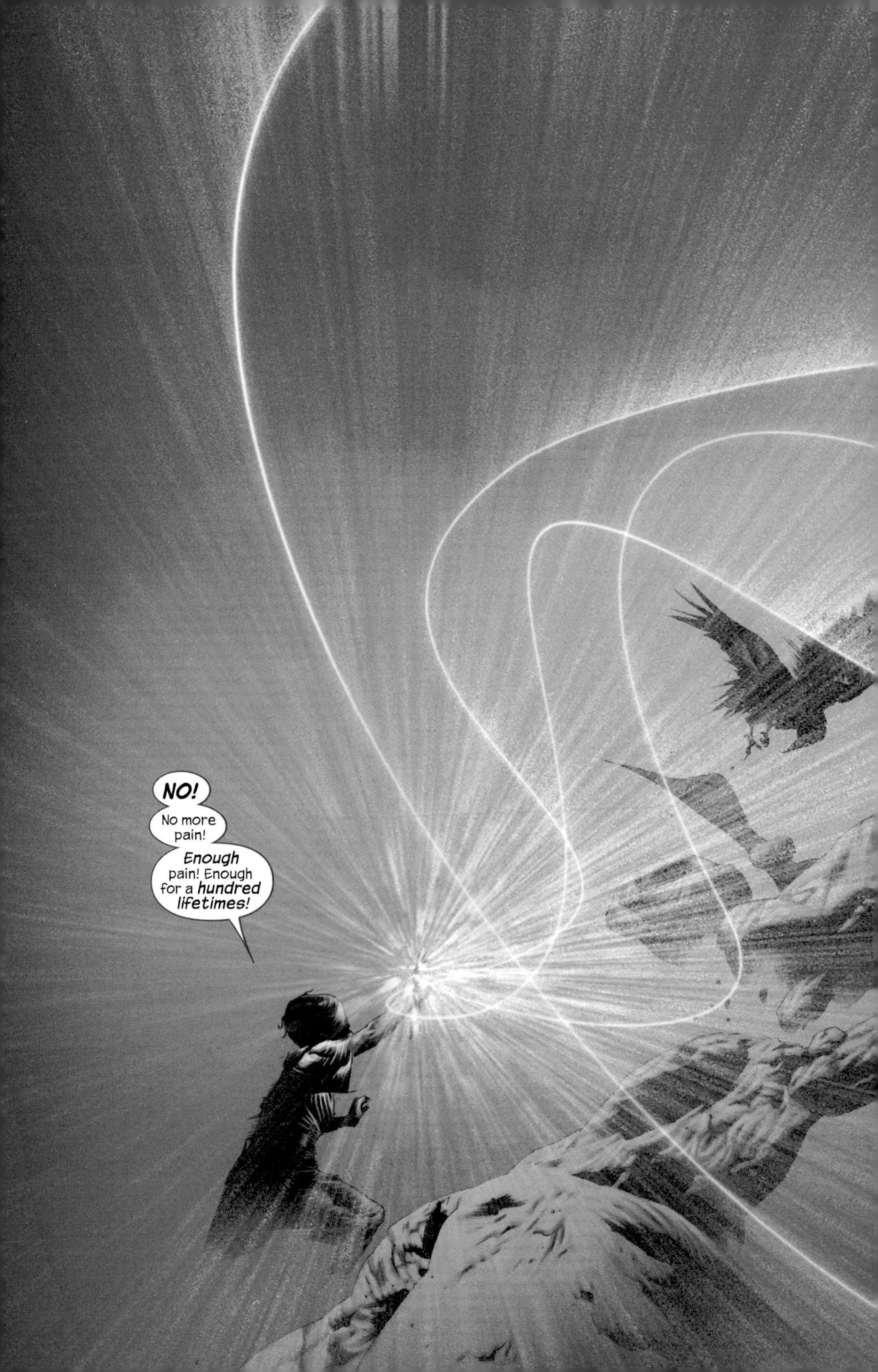
NO!
No more pain!
Enough pain! Enough for a *hundred lifetimes!*

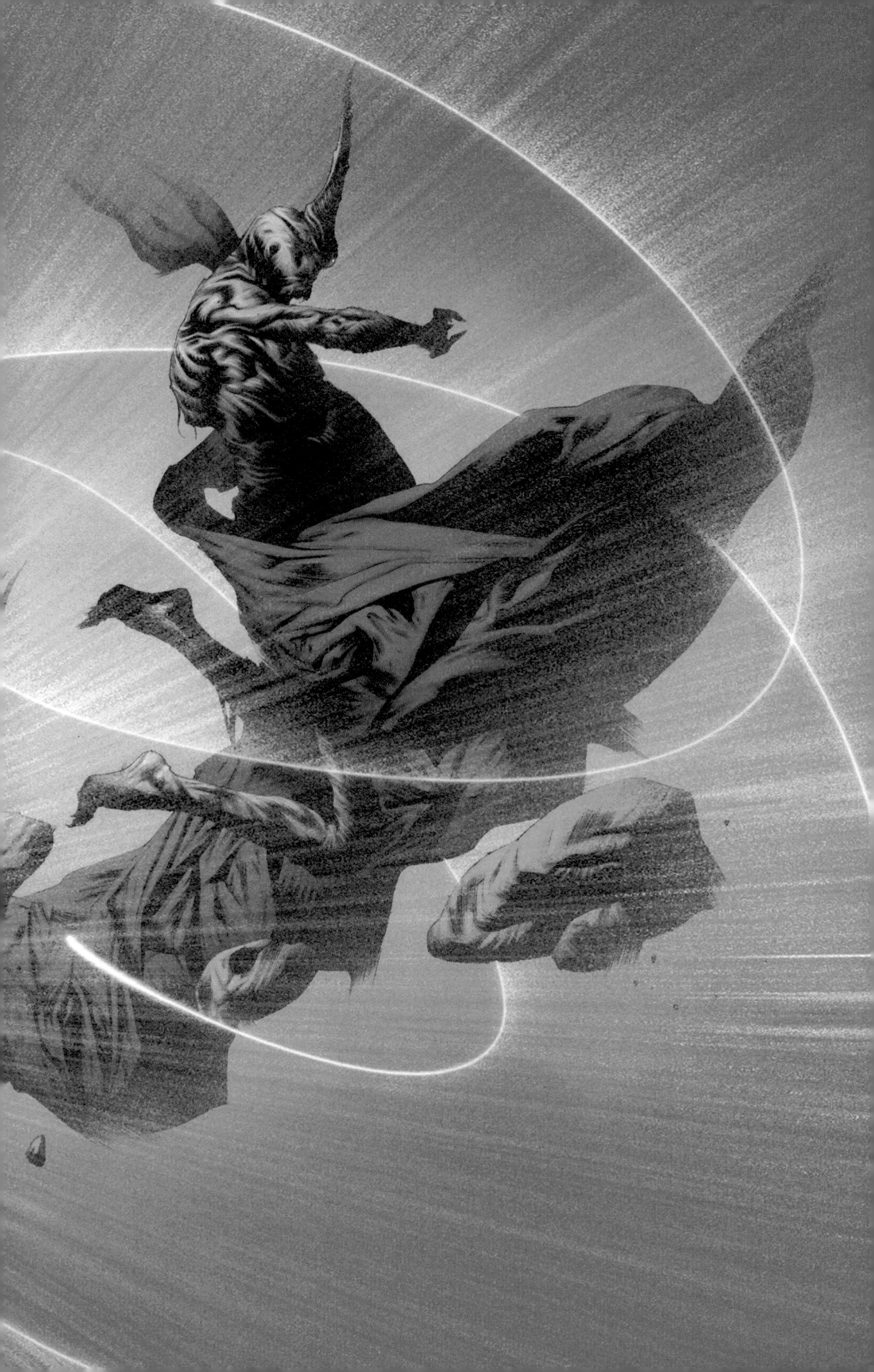

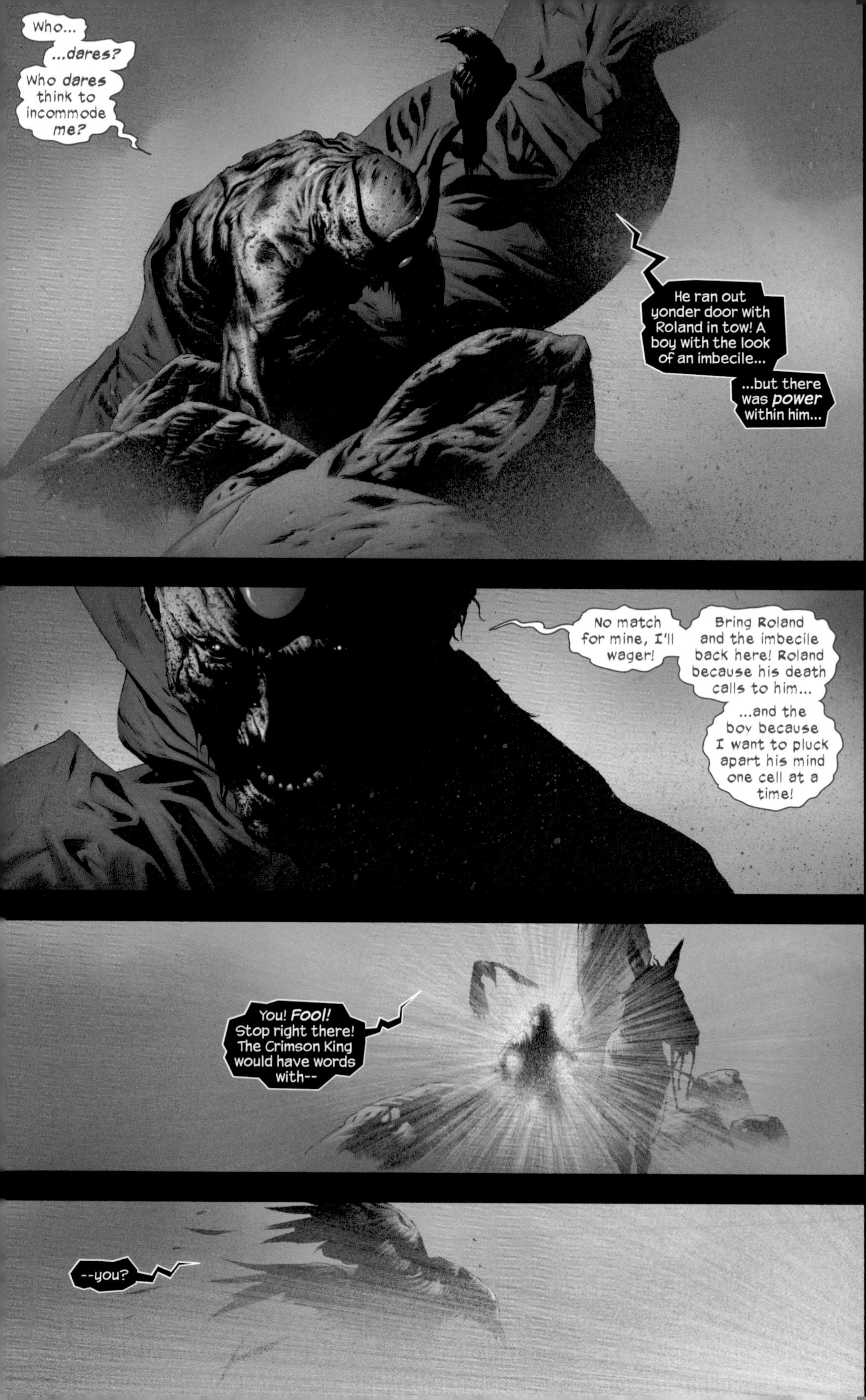

Who...
...dares?
Who dares think to incommode me?
He ran out yonder door with Roland in tow! A boy with the look of an imbecile...
...but there was power within him...
No match for mine, I'll wager!
Bring Roland and the imbecile back here! Roland because his death calls to him...
...and the boy because I want to pluck apart his mind one cell at a time!
You! Fool! Stop right there! The Crimson King would have words with--
--you?

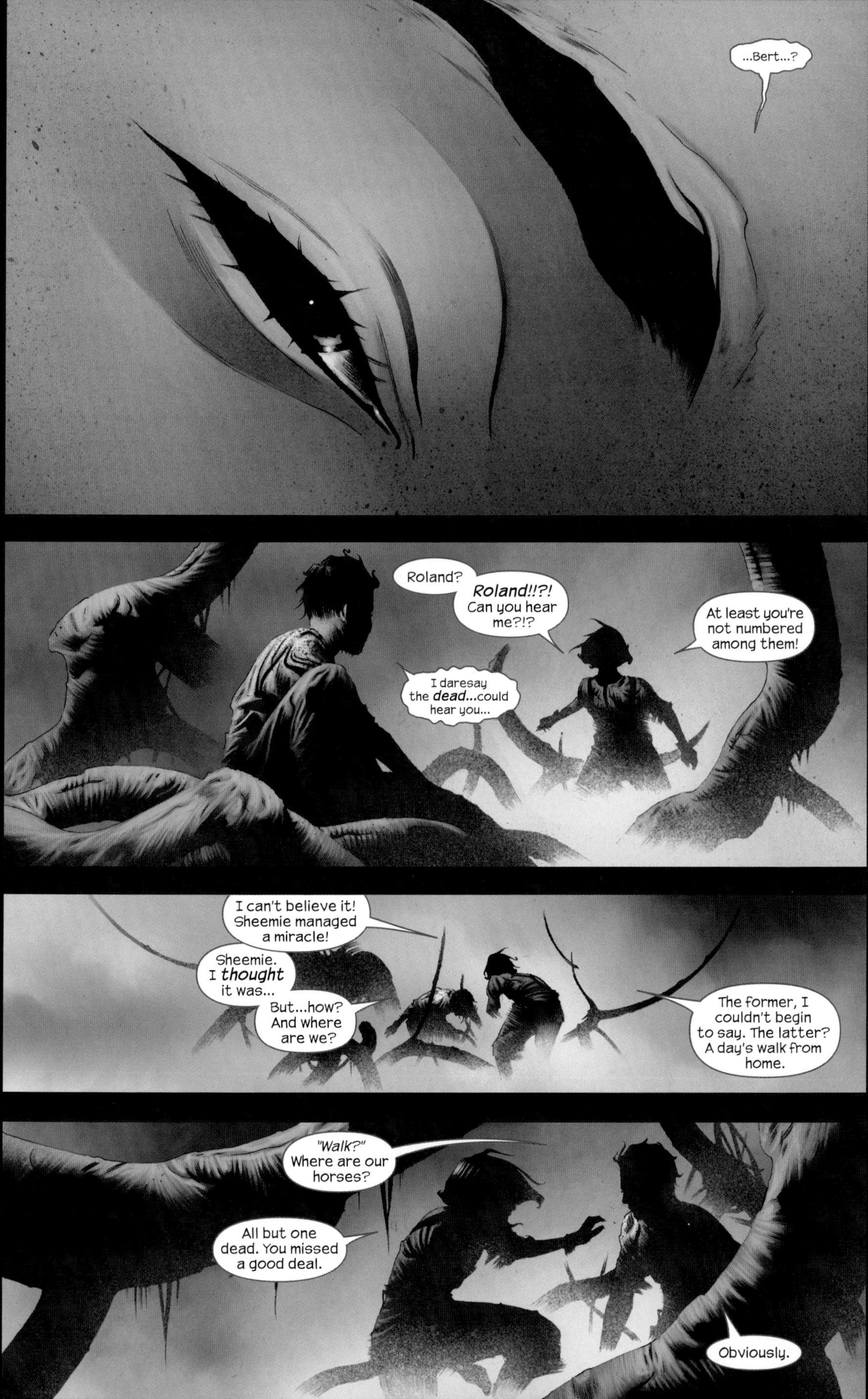
...Bert...?
Roland? *Roland!!?!* Can you hear me?!?
I daresay the *dead...* could hear you...
At least you're not numbered among them!
I can't believe it! Sheemie managed a miracle!
Sheemie. I *thought* it was...
But...how? And where are we?
The former, I couldn't begin to say. The latter? A day's walk from home.
"Walk?" Where are our horses?
All but one dead. You missed a good deal.
Obviously.

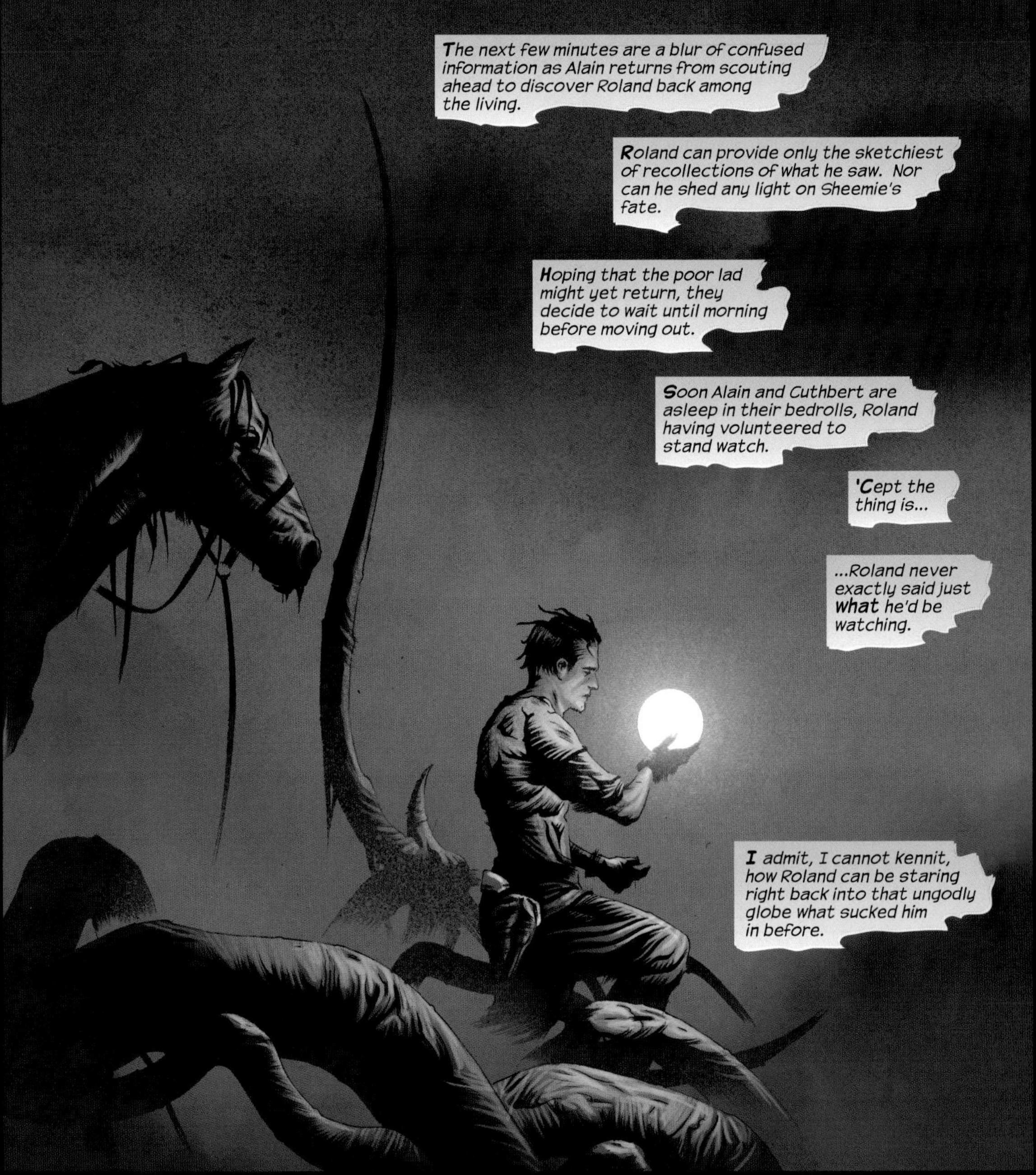
The next few minutes are a blur of confused information as Alain returns from scouting ahead to discover Roland back among the living.
Roland can provide only the sketchiest of recollections of what he saw. Nor can he shed any light on Sheemie's fate.
Hoping that the poor lad might yet return, they decide to wait until morning before moving out.
Soon Alain and Cuthbert are asleep in their bedrolls, Roland having volunteered to stand watch.
'Cept the thing is...
...Roland never exactly said just **what** he'd be watching.
I admit, I cannot kennit, how Roland can be staring right back into that ungodly globe what sucked him in before.

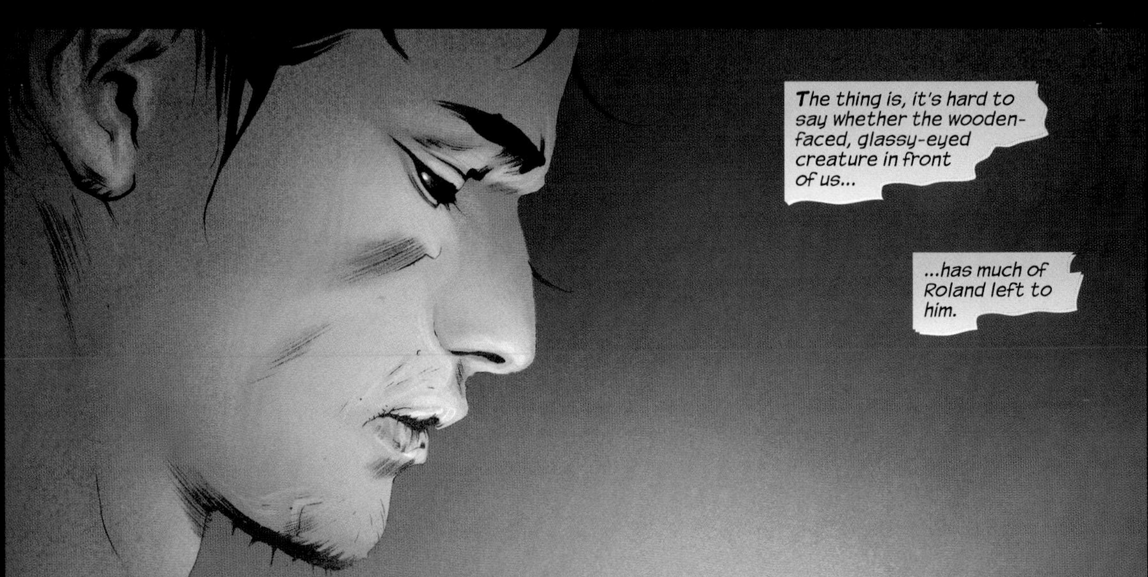
The thing is, it's hard to say whether the wooden-faced, glassy-eyed creature in front of us...
...has much of Roland left to him.

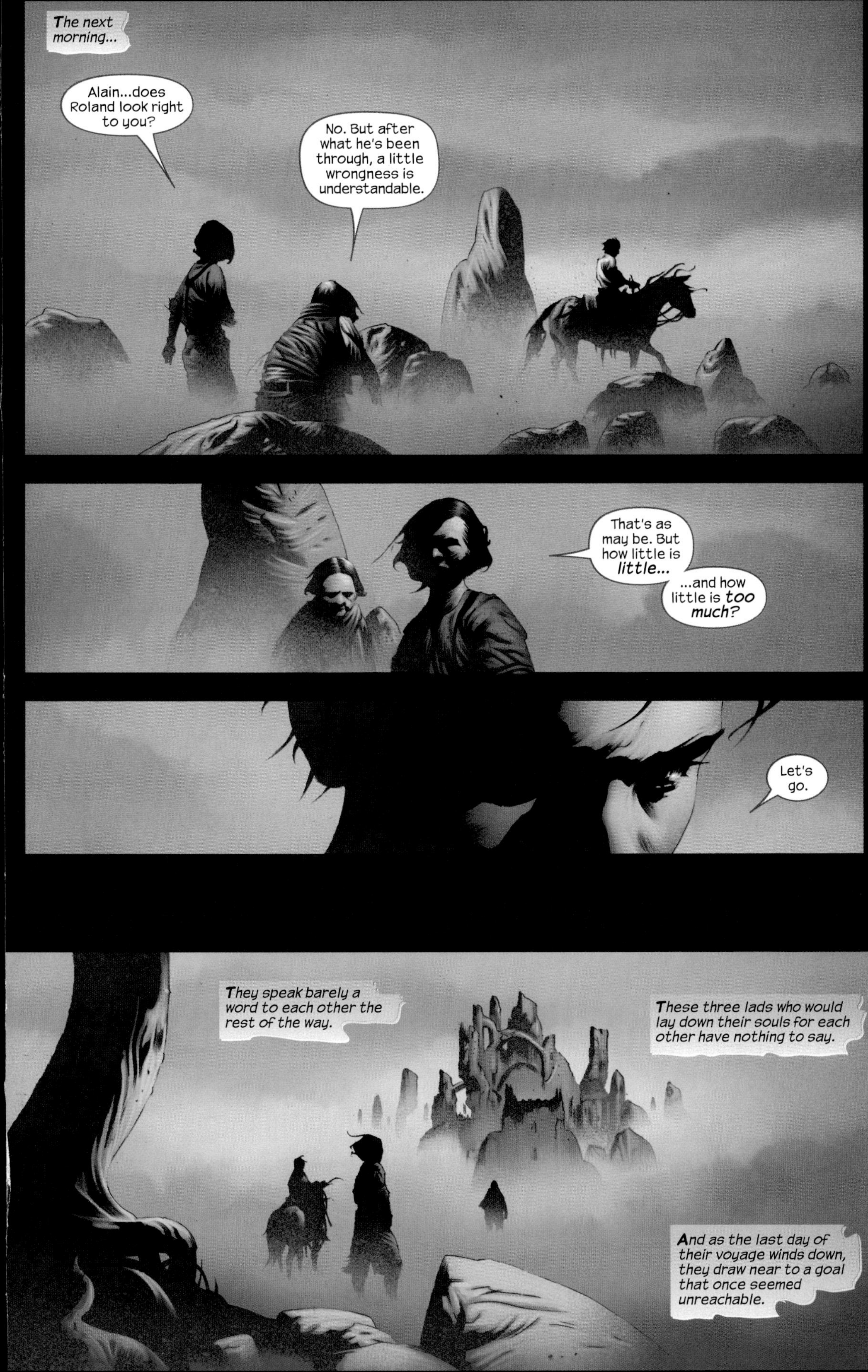
The next morning...
Alain...does Roland look right to you?
No. But after what he's been through, a little wrongness is understandable.
That's as may be. But how little is little...
...and how little is too much?
Let's go.
They speak barely a word to each other the rest of the way.
These three lads who would lay down their souls for each other have nothing to say.
And as the last day of their voyage winds down, they draw near to a goal that once seemed unreachable.

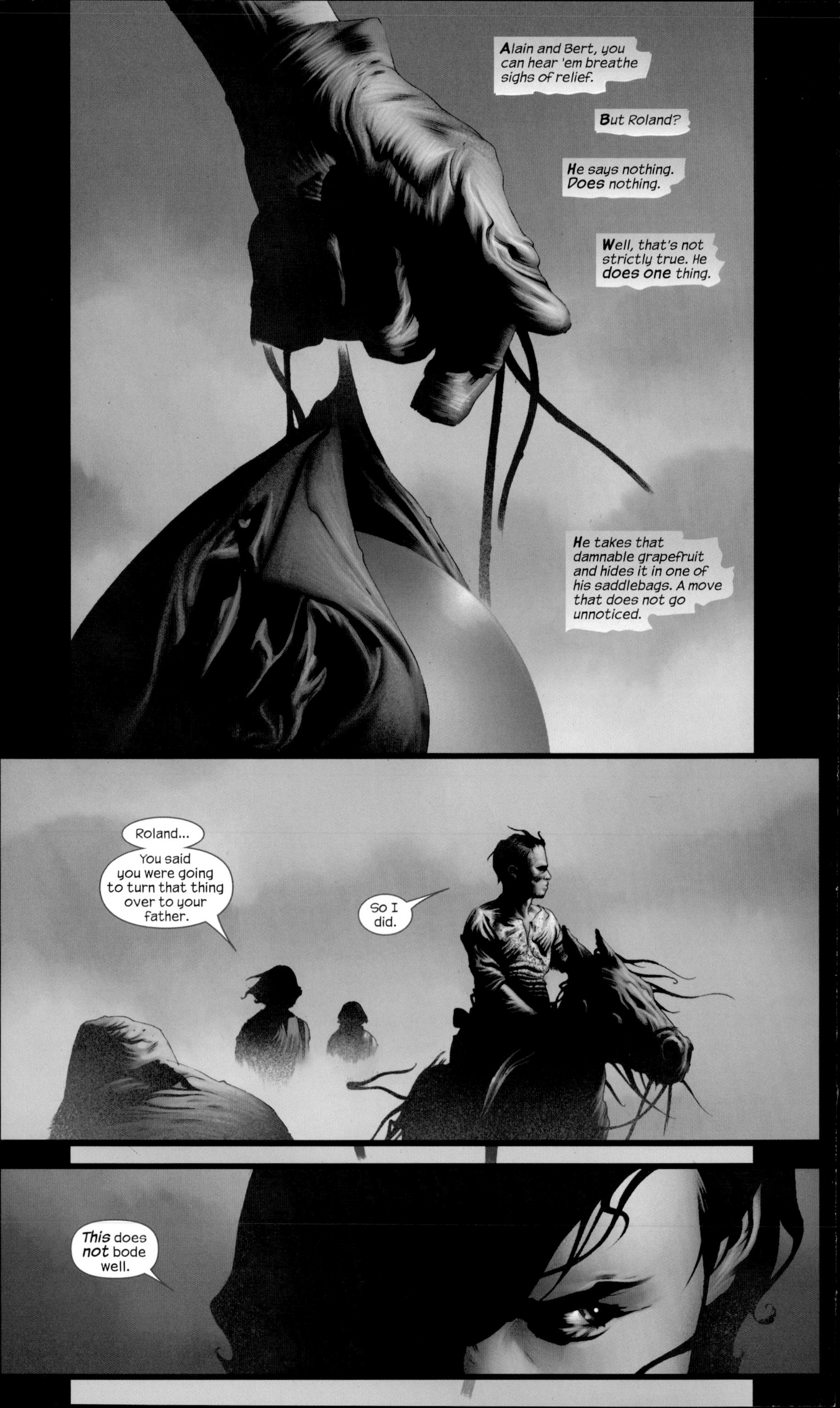
Alain and Bert, you can hear 'em breathe sighs of relief.
But Roland?
He says nothing. Does nothing.
Well, that's not strictly true. He does one thing.
He takes that damnable grapefruit and hides it in one of his saddlebags. A move that does not go unnoticed.
Roland... You said you were going to turn that thing over to your father.
So I did.
This does not bode well.

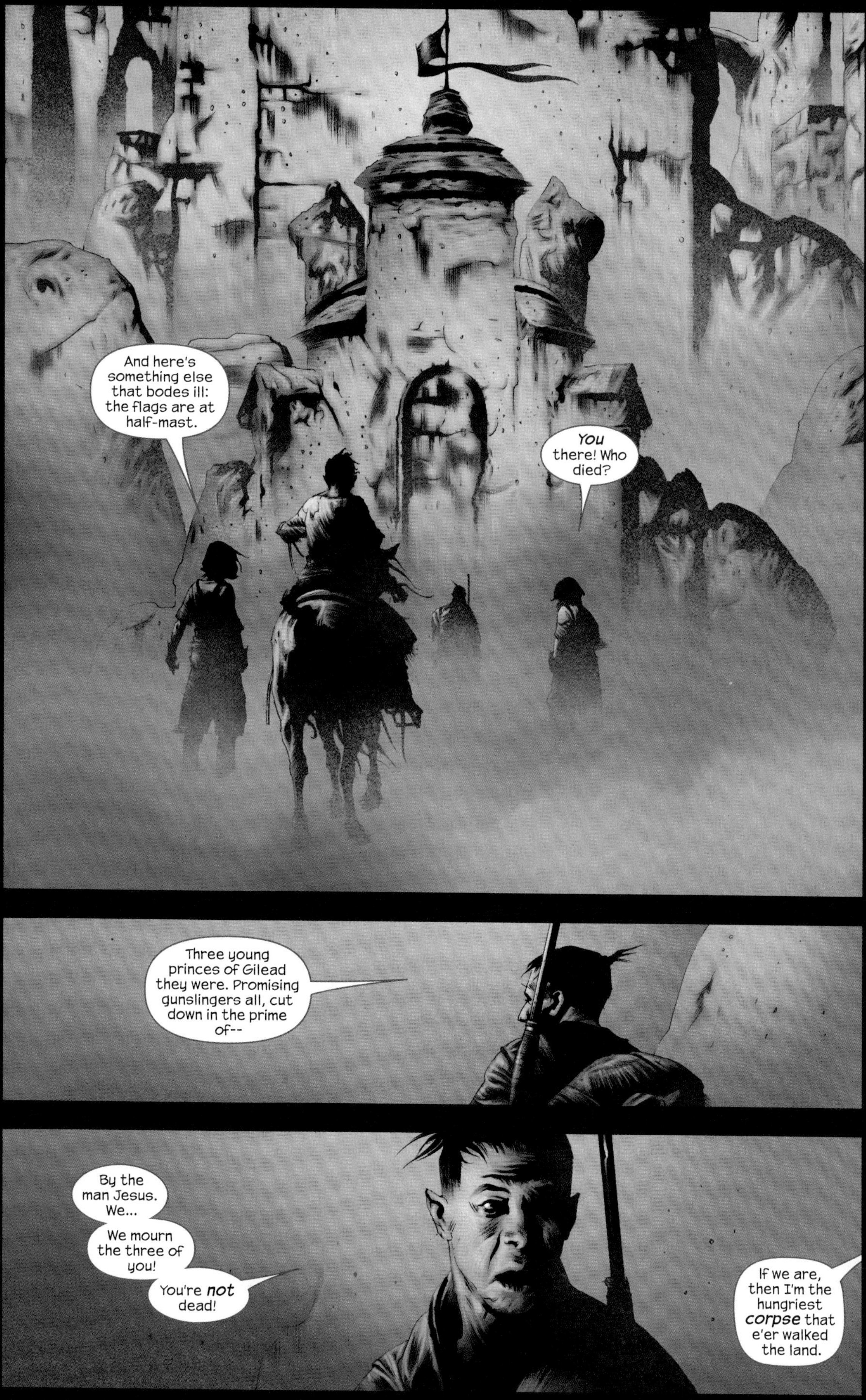
And here's something else that bodes ill: the flags are at half-mast.
You there! Who died?
Three young princes of Gilead they were. Promising gunslingers all, cut down in the prime of--
By the man Jesus. We...
We mourn the three of you!
You're *not* dead!
If we are, then I'm the hungriest *corpse* that e'er walked the land.

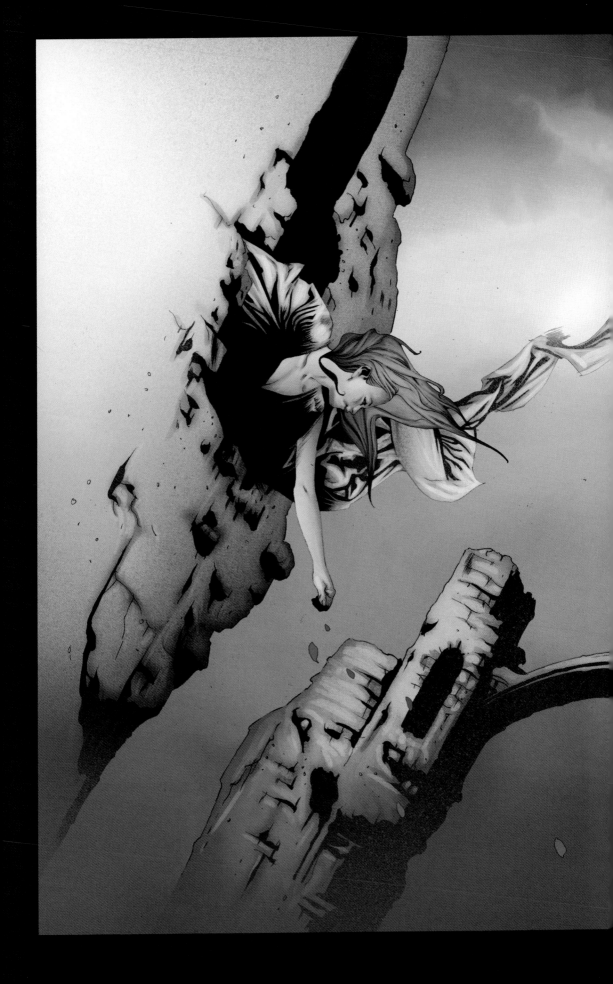

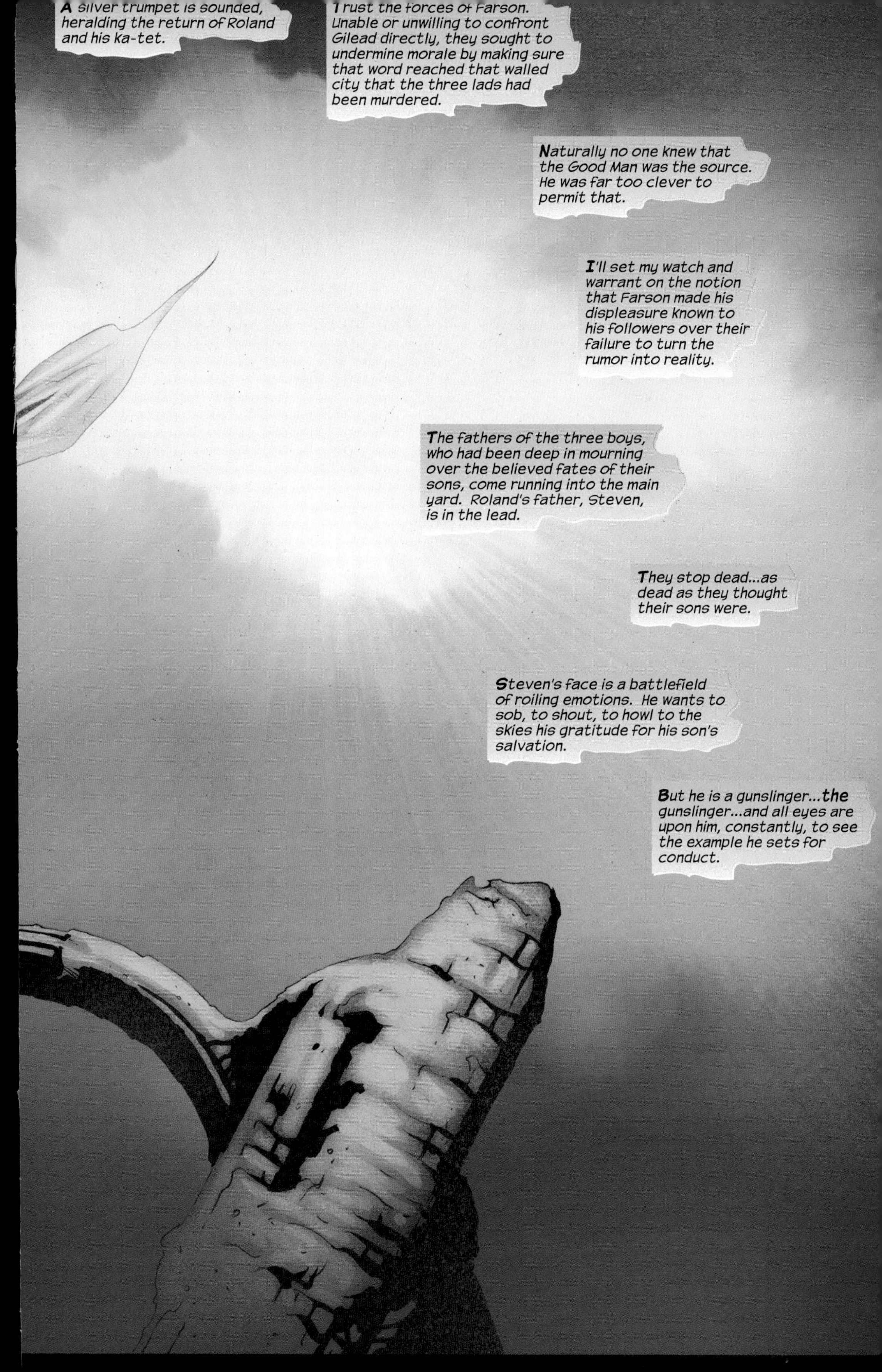
A silver trumpet is sounded, heralding the return of Roland and his ka-tet.
Trust the forces of Farson. Unable or unwilling to confront Gilead directly, they sought to undermine morale by making sure that word reached that walled city that the three lads had been murdered.
Naturally no one knew that the Good Man was the source. He was far too clever to permit that.
I'll set my watch and warrant on the notion that Farson made his displeasure known to his followers over their failure to turn the rumor into reality.
The fathers of the three boys, who had been deep in mourning over the believed fates of their sons, come running into the main yard. Roland's father, Steven, is in the lead.
They stop dead...as dead as they thought their sons were.
Steven's face is a battlefield of roiling emotions. He wants to sob, to shout, to howl to the skies his gratitude for his son's salvation.
But he is a gunslinger...the gunslinger...and all eyes are upon him, constantly, to see the example he sets for conduct.

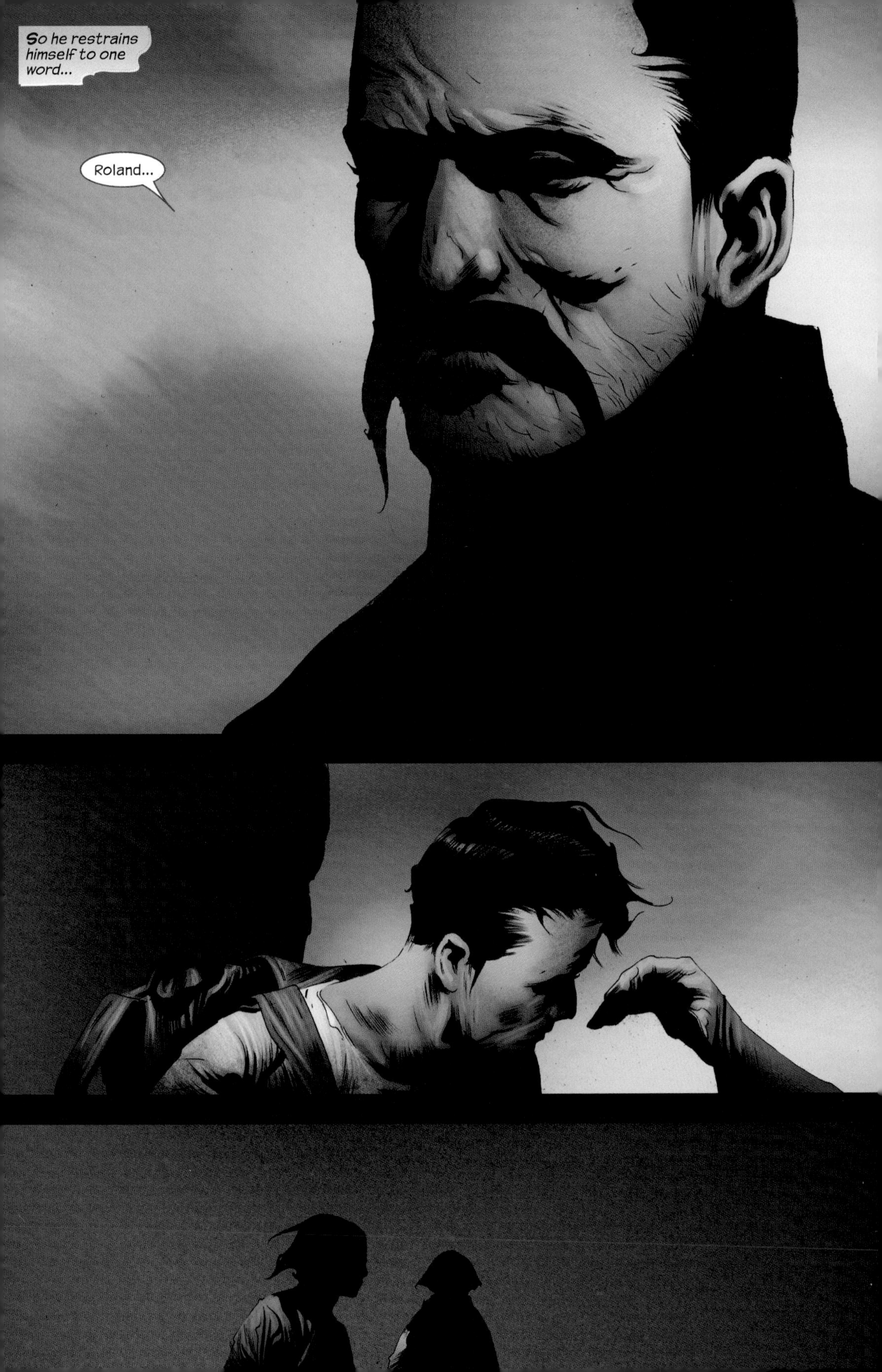
So he restrains himself to one word...
Roland...

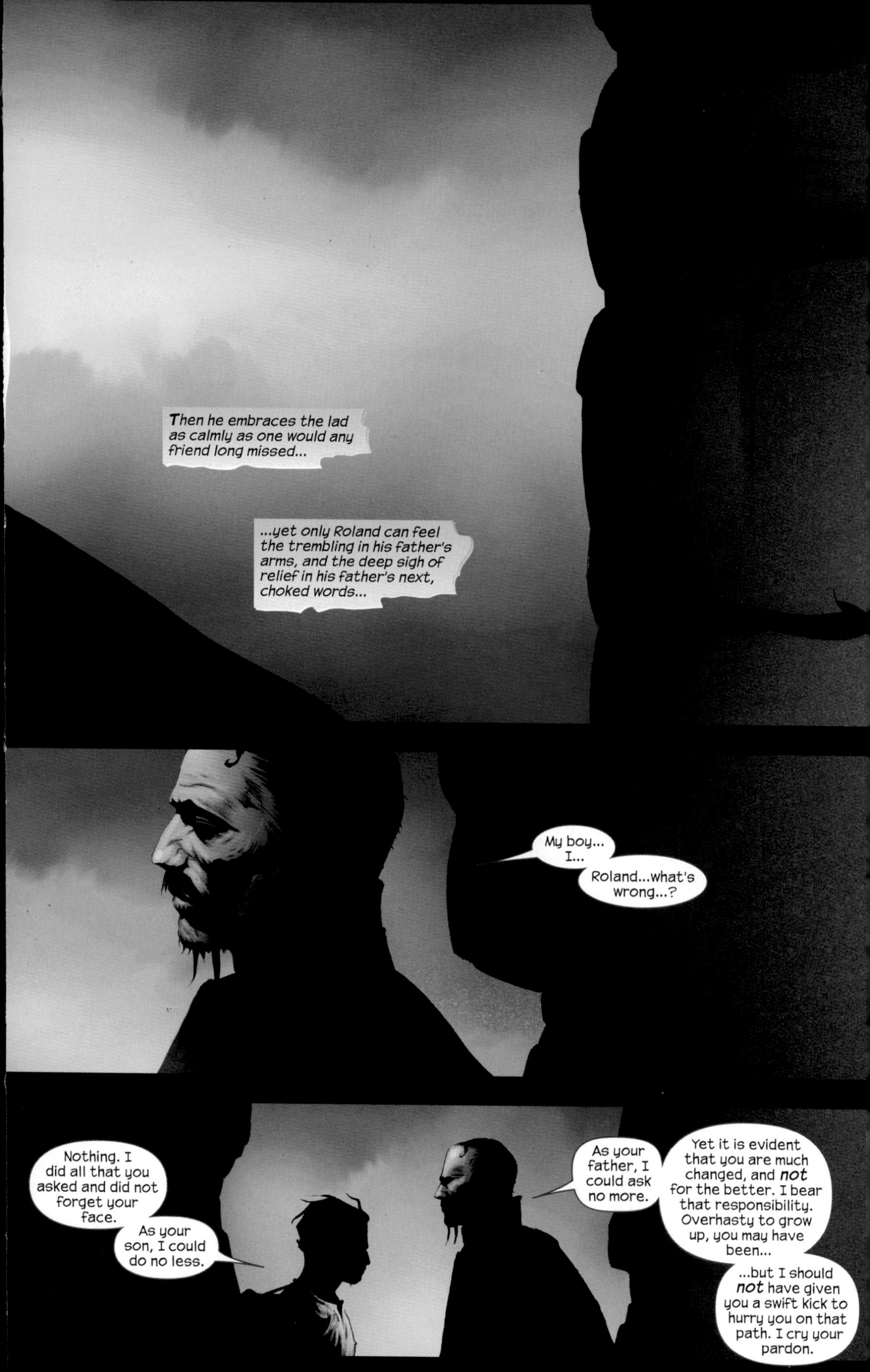

Then he embraces the lad as calmly as one would any friend long missed...
...yet only Roland can feel the trembling in his father's arms, and the deep sigh of relief in his father's next, choked words...
My boy... I...
Roland...what's wrong...?
Nothing. I did all that you asked and did not forget your face.
As your son, I could do no less.
As your father, I could ask no more.
Yet it is evident that you are much changed, and *not* for the better. I bear that responsibility. Overhasty to grow up, you may have been...
...but I should *not* have given you a swift kick to hurry you on that path. I cry your pardon.

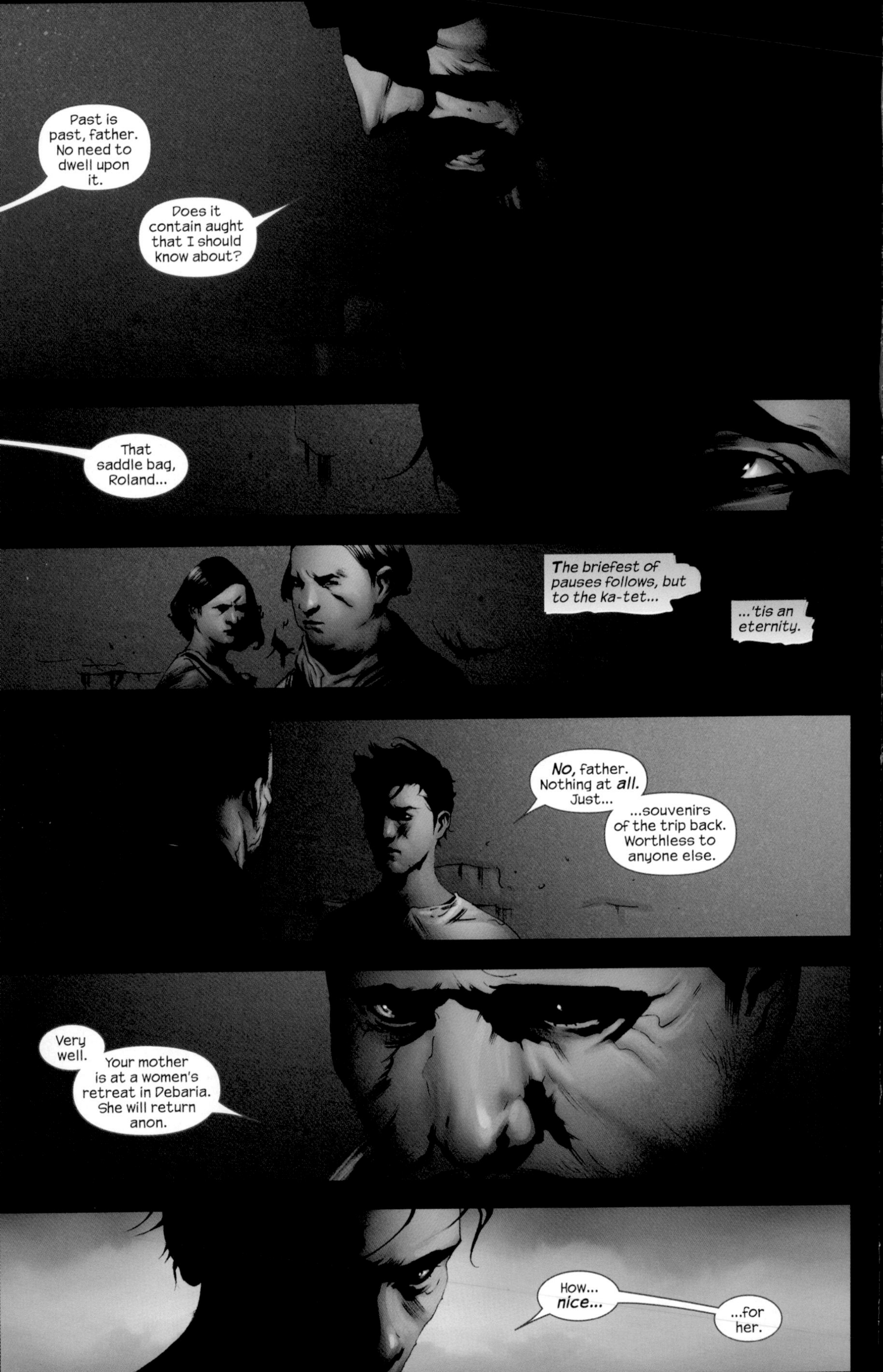
Past is past, father. No need to dwell upon it.
Does it contain aught that I should know about?
That saddle bag, Roland...
The briefest of pauses follows, but to the ka-tet...
...'tis an eternity.
No, father. Nothing at all. Just...
...souvenirs of the trip back. Worthless to anyone else.
Very well.
Your mother is at a women's retreat in Debaria. She will return anon.
How... nice...
...for her.

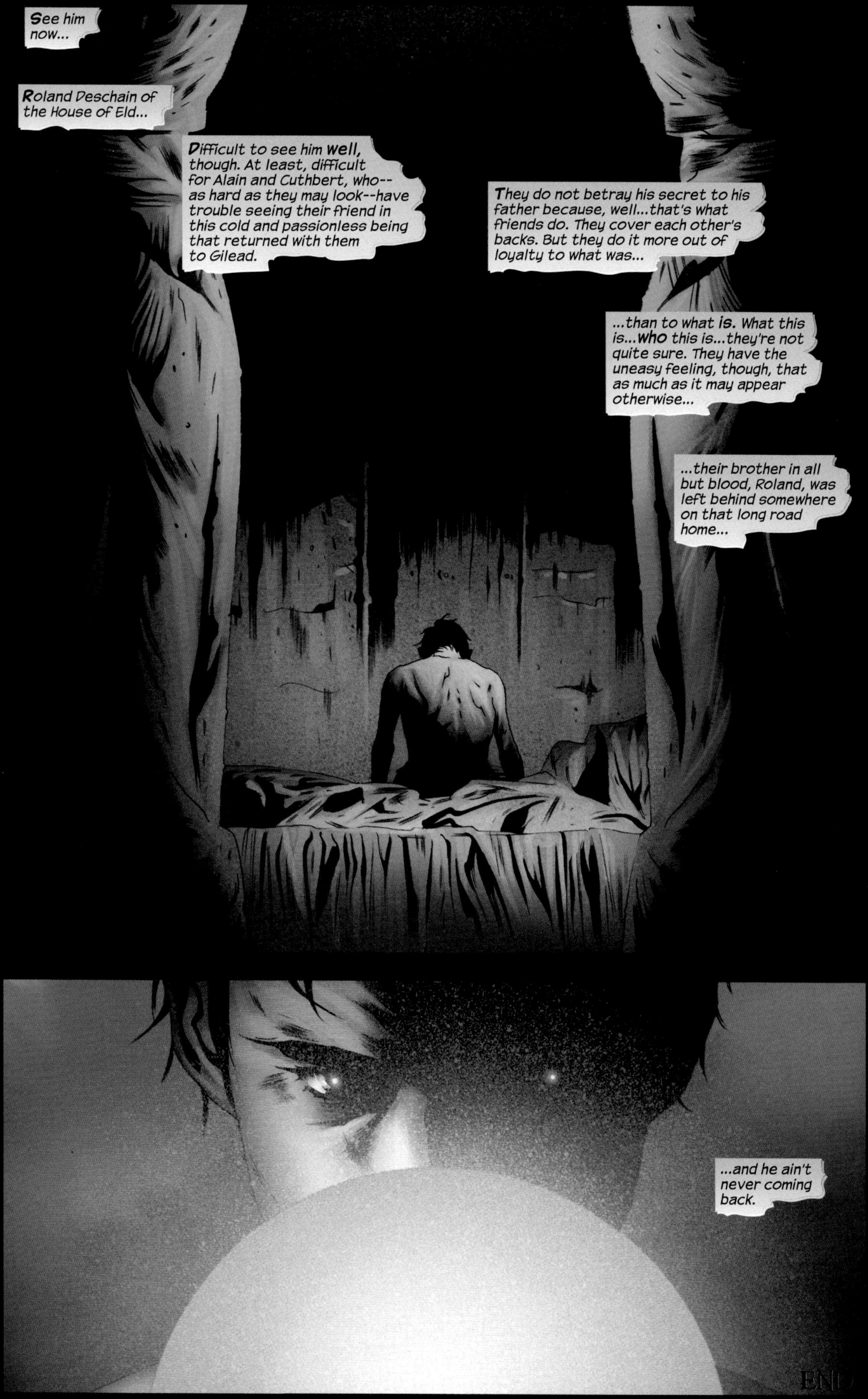
See him now...
Roland Deschain of the House of Eld...
Difficult to see him well, though. At least, difficult for Alain and Cuthbert, who--as hard as they may look--have trouble seeing their friend in this cold and passionless being that returned with them to Gilead.
They do not betray his secret to his father because, well...that's what friends do. They cover each other's backs. But they do it more out of loyalty to what was...
...than to what is. What this is...who this is...they're not quite sure. They have the uneasy feeling, though, that as much as it may appear otherwise...
...their brother in all but blood, Roland, was left behind somewhere on that long road home...
...and he ain't never coming back.
END

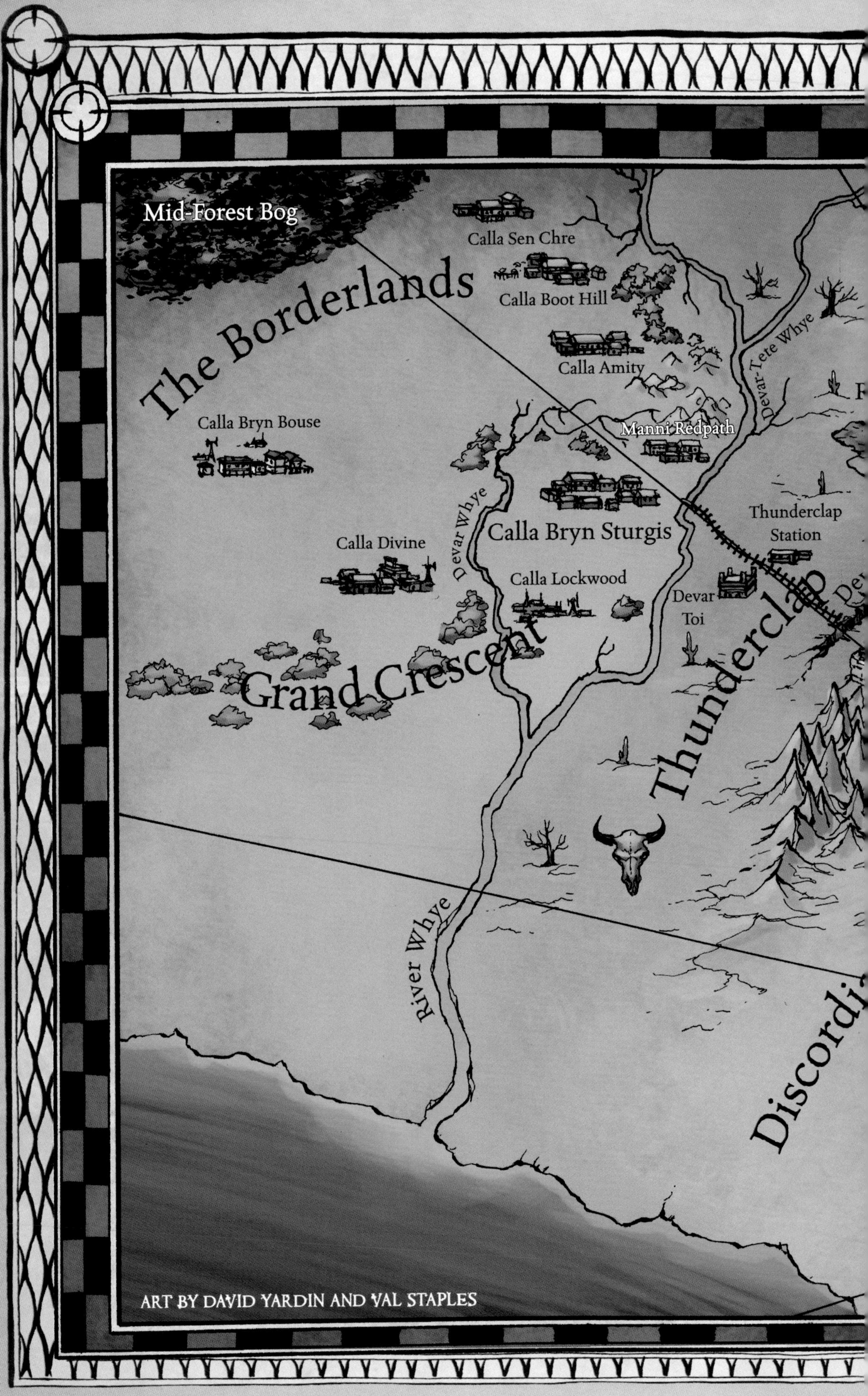
Mid-Forest Bog
Calla Sen Chre
The Borderlands
Calla Boot Hill
Calla Amity
Devar-Tete Whye
Calla Bryn Bouse
Manni Redpath
Devar Whye
Thunderclap Station
Calla Bryn Sturgis
Calla Divine
Calla Lockwood
Devar Toi
Thunderclap
Grand Crescent
River Whye
ART BY DAVID YARDIN AND VAL STAPLES

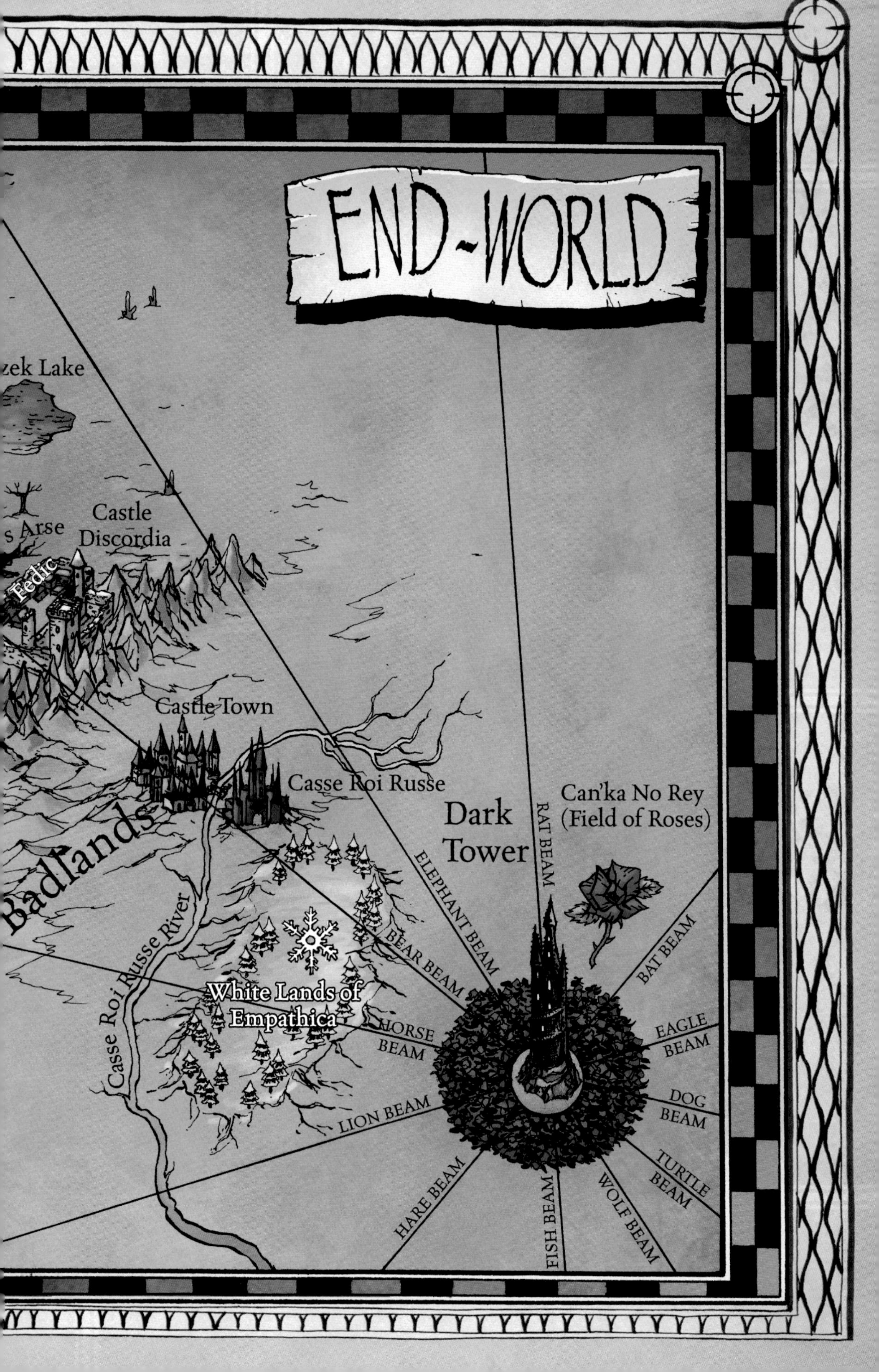
END-WORLD
zek Lake
s Arse
Castle
Discordia
Fedic
Castle Town
Casse Roi Russe
Dark
Tower
Can'ka No Rey
(Field of Roses)
RAT BEAM
ELEPHANT BEAM
BEAR BEAM
Badlands
Casse Roi Russe River
White Lands of
Empathica
HORSE
BEAM
BAT BEAM
EAGLE
BEAM
DOG
BEAM
LION BEAM
TURTLE
BEAM
HARE BEAM
FISH BEAM
WOLF BEAM

Long Road Home #1 Cover by Jae Lee & Richard Isanove

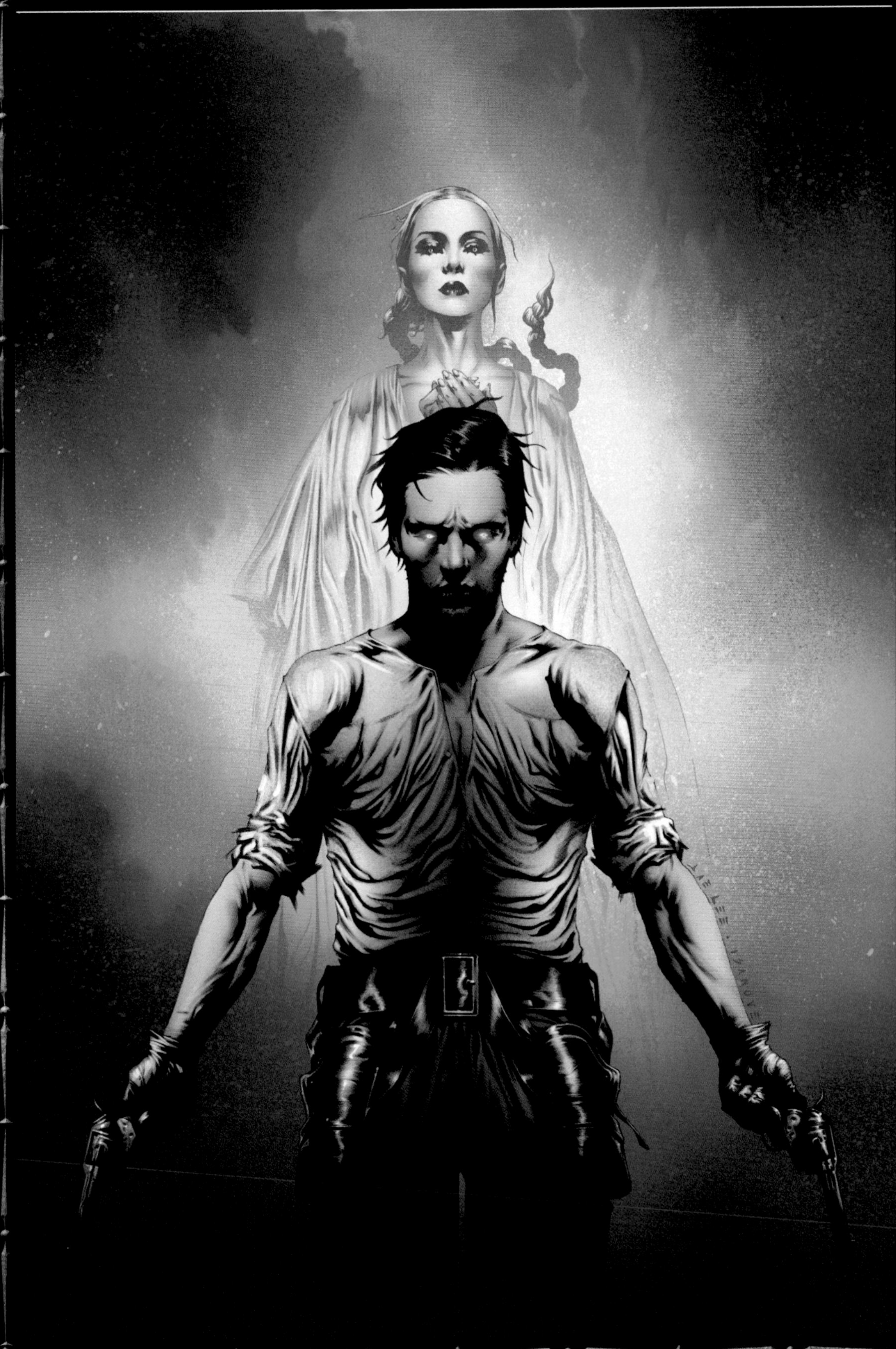

Long Road Home #1 Sketch Variant Cover by Jae Lee

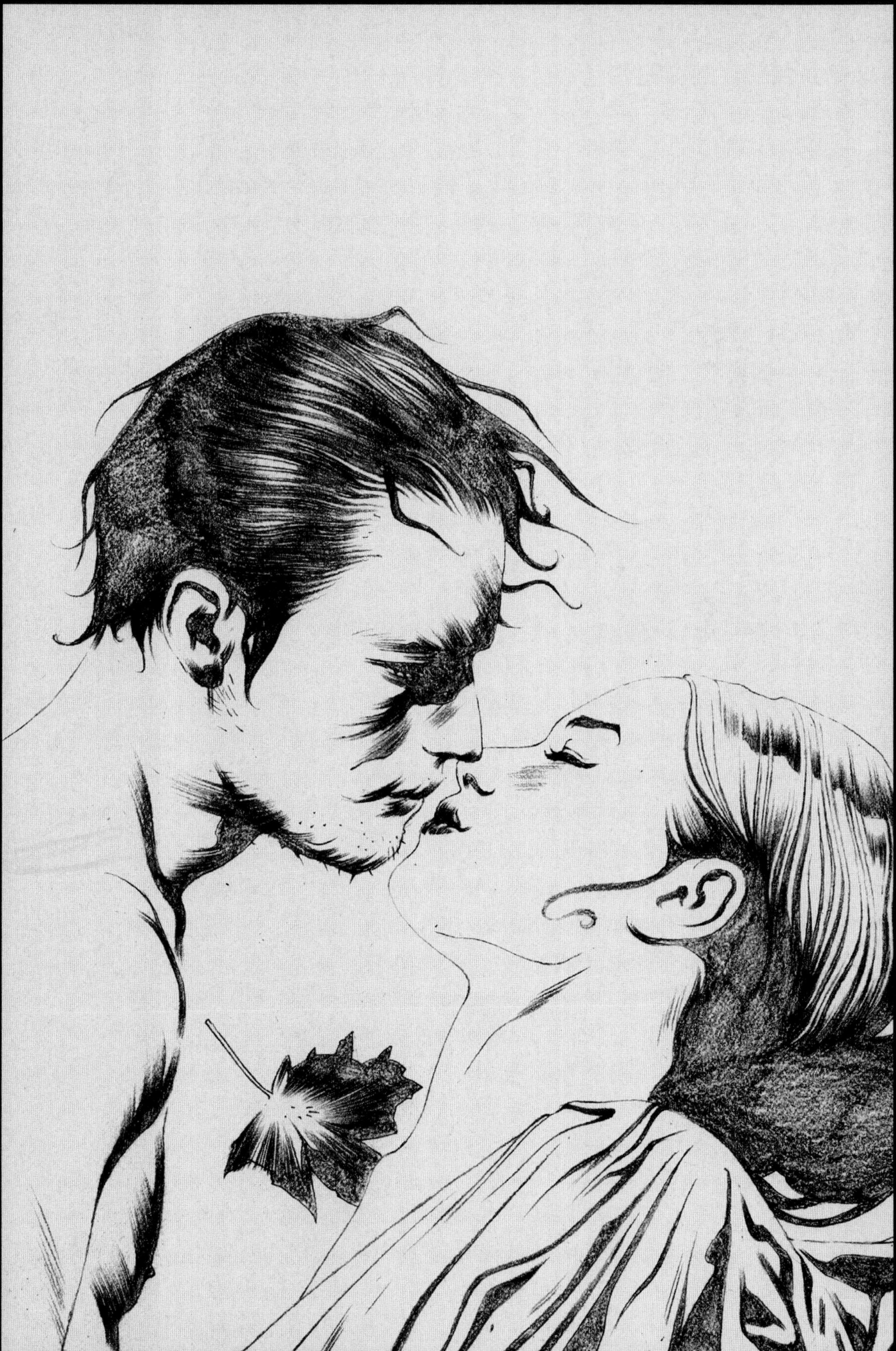

Long Road Home #1 Variant Cover by Mike Deodato & Richard Isanove

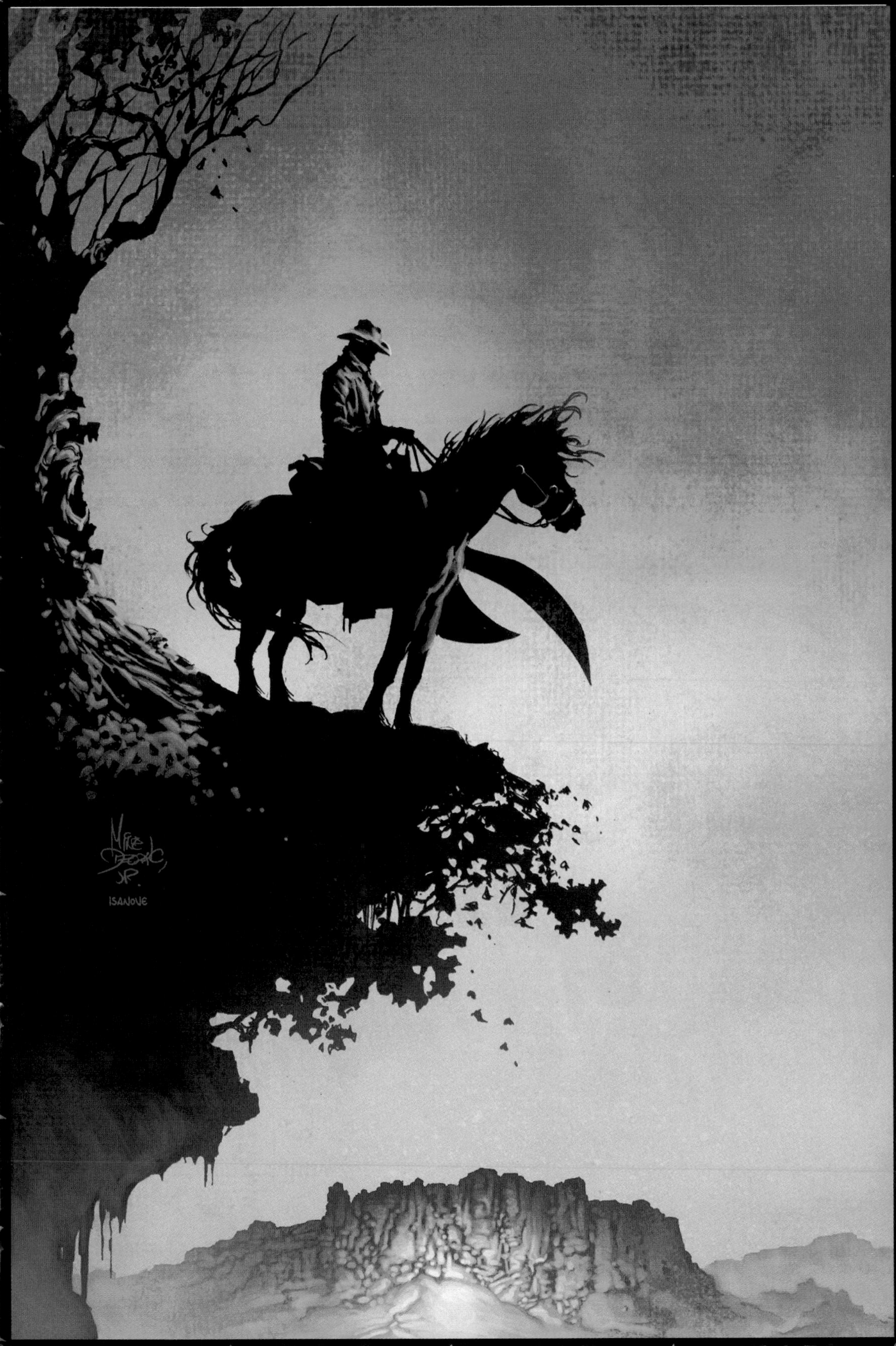
Mike Deodato Jr.
ISANOVE

Long Road Home #2 Cover by Jae Lee & Richard Isanove

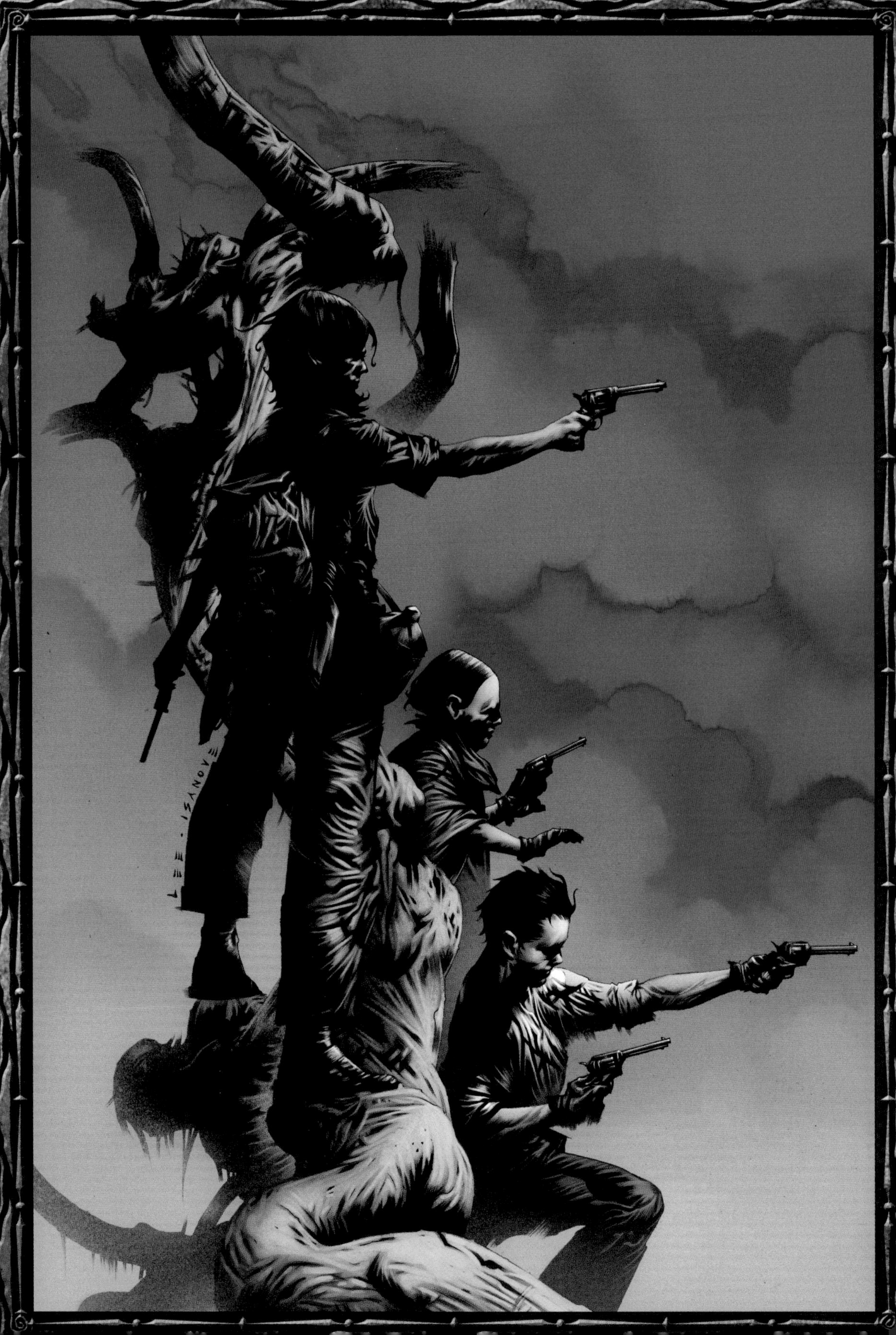

Long Road Home #2 Variant Cover by Joe Quesada & Richard Isanove

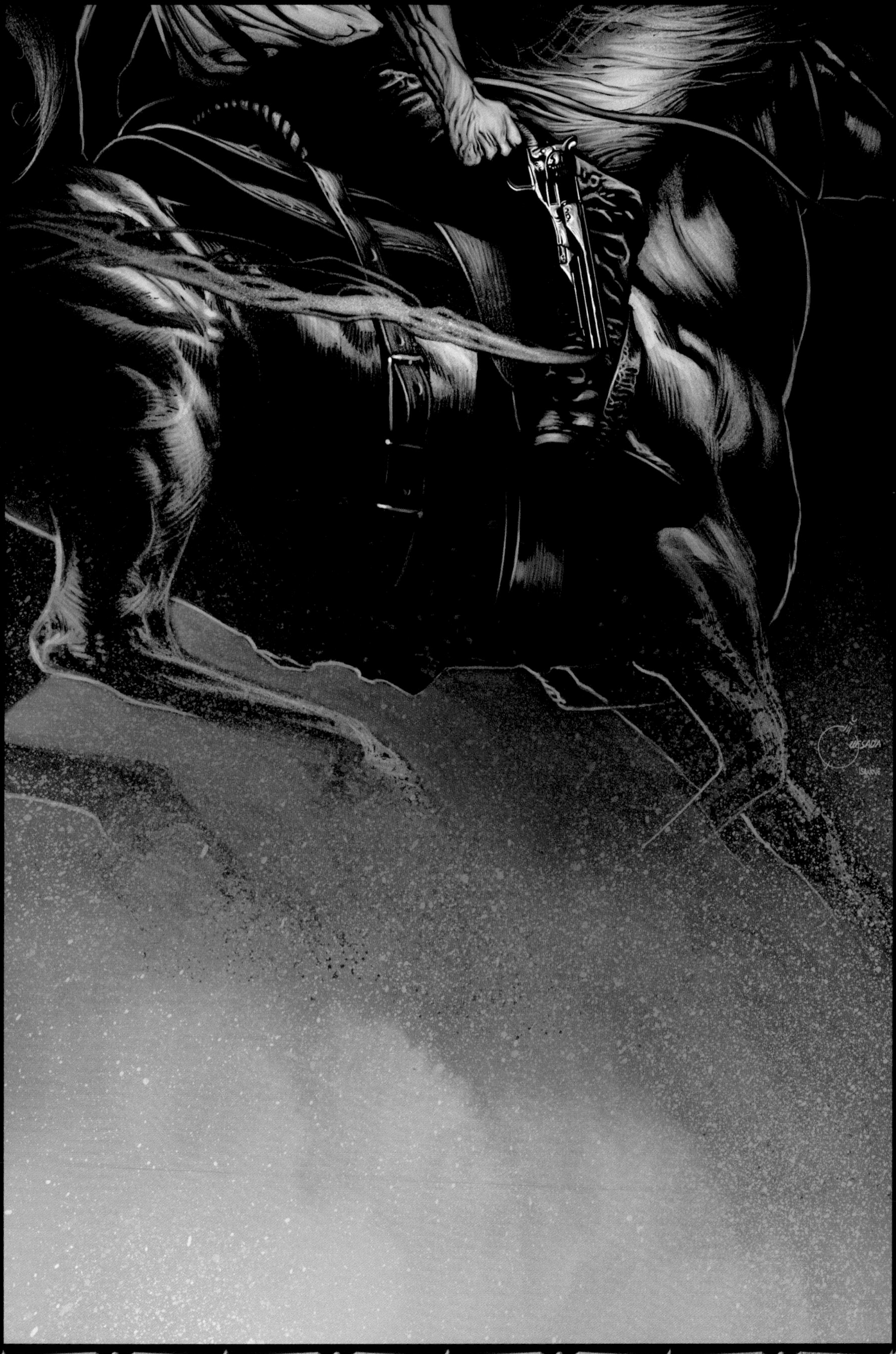
QUESADA
ISANOVE

Long Road Home #2 Variant Cover Art by Joe Quesada

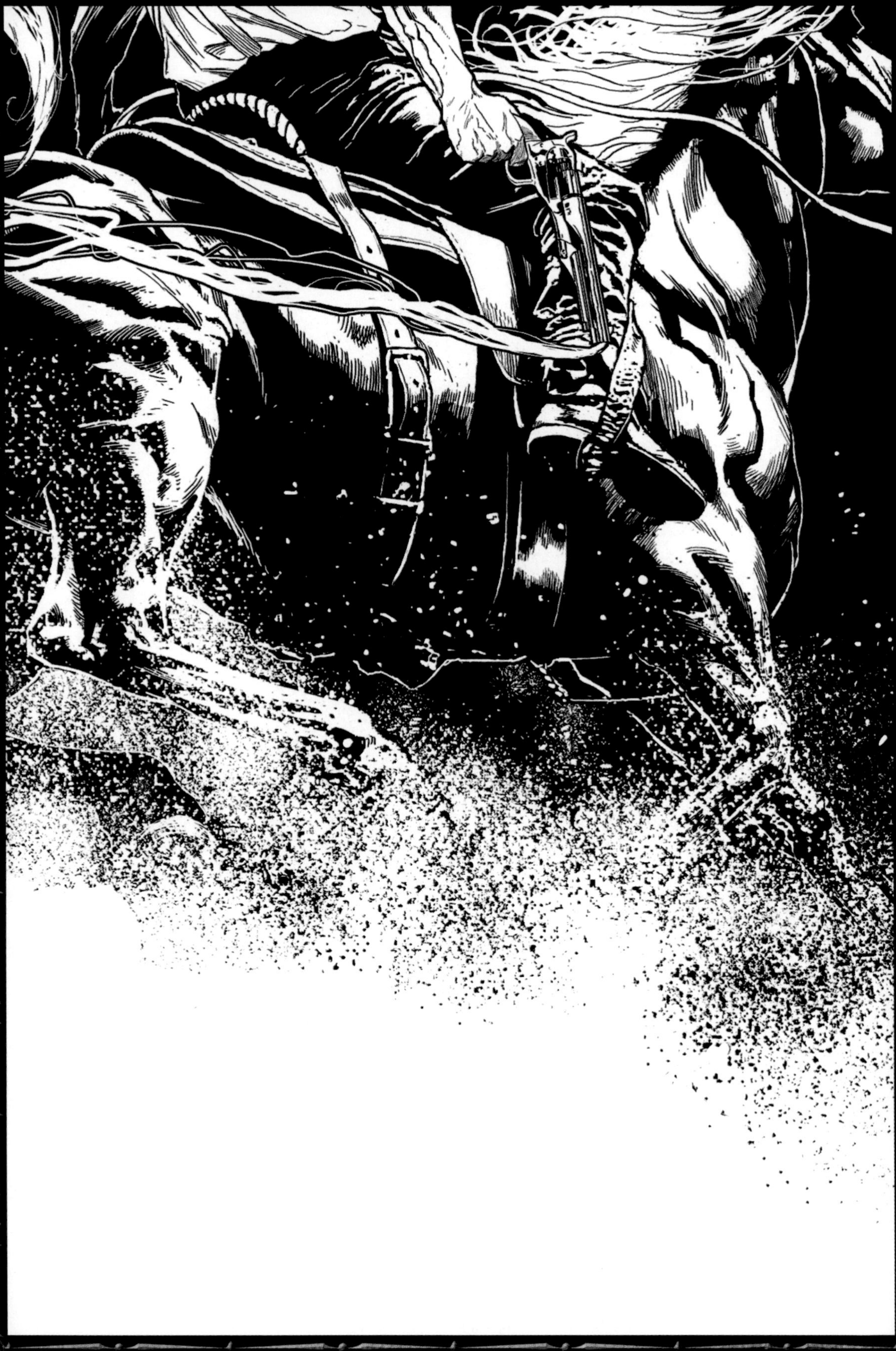

Long Road Home **#2** Sketch Variant Cover by Jae Lee

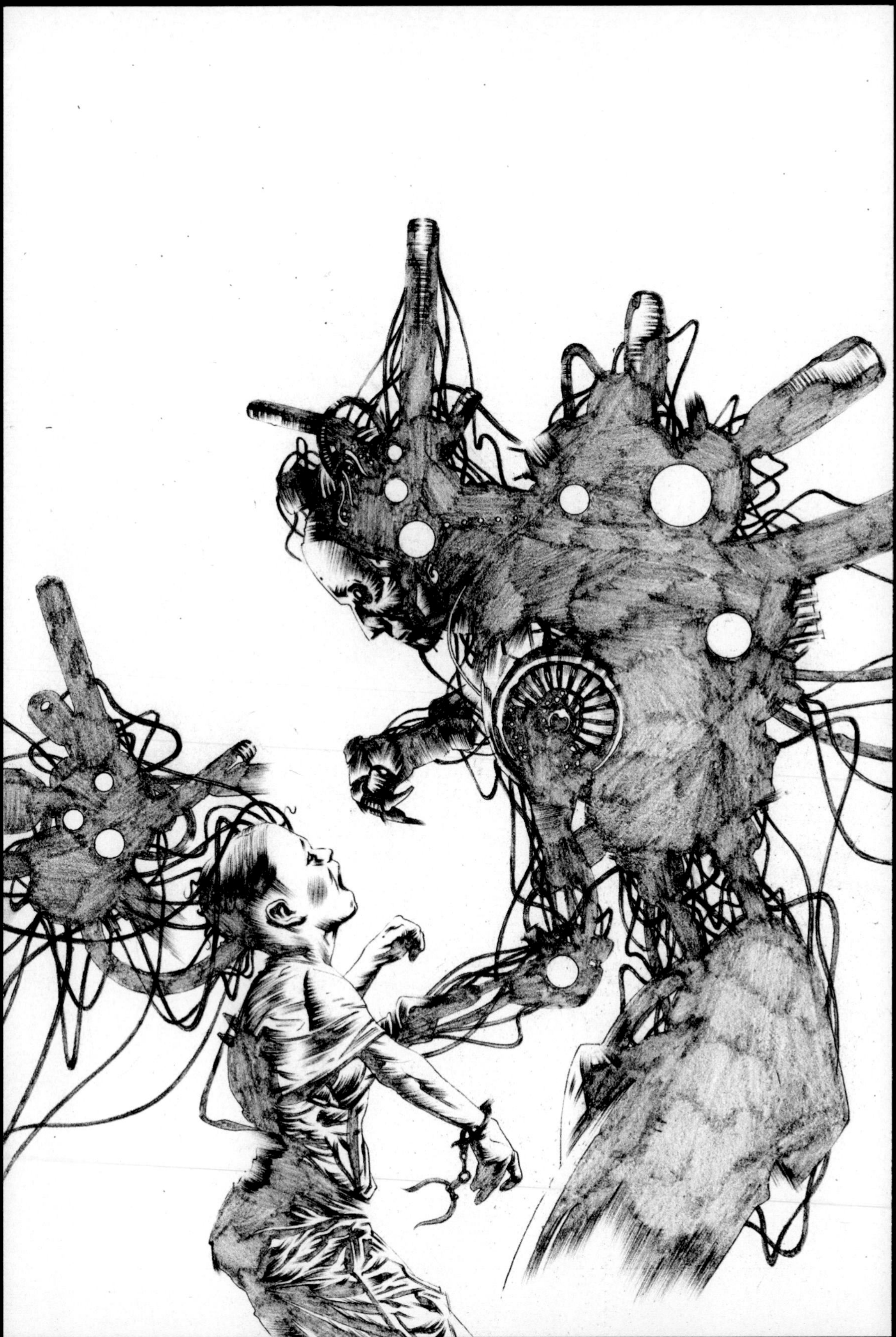

Long Road Home #3 Cover by Jae Lee & Richard Isanove

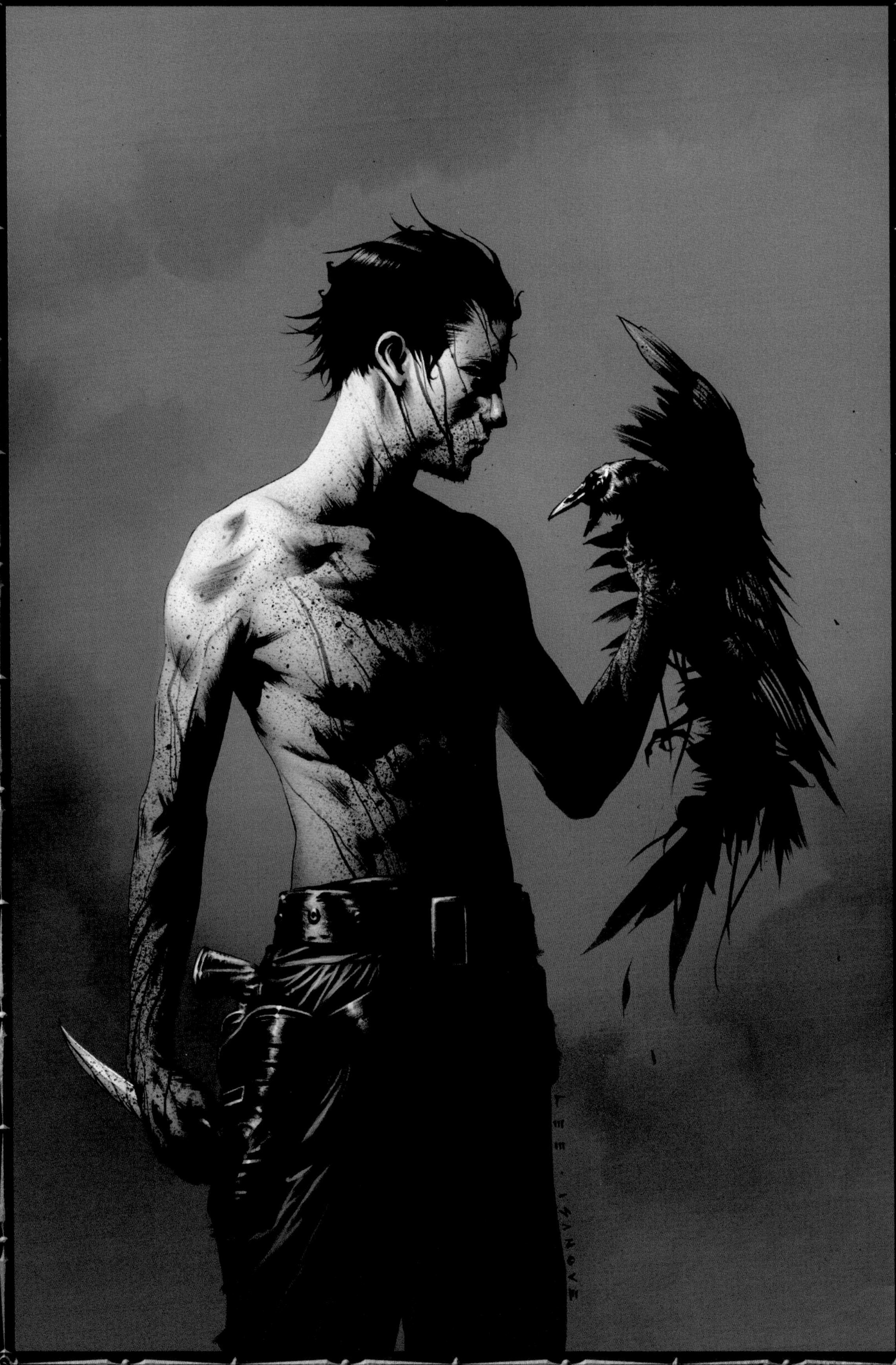

Long Road Home #3 Variant Cover by Marko Djurdjevic

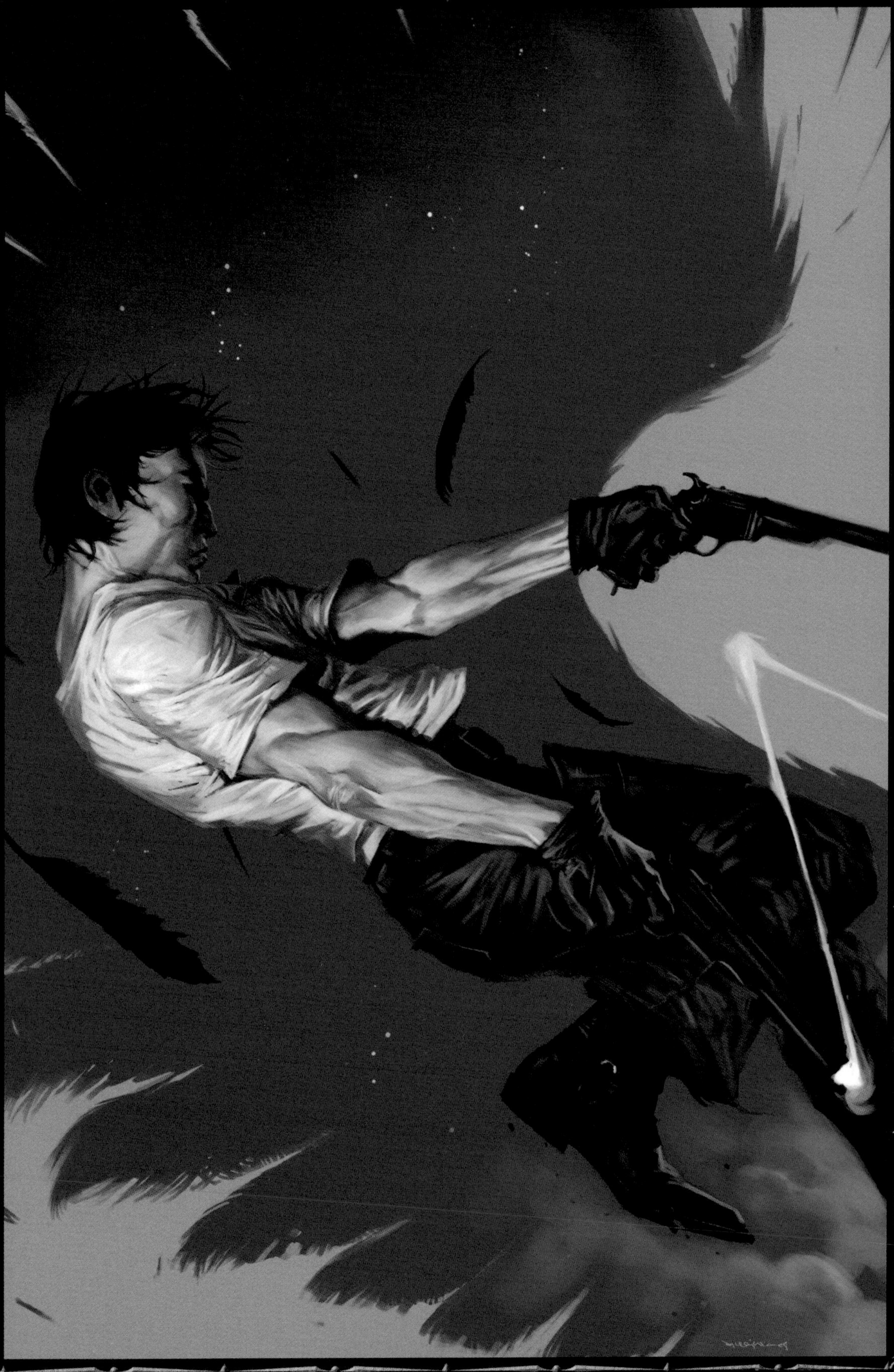

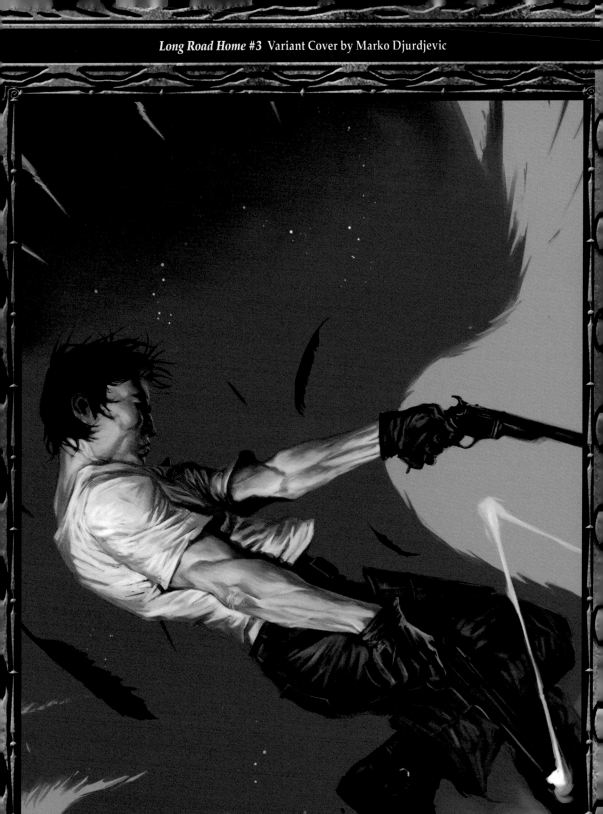

Long Road Home # 3 Sketch Variant Cover by Jae Lee

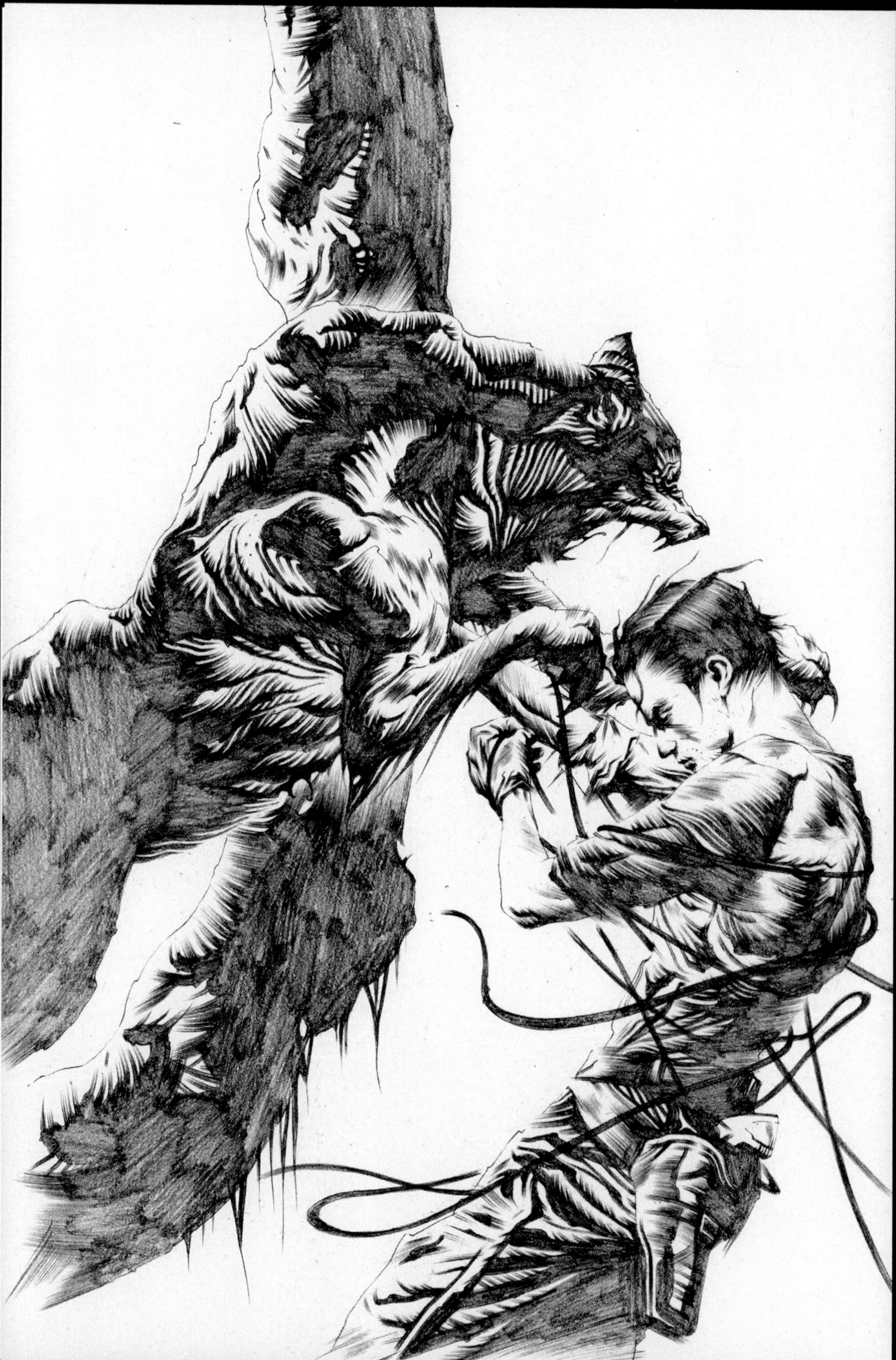

Long Road Home #4 Cover by Jae Lee & Richard Isanove

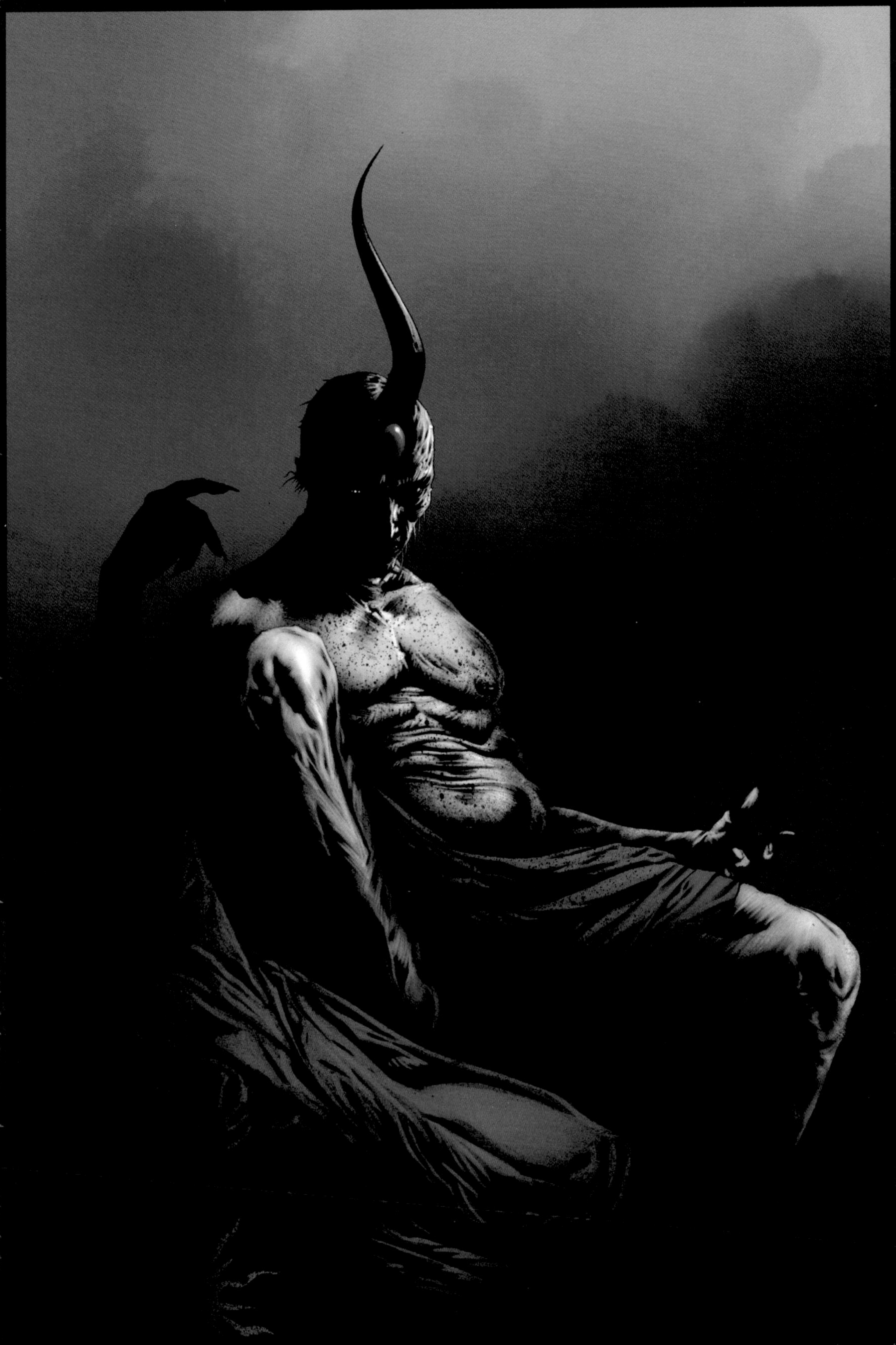

Long Road Home #4 Sketch Variant Cover by Jae Lee

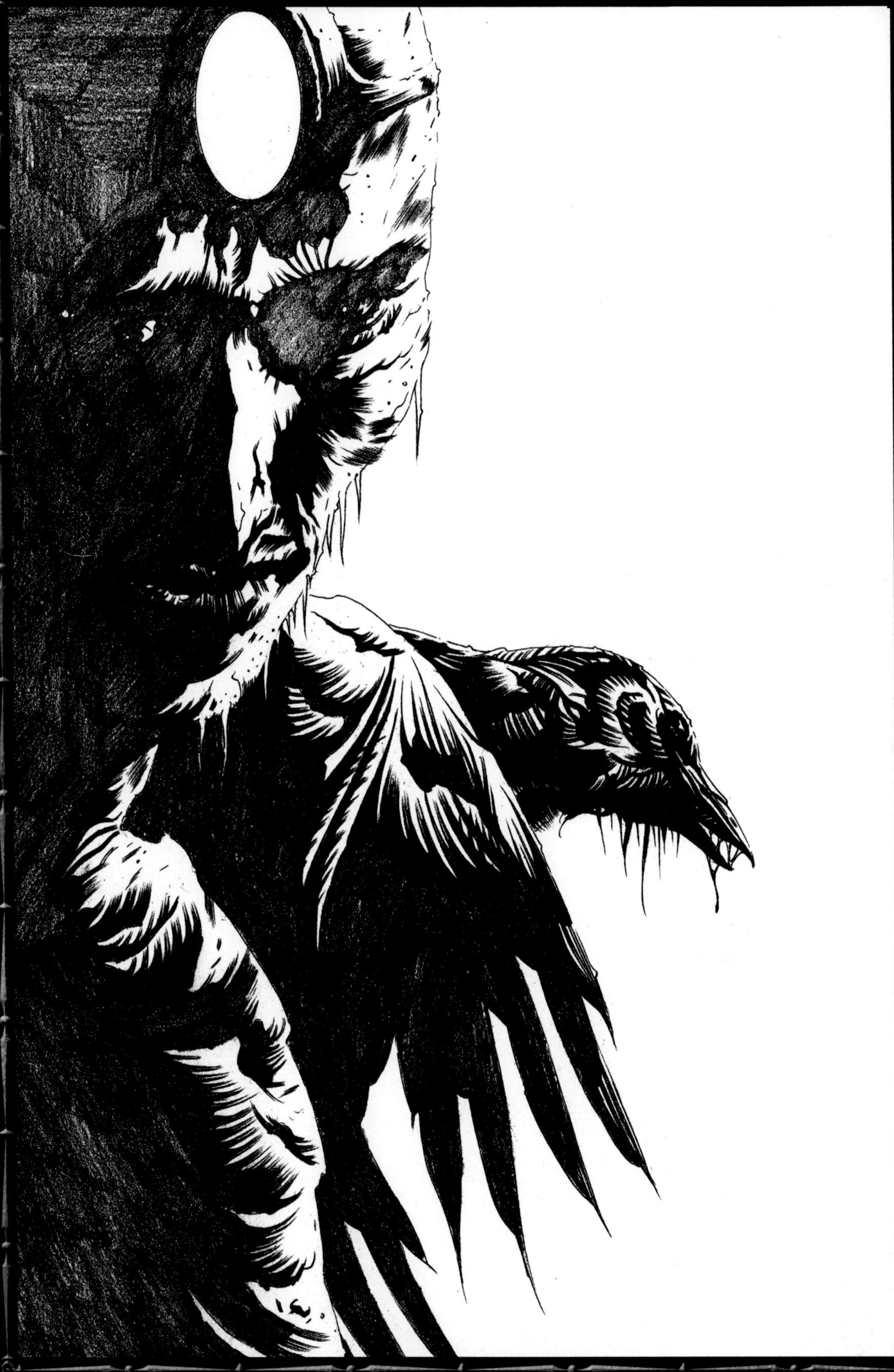

Long Road Home #4 Variant Cover by Ron Garney & Jason Keith

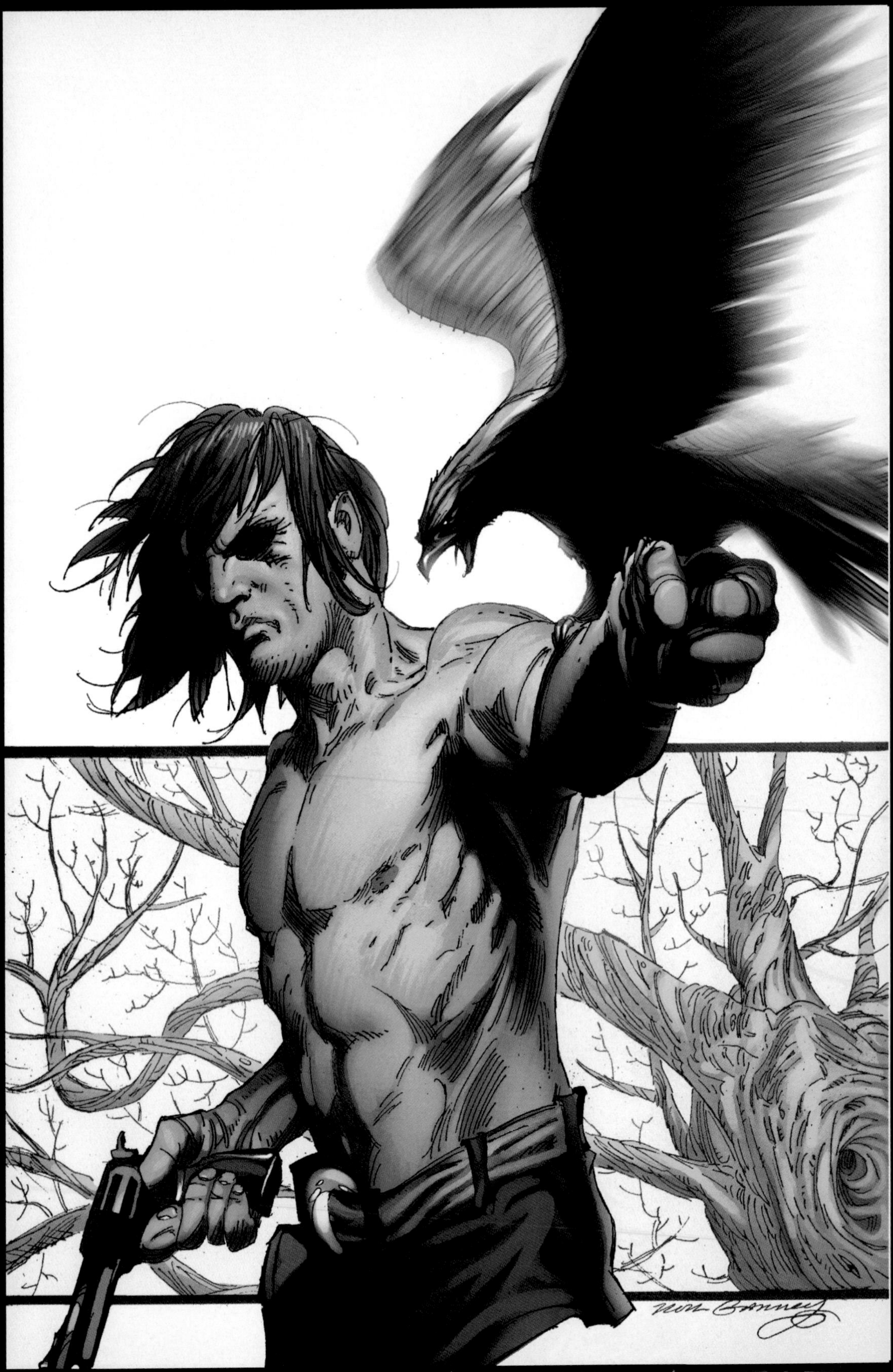

Long Road Home #5 Cover by Jae Lee & Richard Isanove

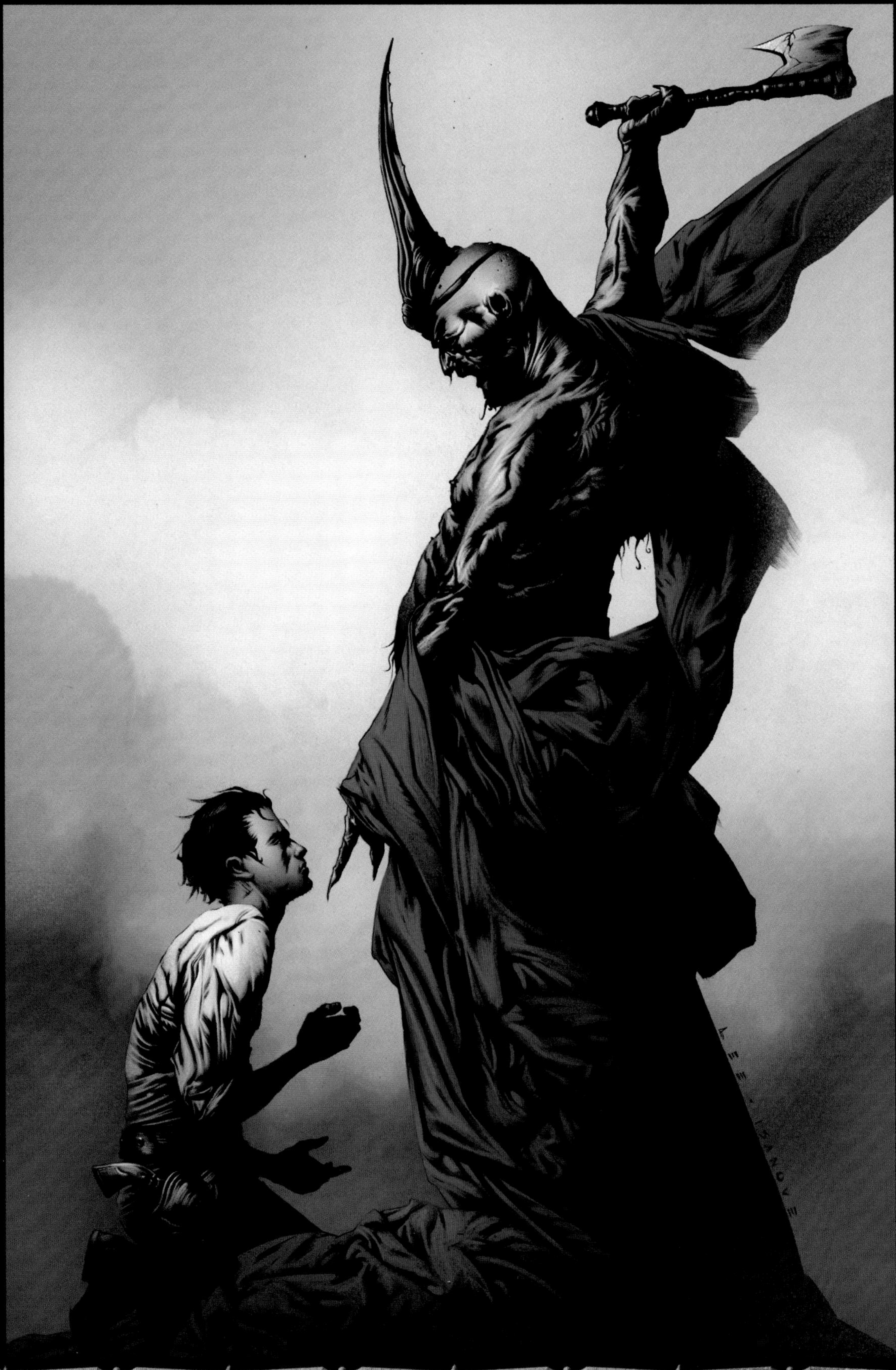

Long Road Home #5 Sketch Variant Cover by Jae Lee

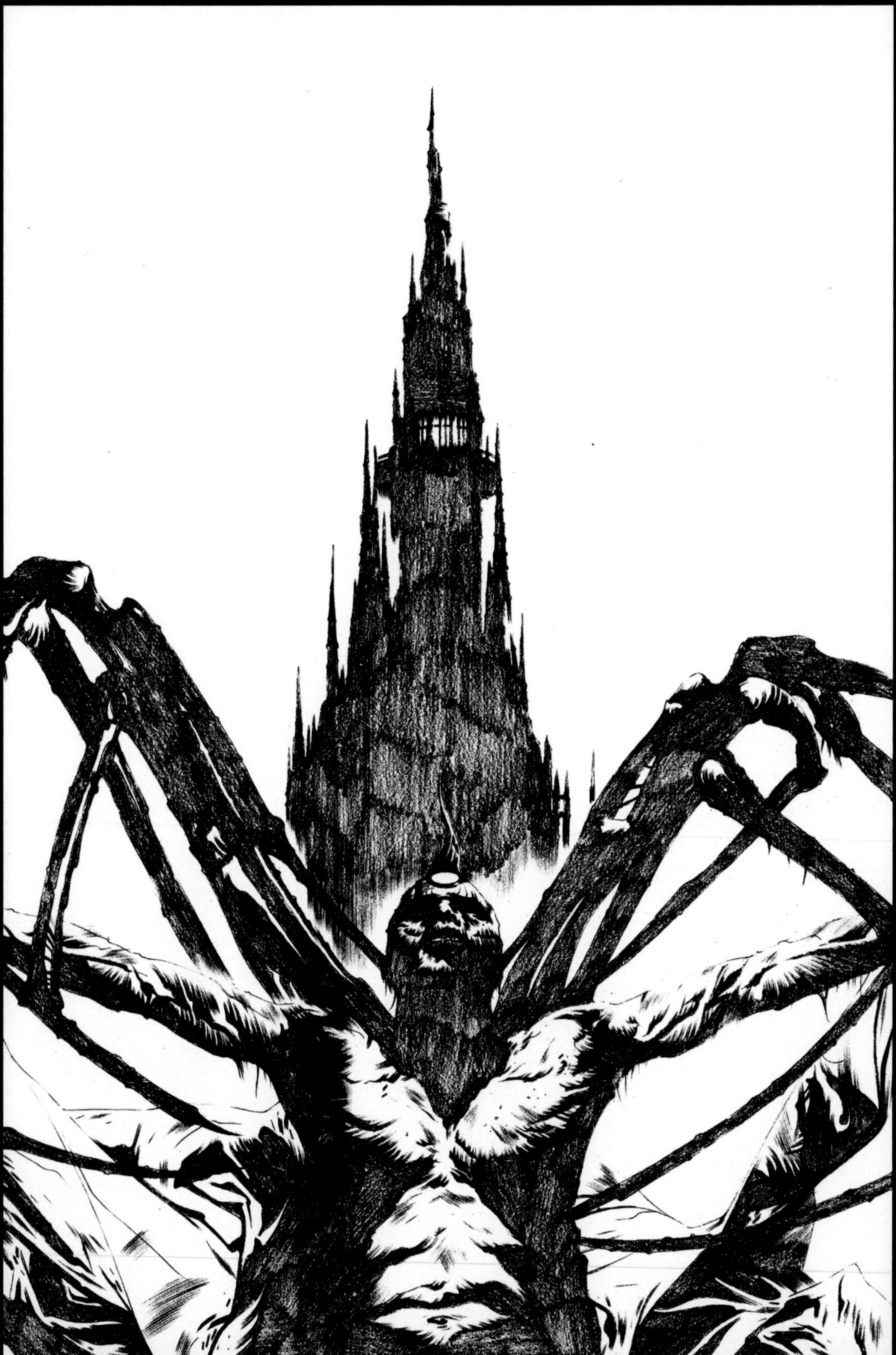

Long Road Home #5 Variant Cover by Lee Bermejo

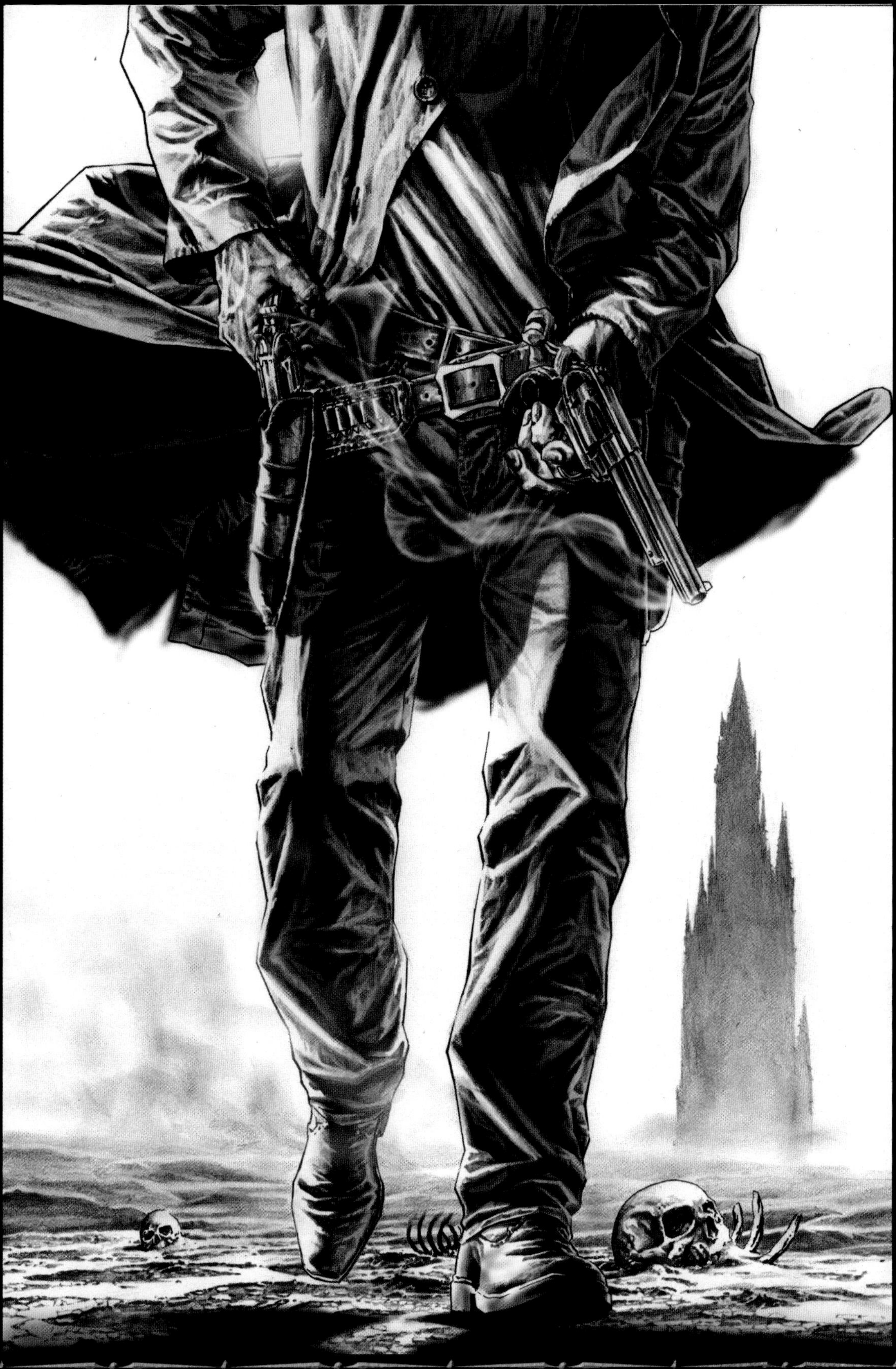

THE MAKING OF A COVER

The cover process begins with Jae Lee's sketch. For this issue, Jae wanted to focus on Roland and the crow (which is Marten in disguise). He e-mailed this sketch to the editors, with the note *"adult roland crushing a crow's guts out (which symbolizes marten) in one hand, a gun in his other."*

After making a few refinements to his initial design, Jae creates a cover in pencil. To the editors, he explains: *"I had originally intended to have the adult Roland, but couldn't make it work. I wanted Roland to look like a butcher doing some bloody work. Seemed odd for him to be doing it with his coat and hat on. When I drew him without those things on, he seemed unrecognizable. So I went with the young Roland which makes more sense anyway because in this issue, the young Roland is trying to kill the crow."*

Richard Isanove's initial painted treatment of the cover was beautiful, but the editors wondered if the red blood would be too graphic. So Richard created an alternate image, this time with the blood done in black.

After seeing both versions, Marvel opted to use the black coloring for promotional purposes, and the red coloring for the printed book that you now hold in your hands.

Long Road Home #1, page 17 Preliminary Pencils by Jae Lee

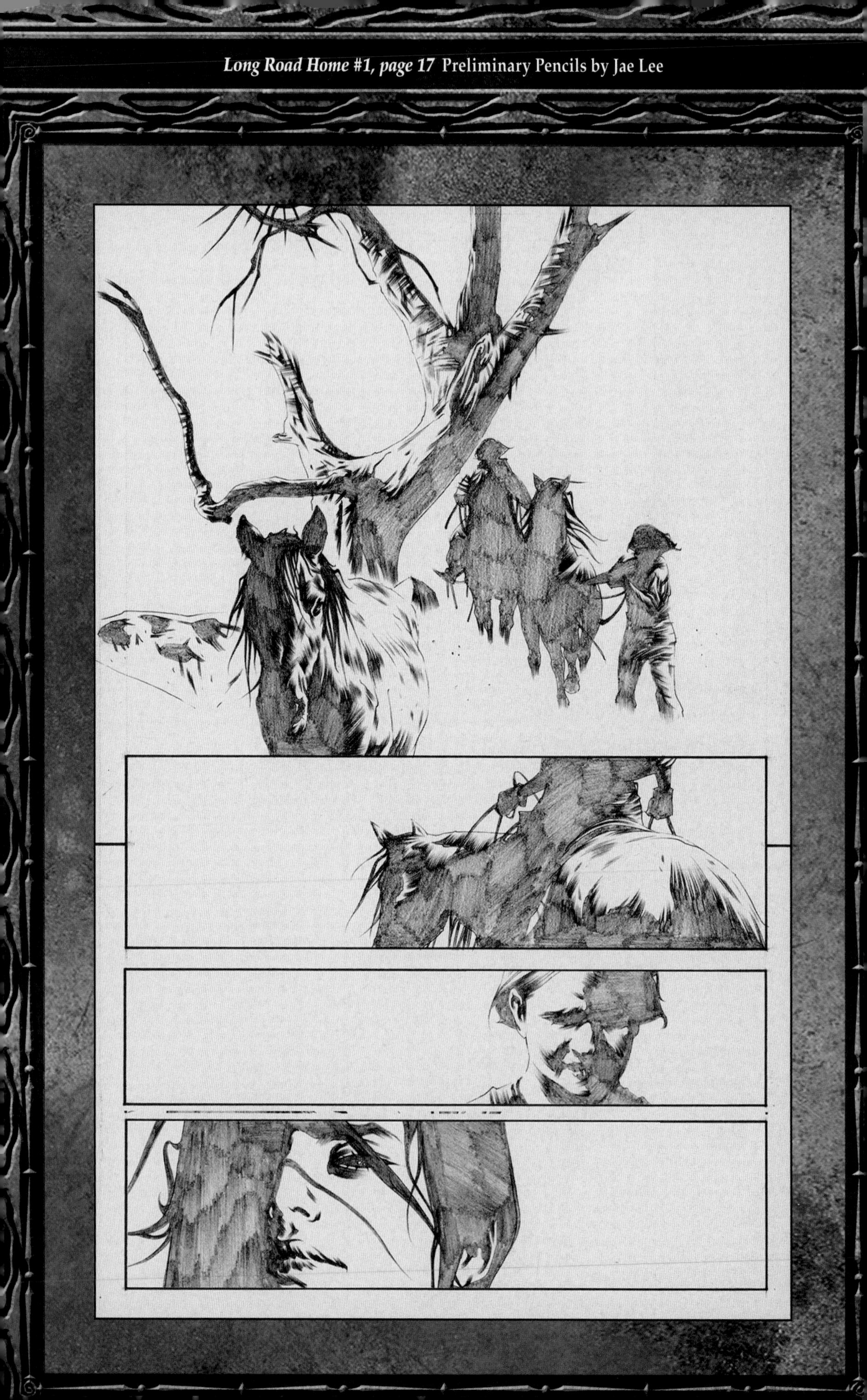

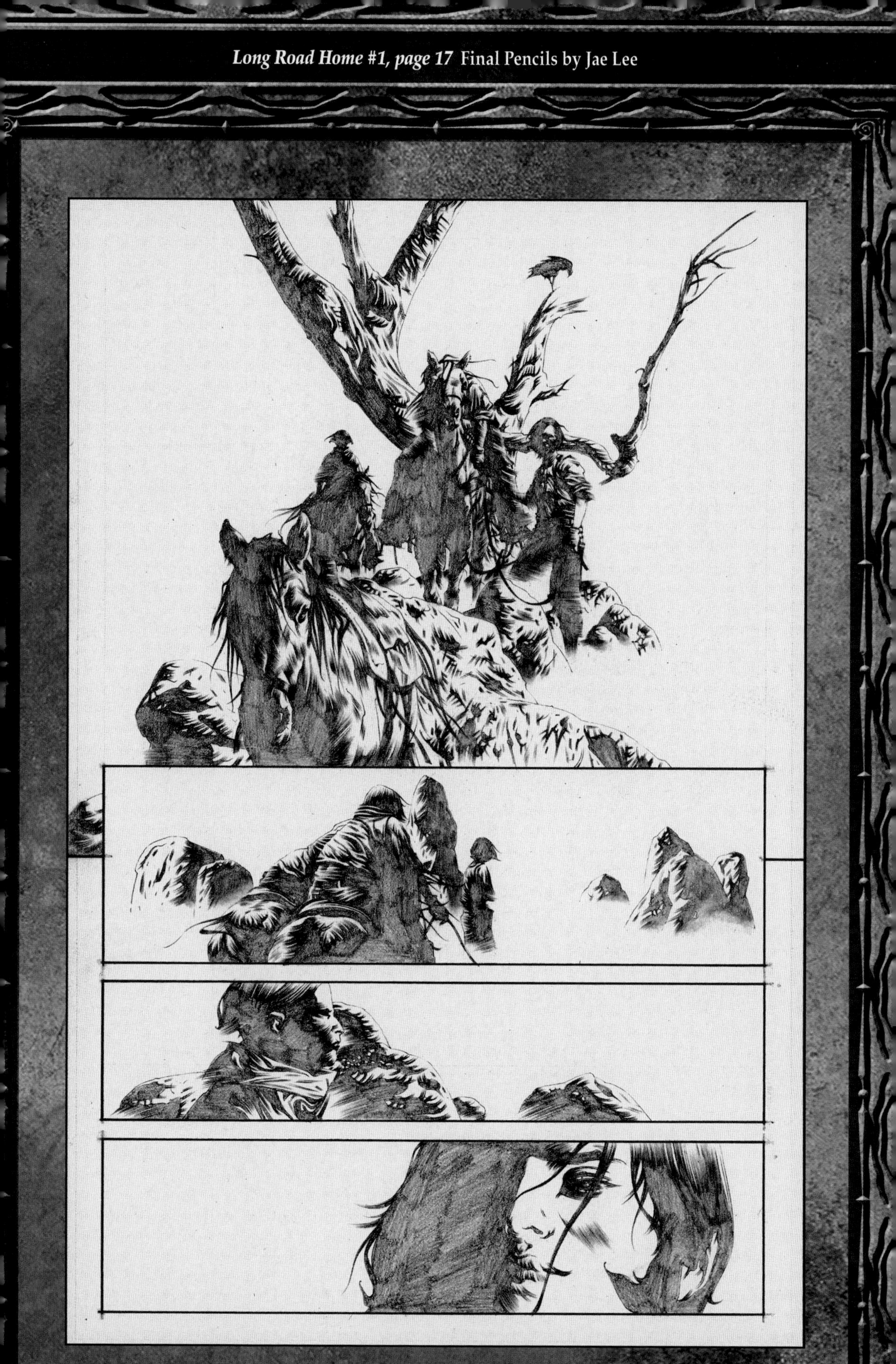

Long Road Home #1, pages 23-24 Preliminary and Final Pencils by Jae Lee

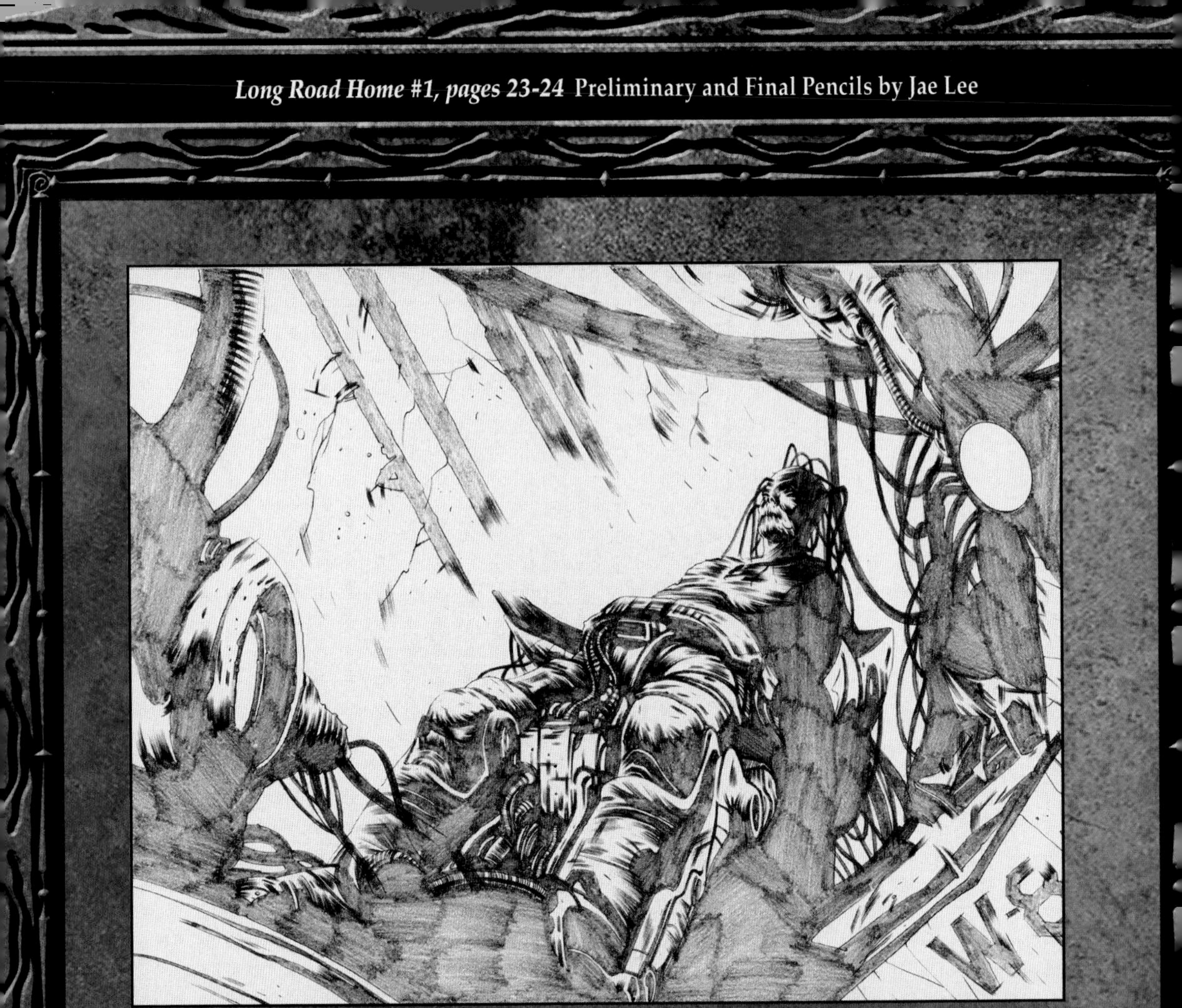

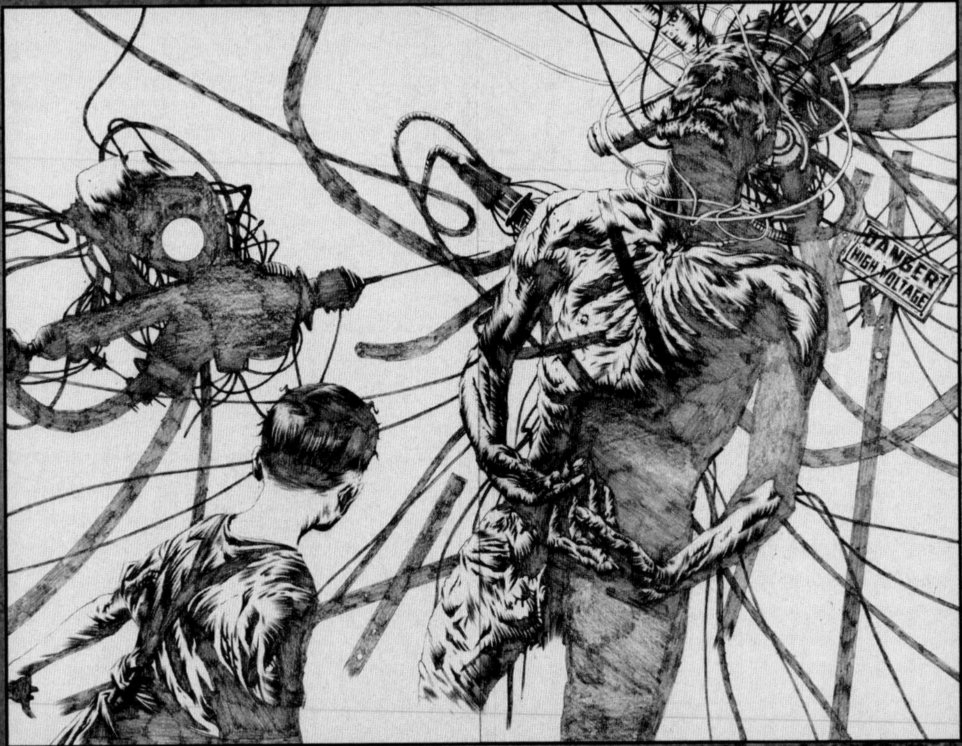
DANGER
HIGH VOLTAGE

Long Road Home #3, page 2 Pencils by Jae Lee

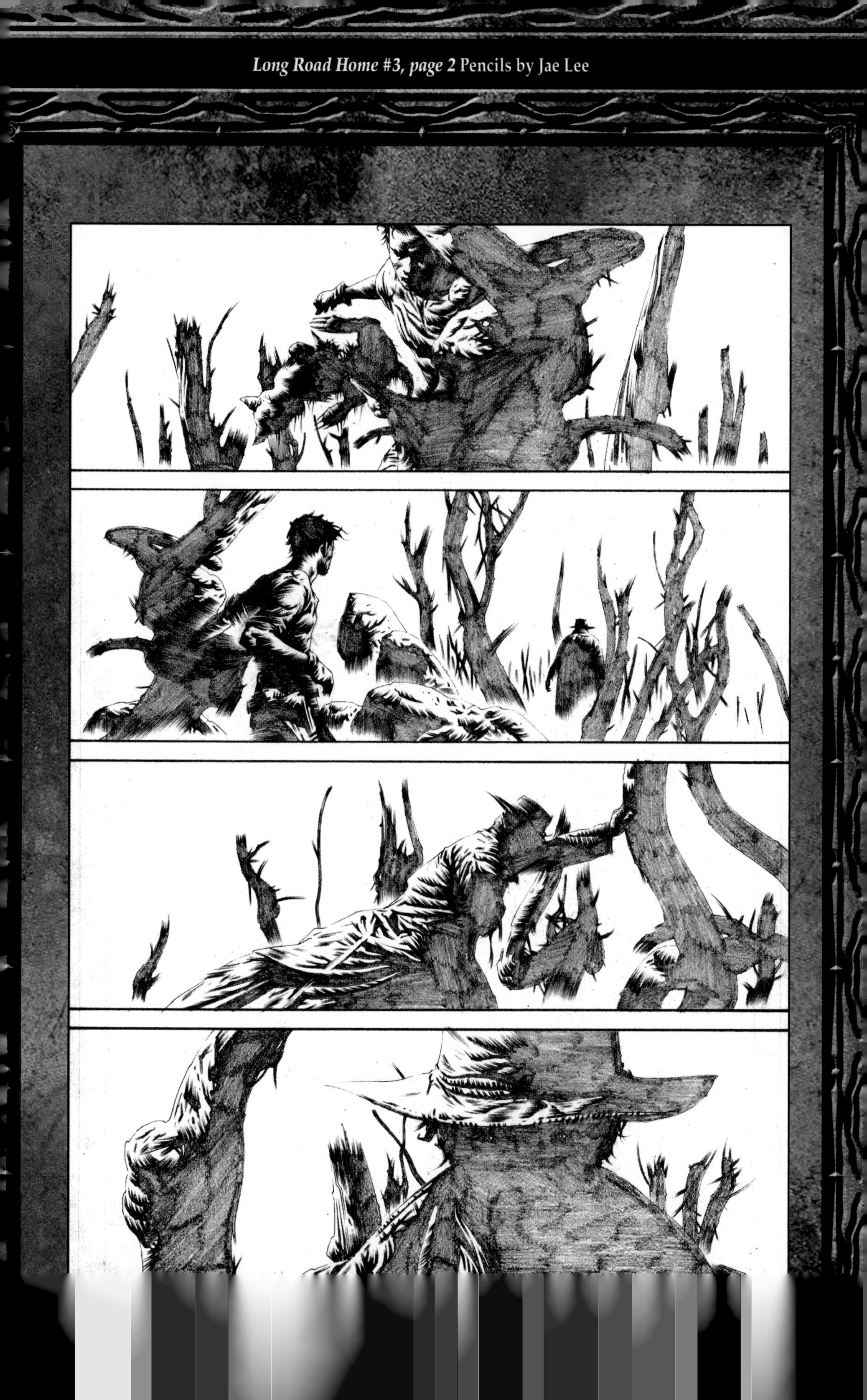

Long Road Home #4, pages 5 and 7-8 Preliminary and Final Pencils by Jae Lee

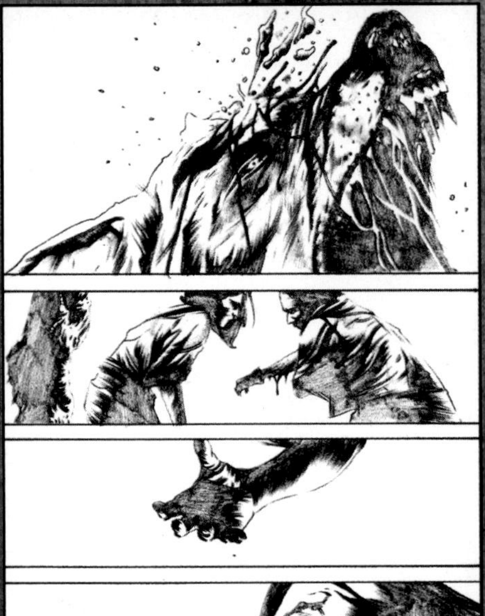

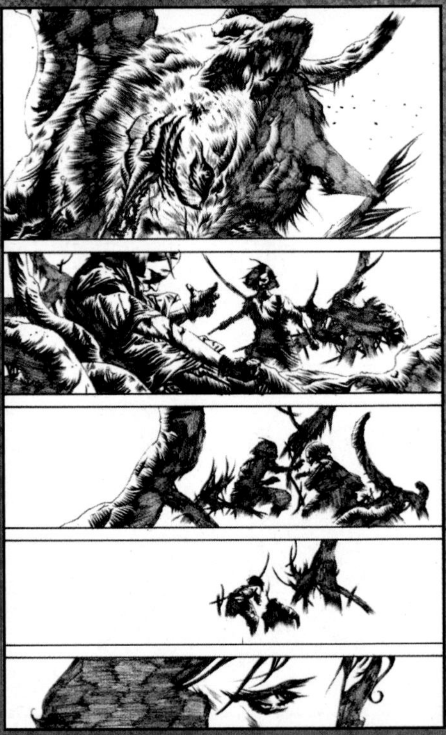

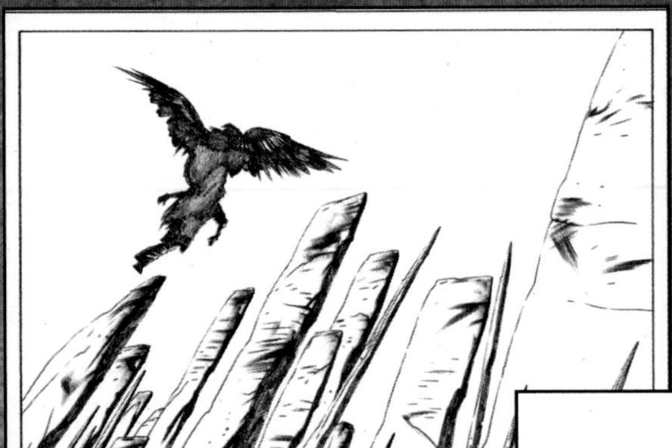

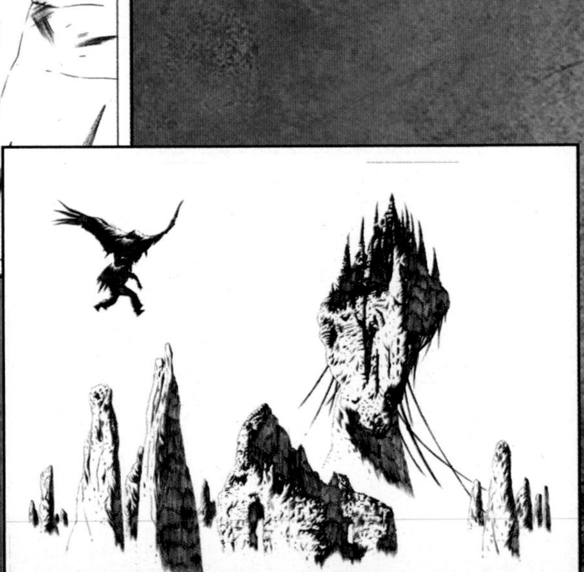

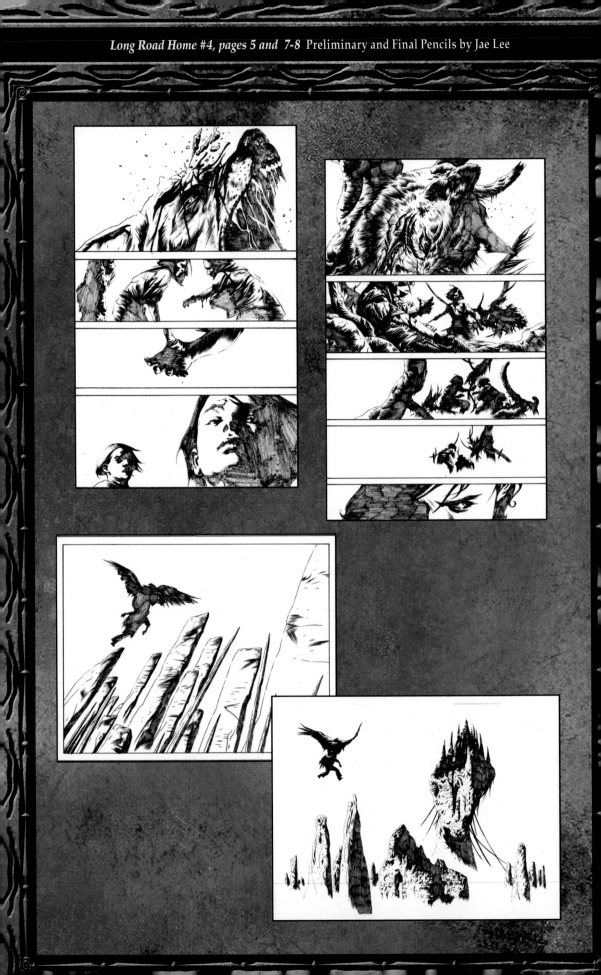

Long Road Home #4, pages 9-10 Preliminary and Final Pencils by Jae Lee

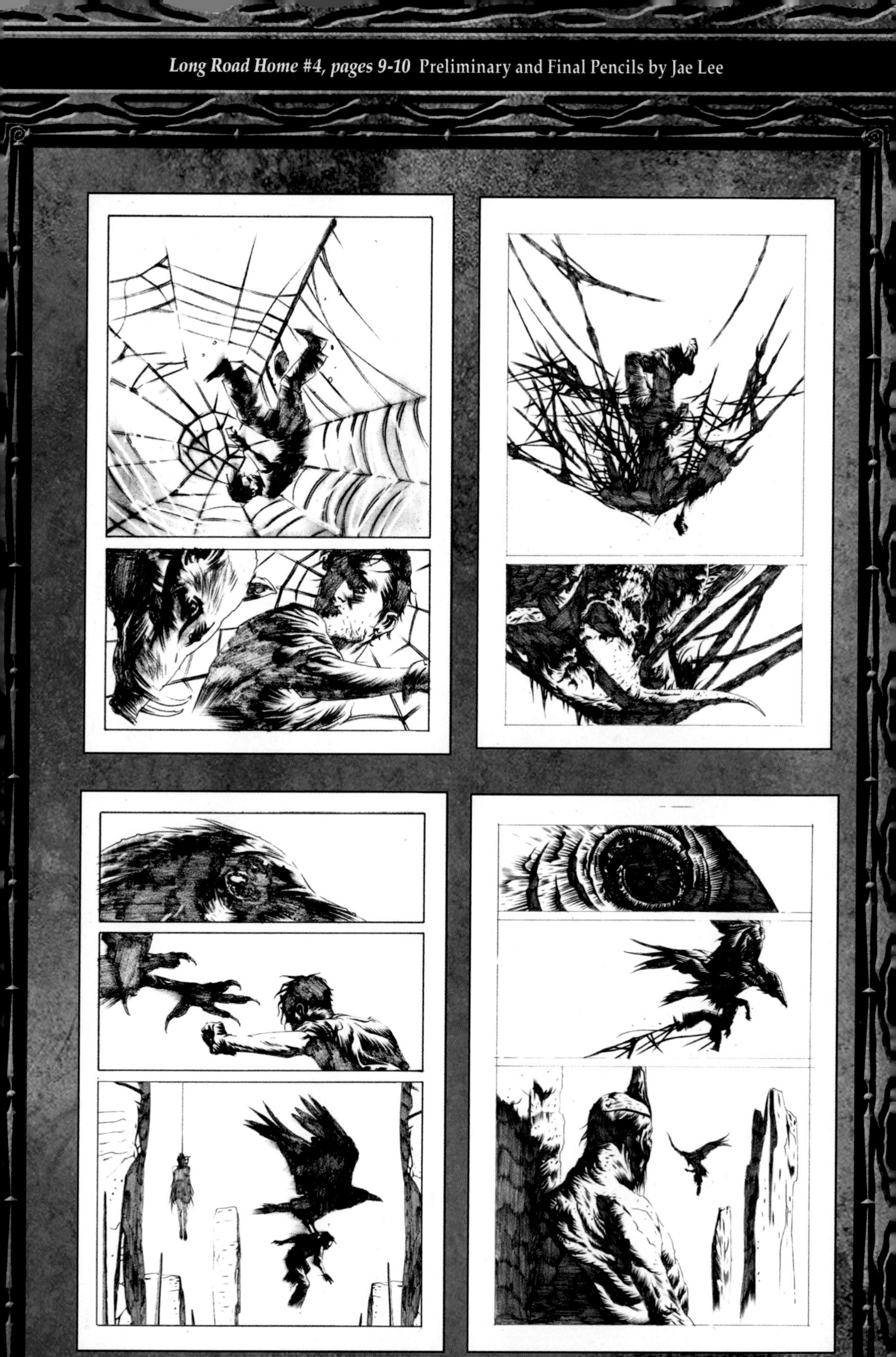

Long Road Home #4, pages 11 and 18 Preliminary and Final Pencils by Jae Lee

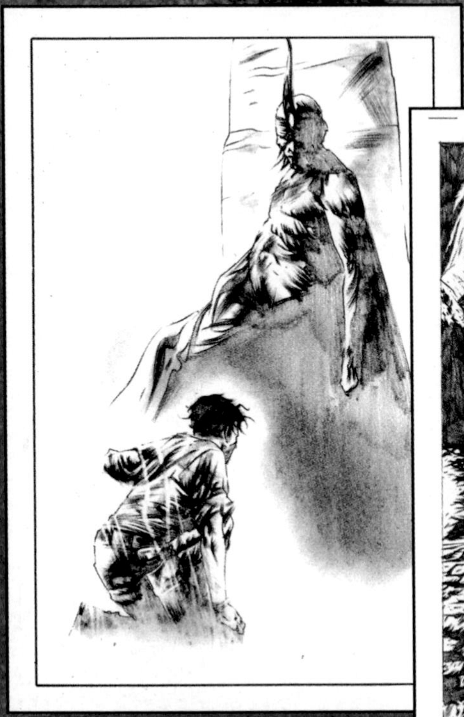

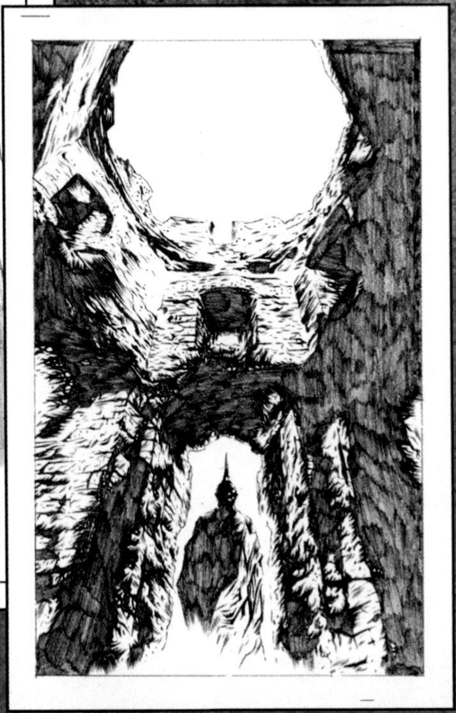

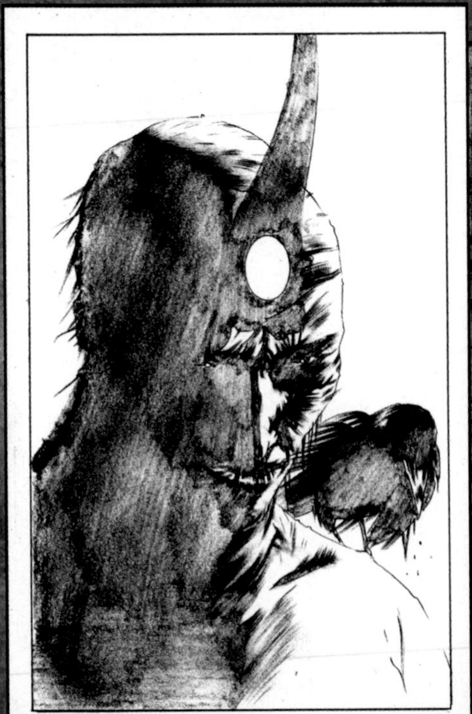

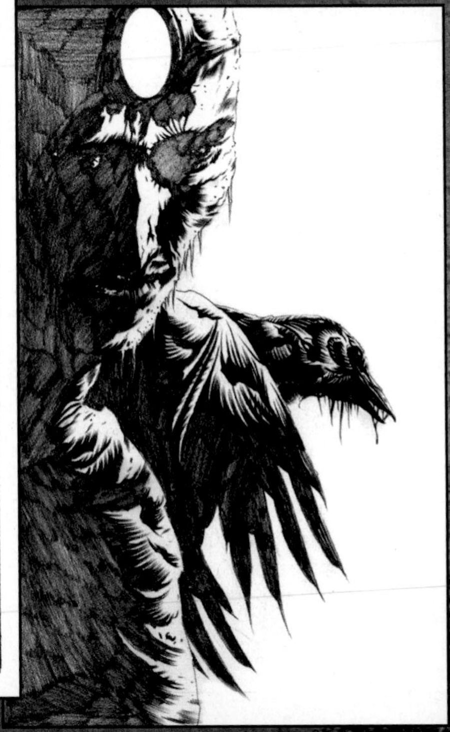

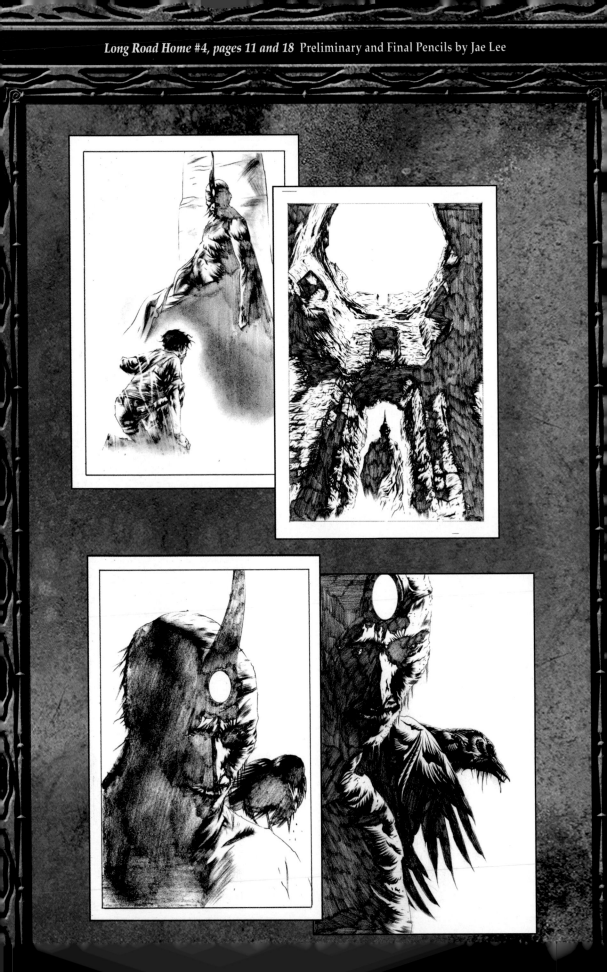

A NOTE FROM ROBIN FURTH

LONG ROAD HOME COMMENTS

Hi everybody, and welcome to the final installment of *The Long Road Home*! I really hope you've enjoyed the series. *The Long Road Home* has a very special place in my heart, since the story you've followed over the past five months began sprouting in my head back in 2001. At the time I was writing up Dark Tower character summaries for Stephen King (I had already begun working on my *Dark Tower Concordance*) and found myself falling in love with Cuthbert and Alain. As I dutifully recorded all of the places, characters, and languages found in *Wizard and Glass*, I couldn't help but wonder what happened to Roland's ka-tet immediately after their Mejis adventures ended. How did Cuthbert and Alain journey all the way back to Gilead with unconscious Roland in tow? What challenges did they face, and where exactly did Roland go while his mind was trapped within the evil seeing sphere known as Maerlyn's Grapefruit?

In *The Gunslinger Born*, my job was to condense *Wizard and Glass* into a tale which Jae Lee and Richard Isanove could then transform into a spectacular visual story. In *The Long Road Home*, I turned to my imagination, and I watched those daydreams of mine unfold into a coherent tale . . .

Thanks to Stephen King, who has been extremely supportive of my storylines, and to Jae and Richard, who have done such a fantastic job with the art. Thanks to Peter, for creating great dialogue, and to all the editors at Marvel who have helped this tale come into being. And finally, thanks to all of you out there who have continued reading Roland's tale.

As they say in Mid-World, long days and pleasant nights.

--Robin Furth

COMMENTS FROM PETER DAVID

You think reading Stephen King can be scary?

Try writing Stephen King.

At any given time, I write for a variety of individuals. First and foremost, I write for myself. If it doesn't entertain me, if I don't find it compelling, it goes no further. Either I keep working at it until it passes muster for me, or it gets scrapped. Second, I write for my wife, Kathleen, my first and most reliable reader. Then comes the editor. Then come you guys, the readership.

Not in the case of *Dark Tower*. I write for one person, and one person only: Stephen King. Oh, sure, there's a level of quality control in my head, a bar that must be cleared. But I am always conscious of the fact that Mid-World's originator will be reading and vetting every word of dialogue. It doesn't paralyze me, obviously. But, having read his book *On Writing* (which I would highly recommend) I scrutinize, consider and weigh every sentence, every word, wondering whether it's (a) in character and (b) necessary.

With all deference to, and appreciation for, the millions of Stephen King fans, you guys don't factor into the equation. If Steve (that's how he introduced himself to the group of us at the 2007 New York Comic Con, so I'm not trying to sound fabulous here) approves of the efforts of Robin Furth and myself as writers, I absolutely don't care what anyone else has to say. Besides, I love the fans, but some can be a smidge tough to please. I've read reviews in which fans declare that I have absolutely no ear for Steve's dialogue, and they cite specific narrative captions to prove it...except invariably the examples they produce were in fact taken verbatim from the original text. So basically they were saying that Stephen King didn't have the knack for writing Stephen King.

On *The Long Road Home*, of course, I don't have that cushion. The trip back to Gilead is not the only journey embarked upon with this new miniseries. Robin and I--with Jae and Richard as our illustrative guides--are now plotting our own course. Yes, Steve is watching us every step of the way, and he's there to catch us if we stumble. But we're walking without his holding our hands in the form of already-written material.

As with all things, this is a double-edged sword. Scripting is now a more time-effective endeavor since I'm not sitting there with copies of *The Gunslinger* or *Wizard and Glass* on my desk, searching for the exact right lines of dialogue to put in Roland's mouth, or the precise descriptive prose to adapt into the running commentary provided by my unseen narrator. However I am now pedaling the Dark Tower bicycle without the aid of training wheels. It's daunting, bordering on presumptuous. But, in the immortal words of Super-Chicken, I knew the job was dangerous when I took it.

It's definitely fortunate that it worked out this way. I know that some readers were a little cranky that we launched with the adaptation of already existing material. However, not only was it necessary for this to be the complete tale of Roland's progress from callow youth to gunslinger--honestly, how can you leave Susan Delgado out of that?--but it was essential for me in finding the voice of Stephen King so that I could replicate it on my own for this new series. There is simply no way that I could have convincingly inhabited the skins of Roland and his ka-tet without having thoroughly immersed myself in the original text the first go-around.

That didn't mean I wasn't nervous the first time I faced Jae's pencils with no King text to guide me. I was. But by the time I was halfway through the first issue, I was feeling a lot better about the idea of carrying on in Stephen King's voice. And whereas I faced this new series with trepidation, I am now nothing but eager to continue with Roland's journey, a journey that will take us all the way to the fabled battle of Jericho Hill.

The results are, of course, ultimately up to you, the reader, to decide. You're the ones who paid the admission price, after all. Rest assured, though, that an audience of one stands between you and me, and as long as he approves our endeavors, then all will be well. Set your watch and warrant on it.

--Peter David